A Foreword to Literature

➤ E R N E S T E A R N E S T ➤

A Foreword
to
Literature

Essay Index Reprint Series

 BOOKS FOR LIBRARIES PRESS
FREEPORT, NEW YORK

Copyright, 1945, by D. Appleton-Century Company, Inc.

Reprinted 1972 by arrangement with
Appleton-Century-Crofts.

Library of Congress Cataloging in Publication Data

Earnest, Ernest Penney, 1901-
   A foreword to literature.

   (Essay index reprint series)
   Includes bibliographies.
   1. Literature.   I. Title.
[PN45.E3 1972]   801   75-167335
ISBN 0-8369-2767-2

PRINTED IN THE UNITED STATES OF AMERICA
BY
NEW WORLD BOOK MANUFACTURING CO., INC.
HALLANDALE, FLORIDA 33009

Preface

This book is not an attempt to discover new truth nor state a new point of view. Rather it tries to explain some of the fundamentals of literary criticism. With as little emphasis as possible upon the jargon of the professional critic, it deals rather simply with such basic concepts of the art of intelligent reading as the recognition of humor, sincerity, restraint, and originality. Since it is designed for college students who are beginning the study of literature, it also tries to present a concise discussion of the forms and functions of the various types of prose and poetry.

That a book of this kind is needed has been a growing conviction of mine. More and more I find myself trying to explain to bewildered students why Chaucer is better than Eddie Guest, or Fielding than Zane Grey. For, in so far as students have literary tastes, they are those of the community, a community trained to accept syndication as the badge of literary excellence.

The fact that so many of our college graduates still retain these tastes is an indication that much of our teaching has failed. The failure, I believe, is frequently the result of the teacher's assumption that students can recognize a good book when they see it. Thus we too often turn Chaucer into a study of linguistics and Milton into a compendium of phrase and fable, forgetting that the student has not necessarily discovered the, to us, self-evident excellence of *The Canterbury Tales* and *Paradise Lost*. The present tendency to pay increasing attention to social backgrounds of literature is commendable. But it is not enough. Literature is one of the arts, and must be studied as an art. The student, however, is not ready for a technical discussion of aesthetic theory; he needs something far more simple: the pointing out of fundamental artistic values in specific works.

Moreover, if students cannot judge even the merits of contemporary literature, they can hardly be expected to recognize excellence when clouded with the film of obsolete literary conventions. Therefore this study tries to go beneath the conventions to the very foundations of art. The examples of the good and bad in literature have been chosen from various periods—even, dangerous as such an attempt may be, from the present. If there is one principle more than any other to which the author subscribes, it is that there are certain essential elements to be found in every work of merit, whatever its age, whatever its form. The book can thus be used profitably in historical survey courses as well as in those designed less conventionally to acquaint the student with types of literature or to teach him how to read. It may also be of use to non-student readers.

An occasional dogmatism must naturally have crept into a book of this sort. But it is hoped that even where the reader disagrees with the specific applications of the principles discussed, he will find the principles themselves useful in helping him to form his own judgments. For my purpose has not been to compile an arbitrary list of good and bad books, but to enable the reader to judge books for himself.

A word of appreciation is due my former colleague, Lieutenant Donald M. Berwick, U.S.N., who, had it not been for the war, would have been a collaborator in this book. I am indebted to him for many things ranging from the correction of inaccuracies to suggestions of viewpoints and ideas which have become an integral part of the work.

E. E.

Contents

		PAGE
Preface		V
CHAPTER		
I.	The Nature of Literature	1
II.	Poetry: Its Nature	17
III.	Poetry: Form and Function	41
IV.	Poetry: Its Interpretation	70
V.	Prose Style	92
VI.	Fiction	125
VII.	Drama	162
VIII.	Humor	201
IX.	Originality and Convention	225
X.	Restraint	248
XI.	Sincerity and Propaganda	267
Exercises		286
Index		321

I

The Nature of Literature

Literature is a much abused word. Politicians send
out "campaign literature"; religious cults and oil
burner companies offer "free literature" to anyone
who will send a penny postcard; and, just to make
the matter complicated, textbooks in English courses
print old ballads and other "oral literature." Most
people, however, when they use the term *literature*
without modifying adjectives have in mind *belles-
lettres*, something written in a more beautiful style
than is, for instance, a college textbook. In other
words, its aesthetic quality is the thing that for many
people distinguishes literature from other sorts of
writing.

The Aesthetic Element

Certainly the aesthetic element is a most important
one in any art—in life itself for that matter. The vast
gulf between the beauty of a medieval cathedral and
a nineteenth-century railway station is produced, not
so much by a difference in engineering and mechanical skill, as by differences in ideals and ideas. Chartres,
built for her who was regarded as a queen in heaven,
was bound to differ profoundly from a building

1

dedicated to "the goddess of getting on." In a like manner, Keats's "On First Looking into Chapman's Homer" differs from a publisher's blurb for *Prisoners of Passion* or *The Corpse on the Curb*.

This is not the place to discuss the nature of beauty nor to develop a theory of aesthetics. Our purposes here will be served by an examination of some of the more concrete problems such as imagery, diction, and music in poetry; and these we shall have to postpone for a time in order to discuss briefly some of the other elements which distinguish works of literature.

For the time being then, let us say somewhat dogmatically that one important mark of good literature is beauty of form or style. Not of all good literature perhaps, but certainly of much of it. This beauty is not superficial, not a mere matter of pleasing words and music nor descriptions of lovely scenery. It is often quite the reverse of prettiness. Macbeth's condemnation of life: [1]

> a walking shadow, a poor player
> That struts and frets his hour upon the stage
> And then is heard no more: It is a tale
> Told by an idiot, full of sound and fury,
> Signifying nothing.

is certainly not pretty, but it has a terrible kind of beauty. Literature can transform despair and disgust into something beautiful, something which conveys despair and disgust without being either despairing or disgusting. In this book we shall study some of the means the writer uses to achieve this transformation.

[1] *Macbeth*, Act V, Sc. 5.

The Ethical Element

Ruskin believed that to be truly great both art and literature must have a moral or an ethical soundness. This idea is not highly regarded by some critics of our day; it is condemned as Victorian. Yet it was once held, and a vast amount of literature was built upon this premise. The Bible, the poems of Cynewulf, Spenser's *Faerie Queene*, Milton's *Paradise Lost*, and Bunyan's *The Pilgrim's Progress* were all to a greater or lesser degree designed for moral and ethical teaching. Wordsworth stated that he never wrote a poem without a worthy purpose. For that matter, *All Quiet on the Western Front* and *The Grapes of Wrath* are both more concerned with ethics than with aesthetics, with truth rather than with beauty.

This is not to deny the great aesthetic element in most of the works mentioned. But because a modern agnostic can read the Psalms or *Pilgrim's Progress* chiefly for beauty of style, it does not follow that this is their chief element. It would be as sensible to say that the body contours and finish are what make a motor car. Some people buy a car on this basis and some people read *Paradise Lost* only for its fine music; but no mere esthete can understand either a motor car or a poem.

We do not have to agree with a particular moral or ethical teaching to understand a work of literature. One does not have to be a Puritan to read *The Pilgrim's Progress* or a Platonist to read Shelley, but unless he knows something of the driving force and the courage of the Puritans or understands the Platonic

concept of unity, he will never have more than a
superficial knowledge of Bunyan or Shelley.

Imagination

The moral or ethical teaching does not make any of
these works literature. It may even spoil a work of
art. Most Puritans wrote no memorable works; and
few sociologists command a style as vivid and clear
as Steinbeck's. Something else is necessary—imagination for one thing. *Imagination* is a vague word, but
the poets themselves often use it to describe a certain element in their work. For Wordsworth it was the
ability to see common things in a new light; for Blake
it meant the power to transcend the ordinary limits
of the five senses and to see realities beyond the material. The dictionary defines it as the creative faculty.
Whichever one of these forms it takes, it is a primary
element in literature. For most people a mosquito is
not a source of poetic inspiration. But here is what a
Thoreau sees in so slight a thing: [2]

Morning brings back the heroic ages. I was as much
affected by the faint hum of a mosquito making its in-
visible and unimaginable tour through my apartment at
earliest dawn, when I was sitting with my door and windows open, as I could be by any trumpet that ever sang
of fame. It was Homer's requiem; itself an *Iliad* and
Odyssey in the air, singing its own wrath and wanderings.
There was something cosmical about it; a standing adver-
tisement, till forbidden, of the everlasting vigor and fer-
tility of the world.

[2] Henry Thoreau, "Where I Lived and What I Lived For,"
Walden or Life in the Woods.

Like Henry Thoreau, Blake was able [3]

> To see a World in a Grain of Sand
> And a Heaven in a Wild Flower,
> Hold infinity in the palm of your hand
> And Eternity in an hour.

And that is no bad definition of imagination.

Intellectual Power

Closely allied to imagination is intellectual power. For Matthew Arnold this was the most important element in literature: for him literature was the record of the best that had been thought and said in the world. Certainly literature contains that. There is a little of Hamlet in all of us; Shakespeare has revealed to us our own souls. A single essay of Plato's, *The Banquet,* has influenced human thought for over two thousand years. Books have often revolutionized the world: the Bible, *The Origin of Species, Das Kapital, Mein Kampf*—for better or worse they have molded our lives.

Any expression of new truth or new theory is almost certain to be included in the body of literature. Thus Plato's *Republic* and Darwin's *Origin of Species* are literature. To some of you this may indicate that literature is poaching in the preserves of political theory or of natural science. Such a point of view grows out of a tendency to classify everything into neat categories, a tendency which by no means ceased with the Middle Ages. Of course, the Bible is a re-

[3] William Blake, "Auguries of Innocence."

ligious work and *The Origin of Species* is scientific, but both are also literature—the record of the best that man has thought and said. William James (a psychologist, by the way) believed that the humanities meant literature primarily, for literature "not only *consists* of masterpieces, but is largely *about* masterpieces," and these masterpieces might be "in almost any field of human endeavor."

Not every statement of new truth or new theory is literature in the usual sense of the term. Some scientists and philosophers have never learned the art of expressing their thoughts. But those thoughts, if they are important and vital, will find expression; someone will translate them into poetry or living prose. It is as Wordsworth stated, "If the labours of men of science should ever create any material revolution, direct or indirect, . . . the poet will sleep then no more than at present, but he will be ready to follow the steps of the man of science. . . . The remotest discoveries of the chemist, the botanist, or mineralogist, will be as proper objects of the poet's art as any upon which it can be employed. . . ." [4]

Then too the literary man more than once has been ahead of the scientist in the statement of new ideas. Shakespeare's understanding of the psychology and treatment of madness as shown in *King Lear* is far beyond that of the medical thought and practice of his time; William Blake was over a century ahead of Freud in explaining the effects of repression: [5]

[4] William Wordsworth, Preface to *Lyrical Ballads.*
[5] Blake, "A Poison Tree."

I was angry with my friend:
I told my wrath, my wrath did end.
I was angry with my foe:
I told it not, my wrath did grow.

And I watered it in fears,
Night and morning with my tears;
And I sunned it with smiles,
And with soft deceitful wiles.

And it grew both day and night,
Till it bore an apple bright;
And my foe beheld it shine,
And he knew that it was mine,

And into my garden stole
When the night had veiled the pole:
In the morning glad I see
My foe outstretched beneath the tree.

Thus Blake says that anger expressed, disappeared harmlessly; anger repressed and brooded upon led to murder, or the wish to murder.

Tennyson as far back as 1842 [6]

. . . dipped into the future, far as
    human eye could see,
Saw the vision of the world, and all
    the wonder that would be;

Saw the heavens fill with commerce,
    argosies of magic sails,
Pilots of the purple twilight,
    dropping down with costly bales;

[6] Alfred, Lord Tennyson, "Locksley Hall."

Heard the heavens fill with shouting,
    and there rained a ghastly dew
From the nations' airy navies
    grappling in the central blue;

Far along the world-wide whisper of the
    southwind rushing warm,
With the standards of the peoples
    plunging through the thunder-storm;

Till the war-drum throbbed no longer,
    and the battle-flags were furled
In the Parliament of man, the Federation
    of the world.

There the common sense of most shall
    hold a fretful realm in awe,
And the kindly earth shall slumber
    lapped in universal law.

These are not isolated instances: Carlyle preached the doctrines of fascism a hundred years before Mussolini and Hitler; Erasmus Darwin, a poet, talked about evolution before his grandson Charles was born; John Milton's remarks on censorship of the press are as true today as they were three hundred years ago. Ever since he has learned to write, man has been recording his most important and most interesting ideas, and the desire to be listened to has driven him to express them in the best form of which he was capable.

Fitzgerald speaks to us of our insignificance in the universe: [7]

---

[7] *The Rubáiyát of Omar Khayyám*, edited by Edward Fitzgerald, Fourth Ed., XLIV–XLVIII.

And fear not lest Existence closing your
Account, and mine, should know the like no more;
The Eternal Saki from the Bowl has pour'd
Millions of bubbles like us, and will pour.

When you and I behind the Veil are past,
Oh, but the long, long time the World shall last,
Which of our coming and departure heeds
As the sea's self should heed a pebble cast.

And David praises God for man's power and glory: [8]

For thou hast made him a little lower than the angels,
and hast crowned him with glory and honor. Thou madest
him to have dominion over the works of thy hands; thou
hast put all things under his feet.

It is one of the mysteries of the universe that both of
these should be true. They represent different sides
of man's own nature.

Both of these excerpts also have the aesthetic quality so characteristic of the finest literature. It is this
rather than originality of idea which causes them to
strike home. Both poems are summings up of old phi-
losophies rather than statements of new ones. Many
a poem or vivid prose line is only a statement of what
we already know in some vague fashion; the vividness of expression clears away the mists of half knowledge. When a person says, "Why, that's what I've
been trying to say," or "That expresses something I've
been thinking about," he testifies to the ability of literature to make him know himself.

[8] Psalms VIII:5–6.

Emotional Power

Man has recorded his emotions also. Lyric poetry is a magnificent record of all that he has felt in the world—the worst as well as the best. Most of us have felt a surge of anger as we read the news of some new act of tyranny or cruelty; so too had John Milton at a massacre of his time; and he has recorded forever his emotions in his sonnet "On the Late Massacre in Piedmont." When the French under Napoleon conquered Switzerland, Wordsworth spoke in his memorable sonnet beginning, "Two voices are there," and Coleridge thundered in "France: An Ode." And when England herself was in danger of invasion, Wordsworth wrote a sonnet which helps us to understand the fortitude of Englishmen a hundred and thirty years later: [9]

> Another year!—another deadly blow!
> Another mighty empire overthrown!
> And We are left, or shall be left alone;
> The last that dare to struggle with the Foe.
> 'Tis well! from this day forward we shall know
> That in ourselves our safety must be sought;
> That by our own right hands it must be wrought;
> That we must stand unpropped, or be laid low.
> O dastard whom such foretaste shall not cheer!
> We shall exult, if they who rule the land
> Be men who hold its many blessings dear,
> Wise, upright, valiant; not a servile band,
> Who are to judge of danger which they fear,
> And honor which they do not understand.

[9] William Wordsworth, "November 1806."

Winston Churchill, facing a like catastrophe, found in Clough's poem written ninety years before, the words in which he expressed his faith: [10]

> For while the tired waves, vainly breaking
>   Seem here no painful inch to gain,
> Far back, through creeks and inlets making,
>   Comes silent, flooding in, the main.
>
> And not by eastern windows only,
>   When daylight comes, comes in the light,
> In front, the sun climbs slow, how slowly,
>   But westward, look, the land is bright.

Poetry, especially lyric poetry, is the most usual place to look for emotional power, but it is by no means the only place. Milton's angry sonnet is matched in prose by Swift's *A Modest Proposal,* where the polished restraint of the style cannot mask the flaming anger of the writer. Suggesting that the poverty-stricken Irish peasants should sell their babies for table delicacies, Swift blandly adds, "I grant this food will be somewhat dear, and therefore very proper for landlords, who, as they have already devoured most of the parents, seem to have the best title to the children." With just such effortless precision does the savage send from his blowgun a dart tipped with mortal poison.

This anger with the stupidities and brutalities of mankind is the complement of another emotion: compassion for human suffering. Out of this emotion come

[10] Arthur Hugh Clough, "Say Not the Struggle Naught Availeth."

such works as Elizabeth Barrett Browning's "Cry of the Children," Dickens' *Oliver Twist,* Harriet Beecher Stowe's *Uncle Tom's Cabin,* and Lincoln's letter to Mrs. Bixby.

Sensitiveness

Sensitiveness to all shades of feeling is one of the most characteristic qualities of literary men. It is because of this compassion, this sympathy (literally "feeling alike") that the literary artist speaks not only for himself, but for all men. It is a rare lover who does not turn to the great love lyrics in order to read his own heart. His act is as natural as turning to a friend who also is in love. And in like manner a person in the agony of bereavement turns to the poets. A nameless Anglo-Saxon poet, "The Wanderer," has told of loneliness and sorrow at the death of friends and kin in phrases that still move the heart: [11]

Then from his slumber he starts lonely-hearted,
Beholding gray stretches of tossing sea,
Sea-birds bathing, with wings outspread,
While hail-storms darken, and driving snow.
Bitterer then is the bane of wretchedness,
The longing for loved one: his griefs renewed,
The forms of his kinsmen take shape in the silence;
In rapture he greets them; in gladness he scans
Old comrades remembered. But they melt in the air
With no word of greeting to gladden his heart.
Then again surges sorrow upon him;
And grimly he spurs on his weary soul

[11] Charles Kennedy, "The Wanderer," *Old English Elegies* (Princeton, Princeton University Press, 1936).

Once more to the toil of the tossing sea.
No wonder therefore, in all the world,
If a shadow darkens upon my spirit
When I reflect on the fates of men—
How one by one proud warriors vanish
From the halls that knew them, and day by day
All this earth ages and droops unto death.
No man may know wisdom till many a winter
Has been his portion.

The sea-birds still dip with wings outspread and the human spirit learns the same wisdom. A man oppressed with present misery can say with the scop, Deor, "That passed away, so may this."

Because the literary artist has developed his sensitiveness and his emotional range, he can develop those of his audience. Thus our sympathies and understanding of humanity are extended. How does a blind man feel about light? Read the opening of Book III of *Paradise Lost*. What emotions has a nun upon taking the veil? Gerard Manley Hopkins has perhaps caught it: [12]

I have desired to go
    Where springs not fail,
To fields where flies no sharp and sided hail
    And a few lilies blow.

And I have asked to be
    Where no storms come,
Where the green swell is in the haven dumb,
    And out of the swing of the sea.

[12] "Heaven-Haven" from *Poems of Gerard Manley Hopkins* (New York, 1931), p. 8. By permission of Oxford University Press.

Would you know how Lincoln's death seemed to those who had worshipped him? You can find it in Whitman's "When Lilacs Last in the Dooryard Bloom'd."

For most of us emotions, like ideas, are formless. Even more is this true of the ideas and emotions of so varied and complex an organism as a nation. Yet more than once some work of literature has gathered these diverse elements into a unity. Shakespeare did it long ago for England, and thereby helped to create England as a nation: [13]

> This royal throne of kings, this scepter'd isle,
> This earth of majesty, this seat of Mars,
> This other Eden, demi-paradise,
> This fortress built by Nature for herself
> Against infection and the hand of war
> This happy breed of men, this little world,
> This precious stone set in the silver sea,
> Which serves it in the office of a wall,
> Or as a moat defensive to a house,
> Against the envy of less happier lands,
> This blessed plot, this earth, this realm, this England.

And as men and women of our day were willing to die for this blessed plot, so in America people strive mightily to preserve an ideal which has being because of literature like Walt Whitman's poems and the "Gettysburg Address." Democracy was once a mere political theory designed to produce a more just government than that furnished by monarchies. If, however, you ask an American what he understands by democracy he is likely to speak of the equality of men,

[13] *Richard II*, Act II, Sc. 1.

of life, liberty, and the pursuit of happiness; of government of the people, by the people, and for the people; of the land of the free and the home of the brave. It is the more eloquent of our writers and speakers—in other words, literature—which has given form to the American dream.

Understanding Literature

An understanding of literature can come so near to giving an understanding of life that one college has made a four-year course out of the study of great books. Science is included, of course, but it is approached through the great books on science. Whether or not literature should be the chief basis of a college course, it will always be one of the most important elements in a genuine education. It can be neglected of course, as it is in the civilization pictured in Aldous Huxley's *Brave New World*. Such a civilization is only possible when literature is forbidden and neglected; Aldous Huxley makes this clear throughout the novel. It is no accident that one of the first acts of the Nazis was the destruction of books. Before he can be enslaved man must first be made blind.

A more subtle way to destroy literature is that practised by those scholastics who turn it into a catalog of dates, types, and sources. Thus Milton's poems are presented as a kind of Herculaneum of classical remains. Parallel passages are traced until the student is led to believe that poems are a kind of mosaic work. Texts are carefully revised to restore every misspelling and obsolete capitalization of the original. The question of dating a poem becomes more important than the idea it contains. Enough man-hours to build Boulder Dam are expended in exhuming forgotten minor works of third-rate poets. Literature becomes a pseudo-science.

One of the chief functions of this book will be to demonstrate that none of these things is fundamental to literature. At best they are but the scaffolding of the true study of literature. Our problem will be to study the architectural and engineering design of the structure. It will be found that this design will reflect the nature of the human mind which created it. These elements we have so far mentioned—love of beauty, the search for moral and intellectual truth, imagination and emotion—all are part of human nature. Literature then is a glass wherein man sees most nearly what he really is. To use it requires as much skill as is needed to handle a microscope or a telescope. It is this skill which this book tries to develop.

II

Poetry: Its Nature

Many people seem to believe that poetry is any form of composition with rhyme. The effusions of contributors to rural newspapers indicate how widespread this notion is. Embarrassed freshmen occasionally approach the instructor with the request that he criticize some "poem" of theirs. The poem usually has rhyme and indentation on alternate lines; yet the student is vaguely aware that something is wrong with the third stanza. The instructor can point out that there is a foot missing, or that there is an extra foot, and can tell the student something about tetrameter, pentameter and ballad meter. The amateur poet, after counting feet on his fingers, repairs the limping stanza, and asks hopefully if everything is now all right.

Everything is not all right, but the faults are difficult to explain to the student, for the explanation involves the discussion of many things the student has never thought of: imagery, diction, emotional content, variety of music, among others. Many students, discouraged, decide to write something they think easier like short stories or the drama. Yet unless they learn something of these fundamentals of poetry, they

are going to find much of literature completely baf-
fling. They will memorize the date of Shelley's birth
and the fact that he wrote "Adonais," and will, in all
probability, write on their examination papers that
Keats wrote "Adonis"—or was it Byron? "What difference does it make anyway?—poetry isn't a practical subject."

Approached as a series of dates and facts poetry is
certainly no more practical than any other set of facts.
The sophomore soon learns that handbooks of literature, or chemistry, or history contain all the facts anyway. He thinks he has thereby put something over on
his instructors. Instead he has taken the first step
toward an education; he has discovered that merely
memorizing facts is a waste of time. His next and more
alarming discovery may be that he is required to understand, to interpret, and to synthesize. Only in those
courses where the "objective" examination obtains
can he transfer the handbook to the blue book without chewing and digesting his material.

When the student gets beyond the handbook stage
in poetry, he discovers it to be a subject so practical
that almost every important idea in the world has at
one time or another been embodied in poetic form;
and that poetry has an emotional content undreamed
of in the neat categories of emotions in the psychology textbooks. For thousands of years men have lived
by the poetry of the Hebrew Psalms and the Sermon
on the Mount. The Anglo-Saxon warrior learned his
courage from the Germanic epics; men have fought
and died to battle songs since the dawn of the race.
The historian who tells us man goes to war solely be-

cause of economic forces seems academic and naïve to him who understands poetry. Economic forces are strong enough in all conscience, but it takes a "Men of Harlech" or a "Battle Hymn of the Republic" to turn farmers and grocery clerks into warriors.

What then is this stuff called "poetry"? Let us admit at once that there are many definitions and that competent judges often disagree about the quality of various poems, or even about the nature of a given piece of work. Thus one critic will describe the "Gettysburg Address" as prose and another as poetry. Yet more astonishing than the disagreements is the unanimity of discriminating persons in this matter. To us, as to the men and women of the fourteenth century, Chaucer's lines are poetry. For example, the dying Arcite is speaking to Emelye: [1]

> "Allas, the wo! allas the peynes stronge,
> That I for you have suffred, and so longe!
> Allas, the deeth! allas, myn Emelye!
> Allas, departynge of our compaignye!
> Allas, myn hertes queene! allas, my wyf!
> Myn hertes lady, endere of my lyf!
> What is this world? what asketh men to have?
> Now with his love, now in his colde grave
> Allone, withouten any compaignye.
> Fare wel, my sweete foo, myn Emelye!"

And so too is this bit by a man whose name is no longer remembered:

> O western wind, when wilt thou blow
>   That the small rain down can rain?
> Christ, that my love were in my arms
>   And I in my bed again!

[1] Geoffrey Chaucer, "The Knight's Tale," *The Canterbury Tales.*

Emotional Intensity

There is an emotional intensity in these which transcends time and place and archaic language. It can often survive translation as in the Twenty-Third Psalm. Obviously then, mere form is not the key. Terms such as *iambic pentameter* or *sonnet*, useful as they are, do not tell us the essential things about a poem. Coleridge was probably the first to call attention to this fact, and to distinguish between verse and poetry—a distinction which has become a fundamental of literary understanding. Verse, as he pointed out, could be anything with rhyme and meter such as "Thirty days hath September." He further pointed out that "poetry of the highest kind may exist without metre." He regarded the first chapter of Isaiah as "poetry in the most emphatic sense."

Coleridge said that the poet—and therefore poetry —"brings the whole soul of man into activity" by means of a synthesizing power which he called "Imagination." Our job will be to analyze and recognize some of the elements in this whole soul of man—remembering always that it is the synthesis of these elements, and not only the elements themselves, which makes poetry.

One of these we have already noted: emotion or emotional intensity. Housman used this as his chief test of a poem. A poem tingled his spine and raised goose pimples—he had to avoid thinking of poetry while he was shaving. For a highly trained literary man like Housman this might be a fairly useful test, but for most of us there are many things which, because of their associations raise goose pimples of pleasure. A trite popular song, for instance, can have terrific emotional effect if you associate it with some emotional moment in your life—like the time you met *her*. Even Housman seems to have been subject to this: he found an emotional intensity in the phraseology of the English prayer book that is often lacking to those not brought up in the Anglican church.

This emotional intensity is far from being the same thing as ranting and sentimentality. These rhinestone articles are discussed in the chapter on restraint. One of the marks of the discriminating person is his ability to distinguish the true from the false emotion. He learns to recognize intensity when, as so often happens, it is expressed in the simplest language and without the panoply of elaborate rhetoric. Wordsworth stated that "the human mind is capable of being excited without the application of gross and violent stimulants." In fact he believed that one person was elevated above another in proportion as he possessed this capability, this emotional sensitivity. It is only the stupid who require three-inch headlines to tell them an event is important. In fact, the relative size of headline type is a fairly accurate sign of the intelligence level of the readers of a given newspaper. And just as sensitivity to good music can be developed, so too can it be developed for good poetry. When, for instance, you can get something of the emotional force of Housman's "With Rue My Heart Is Laden," you have gone far toward the understanding of poetry.

And here are eight lines of Wordsworth's which will do equally well: [2]

> A slumber did my spirit seal;
>   I had no human fears:
> She seemed a thing that could not feel
>   The touch of earthly years.
>
> No motion has she now, no force;
>   She neither hears nor sees;
> Rolled round in earth's diurnal course,
>   With rocks, and stones, and trees.

Music

1. Rhythm. Music is another element fundamental to poetry. This music is a blend of a number of things: rhythm, word-sound, rhyme. Perhaps the most fundamental of these is rhythm. Poetry is the oldest form of literature. It grew out of the rhythmic nature of life itself; breathing, the heartbeat, sleep and waking, walking, polling or paddling a boat, working in a field —all have rhythmic patterns. At times of emotional excitement there is an intensification of rhythm. Thus it becomes a part of religious ceremonies, of celebrations, of impassioned oratory, of funeral chants. Shelley found in this rhythm the origin of poetry: "In the youth of the world, men dance and sing and imitate natural objects, observing in these actions, as in all others, a certain rhythm or order."

This does not contradict Coleridge's statement that poetry might exist without meter, for meter implies a regular, measured rhythm such as tetrameter (four

---

[2] Wordsworth, "A Slumber Did My Spirit Seal."

beats) and pentameter (five beats). Nor is free verse
without rhythm—it simply lacks a regular or easily
counted beat. The Book of Isaiah, which Coleridge
called poetry, will be found to have a high degree of
musical quality.[3]

Come now and let us reason together, saith the Lord:
though your sins be as scarlet, they shall be as white as
snow; though they be red like crimson, they shall be as
wool. If ye be willing and obedient, ye shall eat the good
of the land: But if ye refuse and rebel, ye shall be devoured with the sword: for the mouth of the Lord hath
spoken it.
How is the faithful city become an harlot! it was full of
judgment; righteousness lodged in it; but now murderers.
Thy silver is become dross, thy wine mixed with water:
Thy princes are rebellious, and companions of thieves:
every one loveth gifts, and followeth after rewards: they
judge not the fatherless, neither doth the cause of the
widow come unto them. Therefore saith the Lord, the
Lord of hosts, the mighty One of Israel, Ah, I will ease me
of mine adversaries, and avenge me of mine enemies.

Some lines actually scan into regular verse: [4]

And they/shall go in/to the holes/of the rocks,/and
in/to the caves/of the earth.

Notice the recurrence of the same metrical pattern
of accented and unaccented syllables—in this case
chiefly the anapestic form.
However it is not necessary to find regular patterns
before describing a composition as rhythmic. With
good poetry as with fine music, the rhythmic pattern

[3] Isaiah I:18–24.
[4] Isaiah II:19.

is likely to be varied and subtle. Both *The Merchant of Venice* and *Antony and Cleopatra* are in blank verse, but the later play has considerably less rigidity of metrical form. Compare: [5]

> The quality of mercy is not strain'd;
> It droppeth as the gentle rain from heaven
> Upon the place beneath: it is twice bless'd;
> It blesseth him that gives and him that takes:
> 'Tis mightiest in the mightiest; it becomes
> The throned monarch better than his crown;
> His sceptre shows the force of temporal power,
> The attribute to awe and majesty,
> Wherein doth sit the dread and fear of kings.

with: [6]

> Give me my robe, put on my crown; I have
> Immortal longings in me; now no more
> The juice of Egypt's grape shall moist this lip:
> Yare, yare, good Iras; quick. Methinks I hear
> Antony call; I see him rouse himself
> To praise my noble act; I hear him mock
> The luck of Caesar, which the gods give men
> To excuse their after wrath: Husband, I come!

Not only are there more run-on lines in the second passage, but the end words are less strongly accented. When Cleopatra's lines are spoken on the stage, the audience is scarcely conscious that they are regular verse; the effect is rather that of natural speech with more rhythm than usual. Yet this rhythmic quality helps to give the speech the powerful emotional effect it has upon an audience. Thus Shakespeare retains the

---

[5] *The Merchant of Venice*, Act IV, Sc. 1.
[6] *Antony and Cleopatra*, Act V, Sc. 2.

emotional effect of verse without producing the sense of artificial speech which too regular blank verse often creates.

The recognition of the emotional heightening which verse produces has led many playwrights since Elizabethan times to adopt it. One of the most recent is Maxwell Anderson. The form of his *Winterset* is basically blank verse, but a blank verse even less rigid than that of *Antony and Cleopatra*. We live in an age of less formality of speech than Shakespeare's; therefore poetry must use a less formal verse form and more colloquial diction if conversation is to seem lifelike on the modern stage. Notice how Maxwell Anderson achieves this while retaining the emotional values of poetry: [7]

Suppose one had
only a short stub of life, or held
a flashlight with the batteries run down
till the bulb was dim, and knew that he could live
while the glow lasted. Or suppose one knew
that while he stood in a little shelter of time
under a bridgehead, say, he could live, and then,
from then on, nothing. Then to lie and turn
with the earth and sun, and regard them not in the least
when the bulb was extinguished or he stepped beyond
his circle into the cold? How could he live
that last dim quarter-hour, before he went,
minus all recollection, to grow in grass
between cobblestones?

The poet then can handle rhythm in somewhat the ·same fashion as the musician does. The "Valse Triste"

[7] Maxwell Anderson, *Winterset* (Washington, Anderson House, 1935), Act III.

and "The Blue Danube" are both waltzes, but each has its own individual rhythm over and above the three-quarter time beat. The more technical aspects of this problem are discussed in the next chapter; here we are interested chiefly in the elements which make poetry. The student should practice reading verse aloud, for good verse is always written for the ear. Whenever possible he should listen to poets reading their own work. Some poets mark the beat very distinctly. Wordsworth and Coleridge both read in a kind of chant; so too does James Stephens. Vachel Lindsay used nearly all the sound effects of the human voice, and even gave directions for various types of musical accompaniment in such poems as "The Congo" and "General William Booth Enters Heaven." On the other hand, Carl Sandburg recites in a conversational tone, just slightly heightening the speech rhythms of his verse. Madariaga described Wordsworth's most characteristic rhythm as that of a man walking. That would not be strange, for Wordsworth did much of his composing while he walked in the garden.

2. *Onomatopoeia.* Occasionally poets have tried to imitate very closely the rhythms of the things they are describing. Thus Milton pictures a rooster: [8]

> And to the stack or the barn-door
> Stoutly struts his dames before:

Browning has caught the rhythm of horseback riding, in his "How They Brought the Good News from Ghent

[8] John Milton, "L'Allegro."

to Aix." Tennyson was very fond of this trick, and at times used it superbly as in [9]

> Break, break, break,
> On thy cold gray stones, O Sea!

The device is one form of onomatopoeia: suiting the sound to the sense. Like any other obvious rhetorical trick, it can give the feeling of artificiality if it is overdone.

3. *Unsuitable music.* Even worse, however, is the use of a music unsuited to the mood of the poem. Wordsworth occasionally made this mistake. Thus in "Simon Lee" he uses a meter suited to a humorous or playful mood for sentiments which are quite different:

> But, oh the heavy change!—bereft
> Of health, strength, friends and kindred, see!
> Old Simon in the world is left
> In liveried poverty.
> His master's dead,—and no one now
> Dwells in the Hall of Ivor;
> Men, dogs, and horses all are dead;
> He is the sole survivor.
>
> And he is lean and he is sick;
> His body, dwindled and awry,
> Rests upon ankles swoln and thick;
> His legs are thin and dry.
> One prop he has, and only one,
> His wife, an aged woman,
> Lives with him, near the waterfall,
> Upon the village common.

[9] Tennyson, "Break, Break, Break."

Nothing, perhaps, could more clearly indicate how fundamental to successful poetry is proper rhythm. It is not, as Wordsworth said of metrical language, a beauty superadded; it is part of the whole mood and tone of a true poem. "Simon Lee" deals with a genuine emotional experience, an experience clearly presented to the reader; yet the reader fails to share the poet's emotion because the rhythm is one associated with quite different kinds of emotion.

Another trouble with "Simon Lee" is that its rhythm is too regular. In spite of all changes of fashion in metrical form, we will discover that the better the poem, the more varied, as a rule, will be its rhythms. The regular "ta dum te dum" of inferior verse is one of its most striking characteristics. It makes impossible the subtle emotional effects which belong to the best work.

4. *Word-sound.* Nor is rhythm by any means all there is to poetic music. The sound of the words is a very important element. A ukelele can achieve some of the same rhythms as a harp; it can play some of the same tunes, but they will not sound alike. All good poets, whether consciously or not, have recognized the musical effects of certain words and combinations of words. Keats testified to this when he wrote: "Forlorn! the very word is like a bell. . . ." Milton's Latinic polysyllables are an inseparable part of his sonorous pipe-organ music in such a passage as: [10]

> Him the Almighty Power
> Hurled headlong flaming from the ethereal sky,

[10] Milton, *Paradise Lost*, Book I.

With hideous ruin and combustion, down
To bottomless perdition; there to dwell
In adamantine chains and penal fire,
Who durst defy the Omnipotent to arms.

On the other hand, notice how the same poet chooses
words with softer sound for a pastoral scene: [11]

Thus sang the uncouth swain to the oaks and rills,
While the still morn went out with sandals gray;
He touched the tender stops of various quills,
With eager thought warbling his Doric lay;
And now the sun had stretched out all the hills,
And now was dropped into the western bay;
At last he rose, and twitched his mantle blue:
To-morrow to fresh woods and pastures new.

To pick out just one element, note the number of short
vowels and front vowels as contrasted with the long
back vowels of *Paradise Lost*. It is a difference like
that between a flute and a pipe organ.

There is no set of rules that can be laid down in
this matter of word-sound. Reading verse aloud is the
best way to increase one's sensitivity. The important
thing is to note that the sound must bear a relation to
the sense. This may take the obvious form of onomatopoeia like Tennyson's [12]

The moan of doves in immemorial elms,
And murmuring of innumerable bees.

and the familiar opening stanzas of Gray's "Elegy."
More often, however, it appears in more subtle forms,

[11] Milton, "Lycidas."
[12] Tennyson, *The Princess*, Part IV.

in the poet's recognition of the emotional connotations of certain sounds.

5. *Rhyme*. Rhyme also has a psychological effect. Just why there is a certain pleasure in the repetition of a sound—a pleasure which may be spoiled by a false rhyme—is beyond the scope of this book. It is probably part of the same psychological mechanism which enables us to enjoy music. As we shall see in the next chapter, internal rhyme or frequent rhyme gives a rapid movement to poetry. Also the amount of emphasis on the rhyming word has much to do with the effect it produces. In some periods, like the pseudo-classic of the eighteenth century, the rhymed words have been heavily stressed; in others, like the present, they have been given less weight. The present tendency to use rhyme sparingly, if at all, results from a desire on the part of writers to give poetry greater naturalness. That is one reason for blank verse, especially in plays—to produce a kind of poetry not too unlike ordinary speech. Some poets, among them Milton, dislike the musical effect of rhyme, particularly in long poems. It is foolish to be dogmatic about rhyme: there are fine poems with it and without it. Like all other poetic elements it must, when it is used, be part of the whole design.

Thus the total musical effect of a poem is a blend of rhythm; word-sound, type and frequency of rhyme, or lack of rhyme. And as with rhythm, the greater the variety and subtlety of all these, the better is the poem likely to be. Obvious and mechanical use of any or all of these usually goes along with obvious and trite phraseology and imagery, and obvious and trite ideas. The *Eroica* symphony cannot be played on the mouth organ, nor can "Tintern Abbey" be transposed in the style of "Mary Had a Little Lamb." Wordsworth tried it, and in "The Tables Turned," you can see what happened:

> One impulse from the vernal wood
> May teach you more of man,
> Of moral evil and of good,
> Than all the sages can.

This is an attempt to state the same philosophy as that in: [13]

> Therefore am I still
> A lover of the meadows and the woods,
> And mountains; and of all that we behold
> From this green earth; of all the mighty world
> Of eye, and ear,—both what they half create,
> And what perceive; well pleased to recognize
> In nature and the language of the sense,
> The anchor of my purest thoughts, the nurse,
> The guide, the guardian of my heart, and soul
> Of all my moral being.

Diction

1. Imagery. Unlike music, however, poetry is not entirely a thing of tones and rhythms, of harmonies of sound; poetry derives much of its character from the images and the connotations of the words used. True the effectiveness of these depends partly upon sound, but it also depends upon meaning and upon visual appeal. Thus poetry combines with music the intel-

[13] Wordsworth, "Lines Composed a Few Miles Above Tintern Abbey."

lectual appeal of prose, and the visual effect of painting and sculpture. At its best it is one of the richest and
most comprehensive of the arts.

One school of poetry, the Imagists such as Amy
Lowell, had as one of their aims the selection of exact
and image-creating words. Of course many poets before them had used such diction, but the Imagists believed that the poetry of their time had somewhat lost
this quality. The amateur writer when he talks of
winter, for instance, is prone to use trite and colorless
phraseology: Old Boreas with his icy breath; biting
winds; blanket of snow; gloomy winter, and so forth.
Shakespeare, however, gave us winter in a series of
concrete and specific images: [14]

>When icicles hang by the wall,
>   And Dick the shepherd blows his nail,
>And Tom bears logs into the hall,
>   And milk comes frozen home in pail,
>When blood is nipped and ways be foul,
>Then nightly sings the staring owl,
>"Tu-whit, tu-who!" a merry note,
>While greasy Joan doth keel the pot.

Before the poet can do this he must observe with
eyes as keen as those of the painter for form and color;
witness Tennyson's "Mariana":

>With blackest moss the flower-plots
>   Were thickly crusted, one and all:
>The rusted nails fell from the knots
>   That held the pear to the gable-wall.
>The broken sheds looked sad and strange;

[14] *Love's Labour's Lost*, Act V, Sc. 2.

Unlifted was the clinking latch;
Weeded and worn the ancient thatch
Upon the lonely moated grange. . . .

Not only visual imagery but sounds, flavors, tactual
sensations and odors are part of the poet's medium.
Keats was especially skilful in this sort of thing. Thus
he takes the generalized concept of autumn and vi-
talizes it in a series of concrete images, scents and
sounds: [15]

Who hath not seen thee oft amid thy store?
    Sometimes whoever seeks abroad may find
Thee sitting careless on a granary floor,
    Thy hair soft-lifted by the winnowing wind;
Or on a half-reaped furrow sound asleep,
    Drowsed with the fume of poppies, while thy hook
    Spares the next swath and all its twinèd flowers:
And sometimes like a gleaner dost thou keep,
    Steady thy laden head across a brook;
    Or by a cider-press, with patient look,
        Thou watchest the last oozings hours by hours.

Where are the songs of Spring? Ay, where are they?
    Think not of them, thou hast thy music too,—
While barrèd clouds bloom the soft-dying day,
    And touch the stubble-plains with rosy hue;
Then in a wailful choir the small gnats mourn
    Among the river sallows, borne aloft
    Or sinking as the light wind lives or dies;
And full-grown lambs loud bleat from the hilly bourn;
    Hedge-crickets sing: and now with treble soft
    The redbreast whistles from a garden-croft;
        And gathering swallows twitter in the skies.

[15] John Keats, "To Autumn."

The extreme accuracy of observation is quite apparent: the exact color of the stubble fields, the behavior of gnats and swallows, the characteristic sounds of late autumn.

2. *Unusual diction.* At times he has used words in most unusual ways to get the exact effect. Thus herald's trumpets are "the silver snarling trumpets" and jellies are "soother than the creamy curd." Keats probably created the word *soother* as Poe created *tintinabulations* to describe a sound for which there was no word. Some modern writers, especially James Joyce, have done this frequently, but like any other striking device it can distract the reader's attention from the image or idea to the word or symbol. For words are, after all, symbols for something else, and it is the something else the poet wishes to create for us. Thus when Browning writes: "Irks care the crop-full bird; frets doubt the maw-crammed beast," [16] we are more likely to be startled by the unusual phraseology, more conscious of the rhetoric, than we are to be interested in the idea. When a beautiful woman wears a bizarre dress, we are more likely to notice the dress than the wearer.

3. *Trite phraseology.* A more common fault is the use of trite phraseology, particularly the use of trite figures of speech. Words alone are less likely to become trite or hackneyed. *Snow* is a perfectly good word, whereas *white as snow* is thoroughly hackneyed. Thus when one says, "It has begun to snow," we immediately get an image, but when someone says, "The tablecloth was white as snow," most of us

[16] Robert Browning, "Rabbi Ben Ezra."

get only the picture of a white tablecloth; the figure of speech has lost its image-making power. But when Keats describes a stained-glass window as like the "tiger-moth's deep damasked wings," anyone who has ever seen a tiger-moth gets a vivid picture. "Stars like diamonds" no longer creates the image of diamonds; it was never a very good comparison. Compare Shelley's "like a swarm of golden bees."

Always, however, the successful figure of speech must not distract us from the thing described; it must make us see it in the terms of the figure, a sort of double image. Thus in Keats's figure we see both the moth and the window. The moth makes us see the stained glass more clearly; the symbol does not take the place of the thing it symbolizes. But when T. S. Eliot describes the evening as a "patient etherized upon a table," most of us will see an operating room instead of evening.

4. *Need for vivid phraseology.* Poetry because of its very nature, its intensity, requires more vivid and compact phraseology than does prose. The ability to use the striking and compact phrase is one of the marks of the skilful poet. In a few intense and vivid phrases Keats sums up a whole chapter of the Book of Ruth: [17]

> when sick for home
> She stood in tears amid the alien corn:

Like many another striking phrase, "alien corn" has become the title for a play. One could compile pages of book and play titles which use a phrase from one

[17] Keats, "Ode to a Nightingale."

of the poets. In other words the phrase was so unforgettable and so meaningful that it stuck in a later writer's memory. The woman who complained that *Hamlet* was too full of quotations was paying ignorant tribute to the way in which Shakespeare's phrases have become part of our daily speech.

It is this element in poetry which led Coleridge to say of a poem that "whatever lines can be translated into other words of the same language, without diminution of their significance, either in sense or association, or in any worthy feeling, are so far vicious in their diction." In other words there is no such thing as an exact synonym in poetry: every word in a fine poem must fit into the design with the precision of the bits of jewelled glass in a cathedral window; a single false shade of color or misfit in proportion can ruin the whole design.

Take for example a line of Hamlet's dying speech to Horatio: "Absent thee from felicity awhile." The dictionary gives as synonyms for *felicity*: "bliss," "happiness." Try either of them and note the result. Or rephrase the whole line, using the same meter: "Remain away from heaven for a time." That is what Hamlet wishes Horatio to do, but the whole emotional content is lost in the paraphrase. On the other hand, substitute *felicity* in Jefferson's famous line, "life, liberty, and the pursuit of happiness," and that too is spoiled. Like a line of good poetry, Jefferson's cannot be paraphrased. The virtue lies not in a word itself, but in its suitability in meaning, association, music, and imagery.

Creative Use of Materials

Earlier in this chapter it was stated that no one element produced a poem; rather a synthesis of many elements was required, among them: emotional intensity, rhythm and music, word-sounds, imagery and connotations of words. Often one or more of these will be found in a composition that is not quite a poem, or in a poem in which the sense of completeness or perfection is lacking. Dorothy Wordsworth, in speaking of a scene, said, "It made me more than half a poet." Now, as any student of Wordsworth knows, Dorothy's brother often took scenes and incidents from her *Journal* as the basis for his poems. This seems to be typical of the poetic process. The poet often uses the bricks and mortar created by others in the building of his own structure.

Coleridge is a case in point. Professor Lowes has discovered sources for image after image and phrase after phrase in *The Ancient Mariner* and "Kubla Khan." Such things as the strange thunderstorm with rivers of lightning and the moon at the edge of one black cloud or the "caverns measureless to man" come from Bartram's *Travels*. Phrases like "ice mast-high" and "green as emerald" come from the old voyagers whom Coleridge had read. But as Lowes points out, one can search until doomsday in these same sources without finding the stanza: [18]

[18] Samuel Taylor Coleridge, *The Rime of the Ancient Mariner*, Part I.

And now there came both mist and snow
And it grew wondrous cold:
And ice, mast-high came floating by,
As green as emerald.

5. *Literary bloodhounds.* If we knew as much about the sources of the work of other poets, we should probably find the same thing. Literary bloodhounds are forever turning up parallels and analogues to phrases and images in famous poems. Far from detracting from the achievement of the poet, these usually furnish excellent testimony to his creative power. For the phrases and images are often buried in a rubble of inferior stuff. The poet has chosen only the significant and the vivid, and he has blended it with a host of other materials. The process is not unlike that of the composer who uses folk tunes in his symphony.

A misunderstanding of this process sometimes leads to confusion about the nature of a poem. A person finds a superb phrase, a vivid image, or emotional intensity in a prose work or even in a second-rate poem. Why, he wonders, are these things not classified as great poetry? He may even suspect that a work must be a hundred years old and by a famous writer to be called a great poem. This attitude has been fostered by graduate schools with their tendencies to call any writer since Wordsworth "a modern" and regard the tracking down of parallel passages as scholarship. Furthermore, there are various definitions of poetry, some of which would classify as a poem any work which contains one or two of the qualities we have been considering.

The purpose of this chapter is not to set up any

one definition of a poem as the only possible one. If a poem is defined as a work having emotional power, then "The Gettysburg Address" and most of the New Testament are poems. It is necessary, however, to note that there are some poetic qualities which these do not have. Some definitions are broad enough to include almost any work with any poetic quality at all; others like George Moore's classification of "pure poetry" (poetry like "Kubla Khan" which neither tells a story nor presents ideas) would rule out all but a very few things. In the matter of definitions there is a wide choice. This chapter has attempted only to indicate a number of the qualities found in good poetry, and to show that the best poems are a blend of several or all of these.

Some critics would demand still other qualities: originality, intellectual power, or moral greatness. Certainly originality of a kind is essential; no one must have said just the same thing, or said it in almost the same way before. As the problem of originality is considered elsewhere, it cannot be discussed fully here. And all three of these are found in both prose and poetry. Therefore, this chapter has been concerned chiefly with those elements peculiar to poetry rather than with those which belong to literature as a whole. The ability to recognize and evaluate these poetic qualities should give new meaning and richness to one's reading. Certainly neither this chapter nor the reading of many books of criticism can give this understanding. Criticism can only point the way; a person must develop understanding for himself. Only by practice can he finally develop it. It will lead to the knowledge of himself and of all mankind, but no one else can do it for him, any more than someone else can breathe for him. Unlike a play or a football game, which is most thoroughly enjoyed in company with an enthusiastic crowd, understanding a poem is a personal, inner experience.

III

Poetry: Form and Function

All art is an attempt to give form to the chaotic material of experience. From the countless sounds in the world, the musician selects and organizes those which will express his meaning; from millions of faces and figures, a painter selects a few; from those faces he selects what he finds significant, and upon a few feet of canvas he may give us the whole mood and character of a civilization. Poetry, as was pointed out in the chapter above, combines the pictorial effects of the painter and sculptor with music, and it has the intellectual resources of all spoken and written language.

Poetic form, therefore, grows out of all these elements: pictorial, musical, emotional, and intellectual. As we shall discover, a particular type of metrical pattern may be chosen for a musical effect, while the choice of stanza form may be due to its fitness for a pictorial effect or the type of idea expressed. In time an element of convention enters: a form, after having been used for a certain purpose often enough, becomes identified with that purpose. This purpose might be better served by means of some untried form,

41

and some new poet may create this better form. Or he may adapt a form from some other period as Spenser reworked the pastoral elegy or the Imagists of the 1920's used some of the methods of Chinese poetry.

It may be that entirely new forms will supplant all those of the past, but that is not our problem here. Our job is to understand the nature and purpose of those forms which for hundreds of years have been the basis of English verse, so that we may better understand what that verse expresses.

Fashions in this matter change. In recent years there has been a breaking down of formal, traditional patterns in all art forms: in painting, in music, in the short story, and in poetry. Thus just as some modern music seems at first cacophonous, so too much recent verse seems lacking in rhythm and music. Usually, however, the music is there; only it is more varied and subtle than that of the traditional type.

Stanza Forms

1. *Ballad meter.* The Anglo-Saxon poet used the half-line and the line as his units of rhythm, each half-line having two strong beats marked by alliteration, and with a pause or "caesura" in the middle of the line. With the introduction of rhyme from France, the line and stanza tended to become the metrical units. The line was measured in feet, each foot usually containing an accented and one or more unaccented syllables. Even people who could not read and write learned to use this form, and composed a great deal of verse in four-line stanzas with a regular succession of four and

three foot lines. This "fourteener" or ballad stanza is still widely used in folk poetry or "hill billy" songs. Thus in the ancient ballad of "Sir Patrick Spens":

> The king sits in Dumferling toune,
>   Drinking the blude-reid wine:
> "O whar will I get guid sailor,
>   To sail this schip of mine?"

And again in the much more recent "Wreck of Old 97":

> They give him his orders at Monroe, Virginia,
>   Sayin' Pete she's runnin' fine.
> This is not 98 but it's old 97;
>   You must put her in Spencer on time.

For the time being we shall not consider the poetic merits of these; they are used here to show a simple rhythmic pattern, and one that has become so much a part of our cultural heritage that many people use it almost automatically when they make up a jingle. It is the basic pattern of "Mary Had a Little Lamb" and of countless other nursery rhymes.

Although a number of different effects can be produced with the same basic poetic form, there is a tendency to identify certain forms with certain ideas and emotions. Thus the old "fourteener" or ballad stanza has been most frequently used for telling a simple story. It has been successfully used also for short, unpretentious lyrics like Wordsworth's "Lucy" poems. Certainly it would not do for a poem like *Paradise Lost*. For one thing it becomes monotonous, even in long ballads. That is one reason Coleridge varied it

with longer stanzas and different rhyme schemes in
The Ancient Mariner.

2. *Tetrameter couplet.* On the whole any meter
made up chiefly of short lines tends to be rapid moving. This rapidity is increased if few pauses are used,
or if rhyme is frequent as in the four-beat (tetrameter)
couplet.[1]

> Listen my children and you shall hear
> Of the midnight ride of Paul Revere
> On the eighteenth of April, in seventy-five;
> Hardly a man is now alive
> Who remembers that famous day and year.

Tetrameter couplets start off with a rush, and move
rapidly throughout. Scott used much the same four-
beat (tetrameter) line rhymed in couplets for his
swift narratives of border warfare; Byron used it for
Mazeppa, the story of a wild horseback ride.

It is the basic pattern too of Milton's "L'Allegro"
and "Il Penseroso" and Coleridge's *Christabel.* However in all these the poets have so varied the pauses
and the metrical pattern that the movement is somewhat slower. Notice the variety of Coleridge's opening
lines: [2]

> 'Tis the middle of night by the castle clock
> And the owls have awakened the crowing cock;
> Tu-whit!—Tu-whoo!
> And hark, again! the crowing cock,
> How drowsily it crew.

[1] Henry Wadsworth Longfellow, "The Midnight Ride of Paul
Revere."
[2] Coleridge, *Christabel.*

3. *Pentameter couplet.* When the lines in a couplet have five beats (pentameter) the movement seems to be considerably slower. Here is the opening of Book III of Pope's *Iliad:*

> Thus by their leader's care each martial band
> Moves into ranks, and stretches o'er the land.
> With shouts the Trojans, rushing from afar,
> Proclaim their motions, and provoke the war:

When the lines are run on, that is when the sentence or clause does not end with the line, the movement is still slower: [3]

A thing of beauty is a joy forever:
Its loveliness increases; it will never
Pass into nothingness; but still will keep
A bower quiet for us, and a sleep
Full of sweet dreams, and health, and quiet breathing.

4. *Heroic couplet.* The iambic pentameter couplet was first used by Chaucer, but because the Restoration heroic dramas were written in this form, it is called the heroic couplet. The name is applied only to the couplet which is complete in itself—not to those quoted from *Endymion.*

Dryden and Pope used it so skilfully for purposes of satire that it has come to be chiefly associated with that kind of writing. It is ideally suited to the epigram and the witty remark—remarks such as Pope intended should be quoted in the coffee houses: [4]

> The hungry judges soon the sentence sign,
> And wretches hang that jurymen may dine;

[3] Keats, *Endymion*, Book I.
[4] Alexander Pope, *The Rape of the Lock*, Canto III.

Note how one line is balanced against the other, and how within the last line there is a rise and fall:

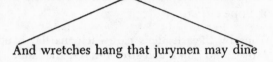

And wretches hang that jurymen may dine

Over and over Pope used variations of this pattern as did his imitators. Thus Goldsmith writes: [5]

> Ill fares the land, to hastening ills a prey,
> Where wealth accumulates, and men decay.

with the same balance; the same rise and fall. In the hands of its best practitioners this couplet had something the effect of a rapier thrust. And it was wonderfully easy to remember.

5. *Quatrains.* For descriptive passages, however, many poets have preferred a larger stanza for much the same reason that one uses longer paragraphs for description. One of the commonest stanza forms is the quatrain of five-beat lines (pentameter) rhyming in one of a number of ways. Gray's "Elegy" is in this form:

> The Curfew tolls the knell of parting day,
>   The lowing herd wind slowly o'er the lea,
> The plowman homeward plods his weary way,
>   And leaves the world to darkness and to me.

The Rubáiyát is in the same form but with a different rhyme scheme: [6]

[5] Oliver Goldsmith, "The Deserted Village."
[6] *The Rubáiyát of Omar Khayyám,* XXXIII.

> Earth could not answer; nor the Seas that mourn
> In flowing purple of their Lord forlorn;
>   Nor rolling Heaven, with all his Signs reveal'd
> And hidden by the sleeve of Night and Morn.

Note that in each case the unit of thought corresponds to the stanza. The quatrain thus lends itself to larger units than does the couplet.

   6. *Spenserian stanza.* A still larger unit is the Spenserian stanza: [7]

And more, to lulle him in his slumber soft,	*a*
A trickling streame from high rocke trickling downe,	*b*
And ever-drizling raine upon the loft,	*a*
Mixt with a murmuring winde, much like the sowne	*b*
Of swarming Bees, did cast him in a swoune:	*b*
No other noyse, nor peoples troublous cryes,	*c*
As still are wont t'annoy the wallèd towne,	*b*
Might there be heard: but careless Quiet lyes,	*c*
Wrapt in eternall silence farre from enemyes.	*c*

This is obviously all in one tone: a single mood or impression is created. The last line, which will be found to contain six beats serves notice to the reader that one unit of thought has been brought to a close. So suitable was this stanza for descriptive poems or those where a particularly rich musical effect was desired that it has been often used—in Keats's "Eve of St. Agnes," in Shelley's "Adonais," and in Tennyson's "Lotus Eaters" among others. The musical effect is in part due to the elaborate rhyme scheme, in part to the hexameter concluding line, and in part to the Spenserian tradition of a lush, musical diction. For as with

[7] Edmund Spenser, *The Faerie Queene,* Book I.

many other verse forms, the Spenserian stanza has
gathered around itself certain traditions and associations, so that when a writer uses it, he usually wishes
to arouse those associations. For a stanza form is itself
a kind of convention, and like every convention is
closely bound up in our minds with a certain mood.

7. *The sonnet.* This is particularly true of the sonnet, a stanza which is large enough to be used as a
whole poem. Usually it is a love poem, although Milton and some other poets have used it for different
purposes. But even they usually kept it as a lyric—a
poem expressing personal emotion. Wordsworth's
"Sonnets upon the Punishment of Death," written in
favor of hanging, are outside the normal sonnet tradition. In fact they are not usually regarded as poetry.

There are in English two basic forms of the sonnet:
the Petrarchan or Italian, and the English or Shakespearian. Both have been widely used and are still
current. Not only is the rhyme scheme different, but
the plan, the presentation of the ideas, is different.

The Italian sonnet usually divides into the octave
and sestet. Often the first eight lines present the idea,
and the remaining six comment upon it or shift the
emphasis. Note the shift from summer to winter in
Keats's "On the Grasshopper and Cricket":

The poetry of earth is never dead:
When all the birds are faint with the hot sun,
And hide in cooling trees, a voice will run
From hedge to hedge about the new-mown mead;
That is the Grasshopper's—he takes the lead
In summer luxury,—he has never done
With his delights; for when tired out with fun

He rests at ease beneath some pleasant weed.
The poetry of earth is ceasing never:
On a lone winter evening when the frost
Has wrought a silence, from the stove there shrills
The Cricket's song, in warmth increasing ever,
And seems to one, in drowsiness half lost,
The Grasshopper's among some grassy hills.

Here are two contrasting sides of the same idea; the sonnet is one unit, not two.

The rhyme scheme of the Italian sonnet is fitted to this thought pattern.

a		
b		
b		
a		
a		*octave*
b		
b		
a		

c	*c*	
d	*d*	and various
c	*e*	other patterns
d	*c*	
c	*d*	*sestet*
d	*e*	

The English sonnet, made up of three quatrains and a couplet, *a b a b c d c d e f e f g g*, developed because English has fewer rhyming words than has Italian. But its different form also produced a different thought pattern. Shakespeare, who wrote in this form, sometimes used the last two lines to restate the theme of the first twelve; sometimes he gave the idea a new twist, a surprise ending as in: [8]

[8] Shakespeare, Sonnet CXXX.

My mistress' eyes are nothing like the sun;
Coral is far more red than her lips' red;
If snow be white, why then her breasts are dun;
If hairs be wires, black wires grow on her head.
I have seen roses damasked, red and white,
But no such roses see I in her cheeks;
And in some perfumes is there more delight
Than in the breath that from my mistress reeks.
I love to hear her speak, yet well I know
That music hath a far more pleasing sound;
I grant I never saw a goddess go;
My mistress, when she walks, treads on the ground:
    And yet, by heaven, I think my love as rare
    As any she belied with false compare.

Thus form is closely bound up with substance, and a poet chooses his forms with this in mind. Note how often the final couplet in a Shakespearian sonnet is used for a neat or epigrammatic statement just as it is in poems entirely in couplet form. Two rhymed lines coming together seem to force the writer to use them as a neat package for an idea.

8. *Other stanza forms*. There are many other kinds of stanzas: Chaucer's rhyme royal, for instance, in seven lines, rhyming *a b a b b c c*. This was an ancestor of the Spenserian stanza, and has somewhat the same effect. Like the Spenserian stanza it has been very successful for long narrative poems containing considerable description. Chaucer used it for *Troilus and Criseyde*. Then there is the eight-line stanza borrowed from the Italian, and having the pattern *a b a b a b c c*. Byron, having tried the Popean couplet for a satirical poem and found it too cramping for his rough and tumble manner, adopted this *ottava rima* for

his *Don Juan, Beppo,* and *The Vision of Judgment.*
Notice how, instead of striving for compactness of
expression as did Pope, Byron plays with an idea, then
winds up like a baseball pitcher and lets it go: [9]

> Milton's the prince of poets—so we say;
>   A little heavy, but no less divine:
> An independent being in his day—
>   Learned, pious, temperate in love and wine;
> But his life falling into Johnson's way,
>   We're told this great high priest of all the Nine
> Was whipped at college—a harsh sire—odd spouse,
> For the first Mrs. Milton left his house.

The point is not that Byron's form is better or worse
than Pope's; it is that different verse forms are suited
to different effects. Thus many poets have invented
forms of their own to produce some particular music
or fit some idea which seemed not adaptable to an
existing stanza. Here is one created by William
Blake: [10]

> The sun descending in the west
> The evening star does shine,
> The birds are silent in their nest
> And I must seek for mine,
> The moon, like a flower
> In heaven's high bower,
> With silent delight
> Sits and smiles on the night.

Browning got an entirely different effect with a different sort of eight-line pattern: [11]

[9] George Noel Gordon, Lord Byron, *Don Juan,* Canto III.
[10] Blake, "Night."
[11] Browning, "Home-Thoughts from Abroad."

Oh, to be in England,
Now that April's there,
And whoever wakes in England
Sees, some morning, unaware,
That the lowest boughs and the brush-wood sheaf
Round the elm-tree bole are in tiny leaf,
While the chaffinch sings on the orchard bough
In England—now!

9. *Blank verse.* It is of course impossible to discuss every sort of stanza form used in English. One which is not properly a stanza at all, but a single line unit, is blank verse—unrhymed, iambic pentameter. (*Iambic* will be explained later.) This, sometimes combined with rhymed couplets, is the form of Elizabethan drama, of Milton's *Paradise Lost*, of Wordsworth's *Prelude* and *The Excursion*, of Tennyson's *Idylls of the King*, and more recently of Edward Arlington Robinson's *Tristram* and Maxwell Anderson's *Winterset*. As has been shown (pp. 24–26), the basic pattern permits considerable variation, all the way from regular, end-stopped lines to run-on lines with all sorts of metrical variations. Compare, for instance, a passage from Marlowe's *Tamburlaine* with the invocation to the muse at the start of *Paradise Lost*. Because of this great flexibility of blank verse it has been used for all sorts of ideas: for comedy or tragedy; for conversation, for narrative, for description, even for lyrics as in Eve's love lyric in *Paradise Lost:* [12]

With thee conversing, I forget all time,
All seasons, and their change; all please alike.
Sweet is the breath of Morn, her rising sweet,

[12] *Paradise Lost,* Book V.

With charm of earliest birds; the pleasant Sun,
When first on this delightful land he spreads
His orient beams, on herb, tree, fruit, and flower,
Glistering with dew; fragrant the fertile Earth
After soft showers; and sweet the coming on
Of grateful Evening mild; then silent Night,
With this her solemn bird, and this fair Moon,
And these the gems of Heaven, her starry train:
But neither breath of Morn, when she ascends
With charm of earliest birds; nor rising Sun
On this delightful land; nor herb, fruit, flower,
Glistering with dew; nor fragrance after showers;
Nor grateful Evening mild; nor silent Night,
With this her solemn bird; nor walk by moon,
Or glittering star-light, without thee is sweet.

Even without rhyme that has a certain pattern;
there is a balance within the lines, and a balance of
one half of the lyric against the second half. The
whole thing is a unit almost like a sonnet with the
first eleven lines handled like the octave; the next
seven like the sestet. The significance of this is that the
verse form alone does not determine the nature of a
poem. There are other elements to form besides those
of the type of foot and the kind of stanza. Because
there is no name for some of these, and they are not
easily classified, they are often omitted in discussions
of versification. At best, then, the names for verse and
stanza forms are only approximations.

Variations Within the Stanza

A skilful poet like Coleridge can take a simple verse
form like ballad meter and give it more varied and
subtle rhythms: [13]

[13] *The Rime of the Ancient Mariner*, Part I.

> "God save thee, ancient Mariner!
> From the fiends that plague thee thus!—
> Why look'st thou so?"—"With my cross-bow
> I shot the albatross!"

The effective use of pauses is one of the things which strikes us first here. Compare it with the mechanical pauses in "Mary Had a Little Lamb." Then note that the rhythms of actual speech are found in Coleridge's stanza, and how at times the rhythmic unit is greater than the single line.

Keats has done the same thing in the Spenserian stanza—a much more complex metrical form to start with. Old Angela is speaking to the young lover, Porphyro: [14]

> "Get hence! get hence! there's dwarfish Hildebrand;
> He had a fever late, and in the fit
> He cursed thee and thine, both house and land:
> Then there's that old Lord Maurice, not a whit
> More tame for his gray hairs—Alas me! flit!
> Flit like a ghost away."—"Ah, Gossip dear,
> We're safe enough; here in this armchair sit.
> And tell me how"—"Good Saints! not here, not here;
> Follow me, child, or else these stones will be thy bier."

With the exception of "here in this armchair sit," the word order is that of natural speech—in other words the rhythm is that of speech, heightened by rhyme and by being fitted to the pattern of the Spenserian stanza.

Shelley took another standard pattern, *terza rima*, but he too worked other rhythms into it—something of the long rise and fall of the wind's sweep: [15]

---

[14] Keats, "The Eve of St. Agnes."
[15] Percy Bysshe Shelley, "Ode to the West Wind."

O, wild West Wind, thou breath of Autumn's being,
Thou, from whose unseen presence the leaves dead
Are driven, like ghosts from an enchanter fleeing,

Yellow, and black, and pale, and hectic red,
Pestilence-stricken multitudes: O, thou,
Who chariotest to their dark wintry bed

The wingèd seeds, where they lie cold and low,
Each like a corpse within its grave, until
Thine azure sister of the Spring shall blow

Her clarion o'er the dreaming earth, and fill
(Driving sweet buds like flocks to feed in air)
With living hues and odors plain and hill:

Wild Spirit, which art moving everywhere;
Destroyer and preserver; hear, O, hear!

1. Quantity. Like stanza forms, the type of foot
does not wholly determine the nature of a verse line.
Here are two lines in iambic meter, the regular recurrence of one accented and one unaccented syllable: [16]

The plow/man home/ward plods/his wea/ry way
It lit/tle prof/its that/an id/le king

Each has the same number of feet and the same kind
of feet; even the lack of a marked pause within the
line is the same; yet the music of the two is entirely
different. One reason is that although we have no way
of measuring it, English verse has quantity. A syllable

[16] Thomas Gray, "Elegy Written in a Country Church-Yard."

like *home* has much greater length than *lit* or *prof* in the second line. A line filled with long *o* and *u* sounds moves more slowly and with a more stately tread than one with short vowels. Contrast the opening stanza of Gray's "Elegy" with: [17]

> Kentish Sir Byng stood for his King
> Bidding the crop-headed Parliament swing;
> And, pressing a troop unable to stoop
> And see the rogues flourish and honest folk droop,
> Marched them along, fifty score strong,
> Great-hearted gentlemen singing this song.

2. *Rhyme.* Of course it is not words only that give the effect here; as in all good poetry they blend with the rhythm to form a musical combination. Furthermore rhyme plays a part. Frequency of rhyme, internal rhyme, or the use of key words in rhyming positions tends to emphasize rhyme sound. Thus a rhyme word in an end-stopped line is likely to have more sound value than one in a run-on line. Compare the emphasis on end words in these couplets: [18]

> A little learning is a dangerous thing;
> Drink deep, or taste not the Pierian spring.

and [19]

> A thing of beauty is a joy forever,
> Its loveliness increases—it will never
> Pass into nothingness.

The rhyme carries still less weight when it falls upon a syllable with only secondary stress or upon an unim-

---

[17] Robert Browning, "Marching Along" from *Cavalier Tunes.*
[18] Pope, *An Essay on Criticism.*
[19] *Endymion,* Book I.

portant word. Shelley often used these methods, thus gaining a flowing music with few heavy beats. Compare the stately tread of Spenser's stanza: [20]

> Led with delight, they thus beguile the way,
> Untill the blustring storme is overblowne;
> When, weening to returne whence they did stray,
> They cannot finde that path, which first was showne,
> But wander too and fro in waies unknowne,
> Furthest from end then, when they neerest weene,
> That makes them doubt, their wits be not their owne:
> So many pathes, so many turnings seene,
> That which of them to take in diverse doubt they been.

with the softer music which Shelley, using the same stanza, produces with run-on lines and rhymes on light syllables: [21]

> He is a portion of the loveliness
> Which once he made more lovely: he doth bear
> His part, while the one Spirit's plastic stress
> Sweeps through the dull dense world, compelling
>   there
> All new successions to the forms they wear;
> Torturing the unwilling dross that checks its flight
> To its own likeness, as each mass may bear;
> And bursting in its beauty and its might
> From trees and beasts and men into the Heaven's light.

This use of light rhymes is not to be confused with the awkward rhymes of unskilled poets, rhymes which force a mispronunciation of a word as in:

> O bury me not on the lone Prairie,
> Where the wild coyote howls mournfully.

[20] *The Faerie Queene,* Book X.
[21] Shelley, "Adonais."

Sometimes a line contains an extra, unaccented syllable called a *feminine ending*. This makes possible a double rhyme, and tends to produce a liquid effect. Chaucer does this unobtrusively by the use of the unstressed final *e*, whereas Swinburne goes in for more ostentatious effects such as: [22]

> Pale, beyond porch and portal,
>   Crowned with calm leaves, she stands
> Who gathers all things mortal
>   With cold immortal hands;
> Her languid lips are sweeter
> Than love's who fears to greet her,
> To men that mix and meet her
>   From many times and lands.

The liquid quality is obvious—too obvious here for modern taste. Like any other special device, double rhyme loses its effect when there is too much of it. It does not become tiresome in Chaucer's verse because his final *e* is a very light sound, but it often does in later verse.

Another special device is internal rhyme. Its usual effect is to give rapidity to a stanza.[23]

> "The fair breeze blew, the white foam flew
>   The furrow followed free:
> We were the first that ever burst
>   Into that silent sea."

In general it can be said that rhymes placed close together tend to produce the effect of rapid movement. The omission of rhyme entirely, as in blank verse

[22] Algernon Swinburne, "The Garden of Proserpine" (New York, Harper & Brothers, 1904).
[23] *The Rime of the Ancient Mariner*, Part II.

and free verse, gives still other musical effects. Milton pioneered in a device often used by modern poets: the use of rhyme at varying intervals instead of in a set pattern. In "Lycidas" he often heralds a change of theme or pace by an unexpected rhyme. More and more, poets have come to use rhyme as an auxiliary rather than as a fundamental element in verse. This is almost the reverse of the tendency of the amateur versifier to emphasize rhyme at the expense of everything else. Note how purposeless are the rhymes in: [24]

Over the hill to the poor-house—I can't quite make it clear!
Over the hill to the poor-house—it seems so horrid queer!
Many a step I've taken a-toilin' to and fro,
But this is a sort of journey I never thought to go.

Rhyme is only one element in poetry. As was pointed out in the preceding chapter, the total musical effect of a poem is a blend of rhythm, word sound, type and frequency of rhyme, or lack of rhyme.

Types of Feet

Although, as we have seen, the poet consciously or instinctively uses quantity in achieving his effects, he usually adopts regular patterns of accented and unaccented syllables called "feet." But because of the varying quantities of the syllables, the names of verse forms can be only approximations.

1. *Iamb.* The iamb ⌣ ′ is the most common foot in English verse, probably because English speech has a prevailingly iambic rhythm. The everyday remark:

[24] Will Carleton, "Over the Hill to the Poor-House."

Ĭ dón't bĕlieve ĭt ís,

follows that pattern exactly. It is a basic element in all the stanza forms we have examined.

2. *Trochee.* Less common than the iamb is the *trochee* ‒ ◡. Except for the omission of a final syllable, the following line of Blake's is trochaic:

Tígĕr tígĕr búrnĭng bríght

However, the trochee is much more often used in the opening of an iambic line. The accent coming first gives a strong, challenging beginning; it sometimes has an effect like a herald's trumpet. Both "L'Allegro" and "Il Penseroso" begin with trochees. Trochees are found, of course, at many places other than the opening of a poem, but nearly always they are challenging, a call to attention. Here are two lines from *Paradise Lost,* both beginning with trochees: [25]

Clashed on their sounding shields the din of war, Hurling defiance toward the vault of Heaven.

3. *Anapest.* A quite different effect is produced by the anapest ◡ ◡ ‒. Any considerable sprinkling of anapests will create a lilting or galloping music depending on the accompanying sounds. Thomas Moore was fond of this meter: [26]

But alás/fŏr hĭs coún/trў!—hĕr príde/ĭs gŏne bý And thăt spí/rĭt ĭs brók/ĕn, whĭch nĕv/ĕr woŭld bénd.

For most people that is too regular; anapests can be-

[25] *Paradise Lost,* Book I.
[26] Thomas Moore, "Oh! Blame Not the Bard."

come cloying very quickly. Byron is more successful in: [27]

> The Assyrian came down like the wolf on the fold
> And his cohorts were gleaming in purple and gold;
> And the sheen of their spears was like stars on the sea,
> When the blue wave rolls nightly on deep Galilee.

But even that cloys before long. The best poetry has more variety of music. "Lochinvar" and "The Midnight Ride of Paul Revere" are both full of anapests, but Longfellow took pains occasionally to break the monotony characteristic of that form, even though he was writing for children and Scott presumably for adults. Anapests are probably most successful when used sparingly to give added sweetness to an iambic line as in: [28]

> It ceased; yet still the sails made on
> A pleasant noise till noon,
> A noise like of a hidden brook
> In the leafy month of June,
> That to the sleeping woods all night
> Singeth a quiet tune.

Notice how the anapest in the fourth line lends grace and lightness just where it is needed.

4. *Dactyl.* The dactyl, ˊ ˘ ˘, is more characteristic of Latin verse than of English. Its effect is somewhat like that of the trochee, and the two are often combined. Possibly because it is not natural to the rhythms of English speech, it has for most people a rather odd

---

[27] Byron, "The Destruction of Sennacherib."
[28] *The Rime of the Ancient Mariner*, Part V.

effect in verse. In *Evangeline* Longfellow tried the classic meter, dactylic hexameter:

> Thís ĭs thĕ/fórest prĭ/mévăl. Thĕ/múrmŭrĭng/pínes
> ănd thĕ/hémlŏcks.

Tennyson used dactyls for the "Charge of the Light Brigade" when he wanted a martial, vigorous effect:

> Hálf ă leágue/hálf ă leágue
> Hálf ă leágue/ónwărd

You will note that the accent markings are only approximate; the syllable *league* obviously carries a heavier beat than *a*. The fact is that true dactyls are very rare. Many people, reading the "Light Brigade," have wished that they were still rarer.

5. *Rare types.* There are several types of feet which are used only singly like the pyrrhic foot ‿ ‿ and the spondee ‚‚. A few words like *Egypt* are natural spondees. Thus Antony's speech:

> Ĭ ăm dyíng Egýpt dyíng

contains an unusual number of spondees.

This line brings up an interesting point: line accent may sometimes change word accent. When this is done awkwardly as in amateur verse, the effect is often comic. In fact the humor of a limerick is often dependent upon a shift of accent to make a word rhyme. But in the line spoken by Antony, the shift does not produce a false accent: that is the way in which a man laboring for breath would speak the word *dying*. The important point is that in good poetry word accent and line accent should blend and harmonize.

Pauses

1. *Caesura.* Besides varying the type of foot to express different moods or to suit different materials, the poet has many other effects at his command. He can vary the position of the *caesura,* the pause within the line, or he can have no pause at all. The characteristic rise and fall of the Popean line is largely due to the caesura. Properly handled the caesura not only varies the music, but emphasizes meaning. Notice how this is true of the following stanza: [29]

> A Moment's Halt—a momentary taste
> Of Being from the well amid the waste—
> And lo!—the phantom caravan has reached
> The Nothing it set out from—Oh, make haste!

2. *Catalexis.* Strongly marked pauses are often substituted for syllables. This omission of a syllable, called *catalexis,* may be at the beginning of a line:

> Stay,/the king/hath thrown/the war/der down

or at the end of a line:

> Tiger/tiger/burning/bright

Note how two lines, one with three and the other with seven syllables can be metrically equivalent by the use of pauses:

[29] *The Rubáiyát of Omar Khayyám,* XLIV–XLVIII.

> Break, break, break,
> On thy cold gray stones, O Sea!

Faults in Poetry

These are only some of the many musical effects possible to the poet. He may blend and combine them in countless ways. But there are certain things he may not ordinarily do. Just as we expect him to avoid false word accent, so too we dislike awkward inversions of natural word order or far-fetched rhyme.[30] Whittier, who included all of these undesirable qualities in "Snow Bound," at one point achieved two of them simultaneously:

> Then roused himself to safely cover
> The dull red brands with ashes over.

In his *Essay on Criticism,* Pope complained of similar faults, which he cleverly imitated at the same time:

> While expletives their feeble aid do join;
> And ten low words oft creep in one dull line!
> While they ring round the same unvaried chimes,
> With sure return of still expected rhymes;
> Where'er you find "the cooling western breeze,"
> In the next line, it "whispers through the trees";

Anyone familiar with popular songs will note that inferior poets are still using the same "still expected

[30] Note, however, that some modern poets use false rhyme purposely to try to gain some emotional effect or to avoid being commonplace. The effectiveness of this depends upon the skill of the poet; it is not a device for the amateur. Cf. Louis MacNeice, *Modern Poetry,* p. 31 (New York, Oxford University Press, 1938).

rhymes" and are still padding their lines with feeble words like "do" and "oft."

There are of course truly great poems with one or more of these faults, but more often than not, a weak style goes with flabby thought or diluted emotion. The contrast will be found at times in the work of the same poet, as in the passages cited in the chapter on "Sincerity and Propaganda" (pp. 269–270). Mere correctness does not make a great poem; form is important, but it is always a means to an end.

New Forms

Because of this, artists at times revolt against existing forms. The poet may feel that a form no longer has vitality, that it has become so stereotyped as to fail to move the emotions. That happens constantly to figures of speech which are used too often; it happened to the Popean couplet. During the nineteenth century there was a tendency for poets to rework old ground: the Arthurian tales; Wordsworthian nature worship; sentimental romance; mother, home, and heaven. Some of them like Tennyson and Longfellow did this with great technical skill. In fact so great was Tennyson's technical mastery of all sorts of metrical patterns that he seemed to have left little room for further development of existing forms. And these forms became so closely identified with the stock themes and stock emotions that poets began to seek for new ways to say new things. This led to the development of free verse.

1. *Free verse.* As far back as Milton's "Lycidas" there had been experiments in this direction—a

breaking away from a regular pattern. Wordsworth's handling of the ode had led in the same direction. But in the nineteenth century Arnold in "Dover Beach," Henley in his poems on a hospital, and above all, Whitman broke entirely with the regular patterns such as foot, line, and stanza. This does not mean that there is no pattern at all in free verse. Usually the pattern grows out of the thought instead of a certain musical form. Thus a new form may be used for every new idea. Music is there too, but it is a more varied and less defined music than that of traditional poetry. Here, for instance, is Whitman's "Prophecy of a New Era": [31]

I see tremendous entrances and exits, new combinations,
    the solidarity of nations,
I see that force advancing with irresistible power on the
    world's stage . . .
I see men marching and countermarching by swift mil-
    lions,
I see the landmarks of European kings removed,
I see this day the People beginning their landmarks—all
    others give way—
Never were such sharp questions asked as this day,
New was the average man, his soul more energetic, more
    like a god . . .

What whispers are these, O lands, running ahead of you,
    passing under the seas?
Are all nations communing? Is there going to be but one
    heart to the globe?
Is humanity forming *en masse?* For lo tyrants tremble,
    crowns grow dim,
The earth, restive, confronts a new era.

[31] "Prophecy of a New Era" from *Leaves of Grass* by Walt Whitman. Copyright, 1926, by Doubleday, Doran and Company, Inc.

There is no traditional pattern here, but there is a pattern: the repetition of the same phrases, the balance and antithesis. This pattern produces a certain rhythm, in this case that of sonorous prose or an oration. Sandburg's verse often falls into similar patterns: [32]

Hour by hour the caissons reach down to the rock of the earth and hold the building to a turning planet.
Hour by hour the girders play as ribs and reach out and hold together the stone walls and floors.
Hour by hour the hand of the mason and the stuff of the mortar clinch the pieces and parts to the shape an architect voted.
Hour by hour the sun and the rain, the air and the rust, and the press of time running into centuries, play on the building inside and out and use it.

Even free verse then tends to follow certain forms, and these forms in turn tend to reappear as do stanza forms. At times free verse approaches very closely to blank verse rhythms as in Edgar Lee Masters' *Spoon River Anthology*. At others it approximates traditional lyric effects as in Whitman's [33]

Come my tan-faced children
Follow well in order, get your weapons ready,
Have you your pistols? have you your sharp-edged axes?
    Pioneers! O pioneers!

For we cannot tarry here
We must march my darlings, we must bear the brunt of danger

[32] Carl Sandburg, "Skyscraper," *Chicago Poems* (New York, Henry Holt and Company, Inc., 1916).
[33] "Pioneers! O Pioneers!" from *Leaves of Grass* by Walt Whitman. Copyright, 1926, by Doubleday, Doran and Company, Inc.

We the youthful sinewy races, all the rest on us depend,
  Pioneers! O pioneers!

Form of some kind is indispensable to art; it is what distinguishes art from the chaotic materials of life.

This is perhaps the reason why many poets have turned from free verse to the traditional types. Free verse, as we noted, has form, but the boundaries are so shadowy that they have little restraining power. As a result, free verse often lacks the compactness and vigor of traditional poetry. It often sprawls. When a poet can use as many words as he pleases, he is less constrained to seek for the exact word; when he can arrange words in any order, he loses the added emphasis of rhyme or line rhythm. It is no accident that the most perfect statements, those in which every word fits perfectly, are still to be found in traditional verse. It has yet to be demonstrated that great art of any kind can be produced without the mastery of certain disciplines.

2. *Other experiments.* This does not imply that the traditional line and stanza arrangements are the only good ones possible. Just as in the past Chaucer created the heroic couplet, and Spenser his stanza, so in the nineteenth century Gerard Manley Hopkins developed a type of verse in which there is a kind of additional rhythm beyond that of foot and line. This he described as "sprung rhythm," and as it carries over beyond the line, he said it "roved over." It might perhaps be compared to an overplaid in a fabric. The poem of his quoted on page 13 above uses this form. It is perhaps too difficult a form to be understood by

the amateur, but Hopkins' work has influenced some of the poets of our day like Spender and Auden.

There is no point in trying to settle the old question of the relative importance of form and content. Spenser's value, for instance, is certainly largely dependent upon his technical skill; Wordsworth's, on the contrary, often appears despite poor technique. A powerful emotion or an original idea will often burn through the mists of poor phraseology, and a great musical theme can sometimes be heard though the instruments lack proper range. But the greatest poetry will always be a fusion of the two. Shakespeare's sonnet "When in Disgrace with Fortune and Men's Eyes" or Arnold's "Dover Beach" or Keats's "Ode on Melancholy" are not great because of any one element alone: they have the qualities of music, superb phraseology, emotional and intellectual power, and they have thoroughly satisfying form. Their power is not of any one thing, but of a blend of all.

IV

Poetry: Its Interpretation

Many people find poetry difficult to understand. Such persons are likely to agree with Isaac Newton's statement, "Poetry is ingenious fiddle-faddle." There is probably a literal-minded sort of person who can never enjoy poetry, just as there are tone deaf people who cannot appreciate music. More frequently, however, the trouble lies not in psychological or physiological inadequacy, but in lack of training. No set of directions can supply this training any more than a laboratory manual can make a chemist. The directions can merely point the way.

Some of the reasons for developing this understanding have been suggested in the chapter on the nature of literature. But one may ask why he should bother with poetry if he can get the same thing in prose. The point is that he cannot get the same thing in prose. Good poetry is capable of certain effects, aesthetic and emotional, which are beyond the range of prose. The range of prose might be compared to that of the speaking voice, that of poetry to the trained singing voice. It is one of the tragic limitations of our culture that it is necessary to explain and defend aesthetic values. The great civilizations of the past developed the arts as a normal part of life; the Elizabethan Englishman, for instance, took to poetic drama as naturally as we accept the technique of the movies. This is not to belittle the technique of the movies: it too is an art. But it cannot achieve certain effects any more than a painting can take the place of a symphony.

Poetic Methods

As we have seen in a preceding chapter, the particular quality of poetry is emotional intensity. This is partly due to its musical qualities. These we have discussed. Along with these go certain ways of presenting the theme or thought; these methods differ somewhat from those of prose, and are the cause of much of the difficulty some people find in understanding verse. The difference of method is functional; the poet is often trying to tell us what he has felt, the prose writer what he has thought. In older poetry this difference did not always obtain. Homer told of battles; Chaucer gave us romances, character sketches, bawdy anecdotes, biographies—all kinds of things which are now commonly put in prose form. Milton, Wordsworth, and many other poets put philosophy into verse. Therefore a literate person often has no trouble reading *Macbeth* or *Paradise Lost,* but may find a lyric of Blake's only a pleasant musical incantation, and a poem by T. S. Eliot mere nonsense.

1. Symbolism. Let us examine Blake's well-known: [1]

> Tiger! Tiger! burning bright
> In the forests of the night,

[1] Blake, "The Tiger."

What immortal hand or eye
Could frame thy fearful symmetry?

In what distant deeps or skies
Burnt the fire of thine eyes?
On what wings dare he aspire?
What the hand dare seize the fire?

And what shoulder, and what art,
Could twist the sinews of thy heart?
And when thy heart began to beat,
What dread hand and what dread feet?

What the hammer? what the chain?
In what furnace was thy brain?
What the anvil? what dread grasp
Dare its deadly terrors clasp?

When the stars threw down their spears,
And watered heaven with their tears,
Did he smile his work to see?
Did he who made the Lamb make thee?

Tiger! Tiger! burning bright
In the forests of the night
What immortal hand or eye
Dare frame thy fearful symmetry?

Blake has not, as one critic puts it, confused a tiger
with a small fire. What he has done is to express something in terms of symbols. The tiger here represents
the wrath of God, or more generally, the evil forces
in the universe; the lamb is the love of God or the
forces of good. The problem then is that of all philoso-
phies, how to reconcile these two conflicting forces
which we find everywhere, and especially in our own

natures. Here Blake is not attempting Milton's task of justifying the ways of God to man; he is not trying to solve the problem. Rather Blake is using a series of images and a musical form like an incantation to give a sense of the terrible quality of the evil forces in creation. Elsewhere he has presented his hypothesis about the matter: the theory that "the God of this world must be a very cruel being." Here he gives us the emotional effect of that realization. Blake's prose statement may make an intellectual impression upon us; the poem makes us feel the power of the mysterious and terrible forces in the world. Both methods of presenting an idea have their place. But because man is more strongly influenced by his emotions than by his intellect, he must usually feel something deeply before it influences his actions. People knew there was child labor before Elizabeth Barrett's "Cry of the Children," and that migratory labor was poverty-stricken before Steinbeck's *Grapes of Wrath*. But it was the emotional appeal of such works which led people to take heed of the problems. It is this power which Shelley describes in "To a Skylark":

> Like a Poet hidden
>   In the light of thought,
> Singing hymns unbidden,
>   Till the world is wrought
> To sympathy with hopes and fears it heeded not;

But why does the poet often use symbols to do this? For one thing because we all do. Also they are a way of saying much in a compact form, and they frequently have associations which aid in producing an effect upon our emotions. Human beings are less readily moved by abstract terms like "patriotism" or "Christianity" than by symbols such as the flag or the cross. We use symbols more often than we realize. We talk of the lamp of learning, the torch of civilization; the sword symbolizes war, the pen literature. The more vast and complex the idea, the more need is there for a readily grasped symbol. In "The Tiger" Blake was dealing with complex and abstract ideas; he has translated them into vivid symbols.

One large group of symbols often found in English poetry comes from Platonic and Neo-Platonic philosophy. There is the cave representing life in this world where the soul is thought of as shut away from the reality outside, and gets its knowledge from shadows on the wall. There is the stream representing life, and the ocean of universal being into which it flows, "That immortal sea which brought us hither," of Wordsworth's "Ode on Intimations of Immortality." The steps by which one passes from the love of a person to a more universal love, or from the perception of physical beauty to that of spiritual beauty are often represented as a ladder or staircase. You will find some of these in the poetry of Spenser, Keats, and Shelley, and in many other places.

Symbols, like any other figurative language, can become trite. For that reason poets often seek new ones. First-rate writers today rarely talk about Cupid with his arrows nor of Pegasus, the winged horse representing poetry. This often leads to the use of symbols not familiar to the reader. He must use notes and commentaries in their interpretation. For instance, to

understand the longer poems of Blake one must know
that Urizen represents the rational faculty divorced
from emotion, whereas Los is the imagination. There
are others like these in Blake, and they must be
learned before the poems become intelligible. A similar problem often faces the reader of the poetry of
William Butler Yeats.

However the meaning of many symbols will become clear from their use in a poem. Here, for instance, are two stanzas of Blake's: [2]

> Bring me my bow of burning gold!
> Bring me my arrows of desire!
> Bring me my spear! O clouds unfold!
> Bring me my chariot of fire!

> I will not cease from mental fight,
> Nor shall my sword sleep in my hand,
> Till we have built Jerusalem
> In England's green and pleasant land.

The first two lines of the last stanza help to show the
meaning of the stanza before it. Obviously part of
Blake's meaning in "bow of burning gold," "arrows of
desire," and "chariots of fire" is that he wants to use
all his powers of intellect, imagination, and physical
force. This interpretation is helped by our knowledge
that ever since Elijah showed Elisha the chariots of
fire in the heavens, they have symbolized vision and
imagination. Symbols often derive from the Bible, literature, and legend. In fact legends are often interpreted as symbolic. Therefore to understand symbols
in poetry one must have some knowledge of his cultural heritage.

[2] Blake, *Milton.*

But to return to Blake's poem. Arrows have long signified speed, directness, and keenness as they do here. Gold and golden have a long association with fineness and with joy, witness phrases like "the golden age," and "golden opportunity." The bow of burning gold suggests that Blake means to use his finest and most valuable powers. But why "burning"? Possibly because fire has a long association with inspiration— the idea of divine fire, or the fire of genius.

Blake, then, desires to use his powers of vision and strength to do what? To build Jerusalem. That too is a symbol. It is the holy city of Biblical history, but also the holy city of the future, a heaven or utopia. Thus in the hymn, "Jerusalem the Golden," we have two of the same symbols found in Blake's poem. Blake's meaning seems to be that he desires to use all his powers to help to create a utopia in England, to make England a lovely and holy place. But there is nothing moving about that bald statement of his idea, whereas the poem itself is profoundly moving; it fires the reader with hope and imagination. The symbols have helped. As we saw, one symbol like arrows can carry several meanings at once. After one becomes used to the method, he does not need an elaborate analysis such as this; he catches the mood and the meaning as he reads, just as the chemist recognizes the meaning of his symbols. In a highly complex compound he may need to think out the symbols, but in most formulas he can get it at once. It is the same with poetic symbols. And in both the chemical and the literary symbol there is a wealth of meaning in compact form.

Symbols are closely akin to literary allusions on

the one hand and to metaphors on the other. "Chariots of fire" comes from the Bible, whereas "arrows of desire" is metaphorical. Much modern poetry, notably that of William Butler Yeats and T. S. Eliot, depends greatly upon symbols. Here, for instance, is a passage from Eliot's "Gerontion": [3]

Here I am, an old man in a dry month,
Being read to by a boy, waiting for rain.
I was neither at the hot gates
Nor fought in the warm rain
Nor knee deep in the salt marsh, heaving a cutlass,
Bitten by flies, fought.

It would be a mistake to take literally the "dry month," the "hot gates," the fighting in the marsh. All are symbolic. The speaker means that he is living a dried-up life; he has not plunged into the struggles and turmoil of the world. Gerontion himself is probably a symbol of what Eliot regards as our dried-up civilization. This is not the place to attempt a complete analysis of the poem. It has been interpreted by Ruth Baily in *A Dialogue of Modern Poetry*. The purpose here is only to indicate the methods of symbolism. A justifiable criticism of such poetry is that it requires too much commentary; it does not speak clearly for itself. Yet with all its obscurity, it has a kind of emotional power. This can be seen by reading such a poem as Yeats's "Byzantium" without commentary, and then turning to explanations such as those of Elizabeth Drew [4] or

[3] "Gerontion" from *Collected Poems of T. S. Eliot*. Copyright, 1936, by Harcourt, Brace and Company, Inc.
[4] Elizabeth Drew and J. L. Sweeney, *Directions in Modern Poetry* (New York, W. W. Norton & Company, Inc., 1940), pp. 166–171.

David Daiches.[5] You will find that behind the symbols is an added wealth of thought and emotion.

2. *Connotative use of images.* Closely allied to symbolism is the technique of using images for their connotative effect. One thing is not compared specifically to another as in the simile; the image is simply given to create the appropriate emotion in the reader. We all use the method in some degree. When a man mashes his thumb he may use some such expression as, "Hell fire!" He is not comparing anything to the fires of hell; he is merely using a phrase which carries with it the appropriate emotional connotation. In fact most swearing is the use of this technique of conveying emotion. On a higher level Vaughan's "The World" shows how a poet uses the method:

The darksome statesman, hung with weights and woe,
Like a thick midnight-fog, moved there so slow,
    He did not stay, nor go;
Condemning thoughts, like sad eclipses, scowl
    Upon his soul,
And clouds of crying witnesses without
    Pursued him with one shout.
Yet digged the mole, and lest his ways be found,
    Worked under ground,
Where he did clutch his prey; but one did see
    That policy;
Churches and altars fed him; perjuries
    Were gnats and flies;
It rained about him blood and tears, but he
    Drank them as free.

That is not given as a picture we can visualize, unless we see it as a surrealist painting. The technique is in

    [5] David Daiches, *Poetry and the Modern World* (Chicago, University of Chicago Press, 1940), pp. 181–185.

fact related to surrealism. But anyone reading the poem thoughtfully gets the sense of the deviousness of statesmen, of the blood and tears resulting from their schemes. Phrase after phrase and image after image carries the same connotation: "midnight-fog," "sad eclipses," the mole working under ground, "clutch his prey," "gnats and flies." The effect is cumulative like a series of oaths or name-calling all adding up to the same thing.

Vaughan was a seventeenth-century poet of the school we call "metaphysical." Their aim as described by T. S. Eliot, was that of "trying to find the verbal equivalents for states of mind and feeling." Because this is the aim of many contemporary poets, they have often used the same methods. Here is a satiric stanza by Louis MacNeice, who uses the method somewhat more simply than do some moderns: [6]

It's no go my honey love, it's no go my poppet;
Work your hands from day to day, the winds will blow the
　　profit.
The glass is falling hour by hour, the glass will fall for ever,
But if you break the bloody glass you won't hold up the
　　weather.

Here both the idea of profitless work and that of a falling barometer express the poet's feeling that the present social order is doomed. The idea is put not in the form of logical reasoning but is given by the images.

In "The Hollow Men" T. S. Eliot gives us a series

[6] Louis MacNeice, "Bagpipe Music," *Poems 1925–1940* (New York, 1940). Reprinted by permission of Random House, Inc.

of images designed to carry his mood of disillusion with his own time: [7]

I

We are the hollow men
We are the stuffed men
Leaning together
Headpiece filled with straw. Alas!
Our dried voices, when
We whisper together
 Are quiet and meaningless
As wind in dry grass
Or rats' feet over broken glass
In our dry cellar. . . .

III

This is the dead land
This is the cactus land
Here the stone images
Are raised, here they receive
The supplication of a dead man's hand
Under the twinkle of a fading star. . . .

This is of course only part of the poem. It concludes:

This is the way the world ends
This is the way the world ends
This is the way the world ends
Not with a bang but a whimper.

You will note that Eliot has not tried to give us proof or even examples of the decadence of the civilization he condemns; nor has he tried to present a logical argument based upon cause and effect or philosophical theories. If you look for facts and logic, the poem

[7] "The Hollow Men" from *Collected Poems of T. S. Eliot.* Copyright, 1936, by Harcourt, Brace and Company, Inc.

is incomprehensible. But if you catch the connotations of his imagery: "filled with straw," "wind in dry grass," "cactus land," "stone images," "fading star," you begin to get the meaning of the poem. It gives us a state of mind and feeling. It is of course quite possible that it is not the world which ends with a whimper, but Mr. Eliot.

Contrast this method of picturing a decadent period with Auden's: [8]

Get there if you can and see the land you were once proud
    to own
Though the roads have almost vanished and the expresses
    never run:

Smokeless chimneys, damaged bridges, rotting wharves
    and choked canals,
Tramlines buckled, smashed trucks lying on their side
    across the rails . . .

Far from where we spent the money, thinking we could
    well afford,
While they quietly undersold us with their cheaper trade
    abroad . . .

Shut up talking, charming in the best suits to be had in
    town,
Lecturing on navigation while the ship is going down.

Drop those priggish ways for ever, stop behaving like a
    stone:
Throw the bath-chairs right away, and learn to leave ourselves alone.

If we really want to live, we'd better start to try;
If we don't, it doesn't matter, but we'd better start to die.

[8] W. H. Auden, "Get There If You Can," *Poems* (New York, 1934). Reprinted by permission of Random House, Inc.

Here Auden has given us a realistic, if exaggerated picture of an industrial repression, has suggested the causes, and told us what to do about it. This is an adaptation of the characteristic methods of prose or of Tennyson's "Locksley Hall," from which he borrows (with some mangling) the verse form. It has the advantage of clarity; it is less subtle than the methods of metaphysical poetry. This is not to argue that one method is better than the other; both have been used in good poetry.

3. *Free association.* A recent variant of the metaphysical technique grows out of one of the methods of psychological investigation. This is the use of "free association." An idea or a theme is presented in a series of images and phrases that follow one another in the mind. Like metaphysical poetry the aim is to represent a state of mind or feeling. For instance "moon" might immediately suggest "June," which in turn may suggest "roses"; these may suggest "hay fever." A poet might choose to write about roses, or the moon, or conceivably, about hay fever. He could, by means of his logical faculty, discard some of the related suggestions and give us a poem like Herrick's: [9]

> Roses at first were white
> Till they could not agree
> Whether my Sapho's breast
> Or they more white should be.
>
> But being vanquished quite,
> A blush their cheek bespread;
> Since which, believe the rest,
> The roses first came red.

[9] Robert Herrick, "How Roses Came Red."

Here quite obviously the compliment which the poet had in mind controlled his selection of images and phraseology; he discarded all extraneous suggestion. We have a neatly wrought artistic creation, but do not get the shifting lights and shadows characteristic of human emotion. In Eliot's "The Hollow Men" the images have more of the quality of actual thought processes. Hollow men and stuffed men are logically incompatible, but such a sequence is quite characteristic of the way things follow one another in the mind. Thus Eliot gives us the flow of thought of J. Alfred Prufrock: [10]

I grow old. . . . I grow old. . . .
I shall wear the bottoms of my trousers rolled.

Shall I part my hair behind? Do I dare to eat a peach?
I shall wear white flannel trousers, and walk upon the beach.
I have heard the mermaids singing, each to each.

I do not think that they will sing to me.

Prufrock's dislike of growing old suggests to him the idea of adopting new styles of clothing, of combing his hair differently. But age also suggests to him the need for being careful about what he eats. Walking upon the beach brings up the idea of mermaids. They are a symbol to him of the world of adventure. Prufrock knows he will not go adventuring; elsewhere he has said, "I have measured out my life with coffee spoons." The whole poem gives a superb portrait of

[10] "The Love Song of J. Alfred Prufrock" from *Collected Poems of T. S. Eliot*. Copyright, 1936, by Harcourt, Brace and Company, Inc.

a man bound by social usages, overcareful about trifles, timid, and a bit ironic. All this is given in the flow of images through Prufrock's mind.

4. Suggestion and implied meaning. Such poetry is not always easy reading. The poet does not usually tell us what conclusions to draw; he is not interested in conclusions, but in states of feeling. It is a revolt against the overexplicit moralizing of Wordsworth, Tennyson, and Browning. Many modern poets agree with Keats in his dislike of poetry with too obvious a design upon us. More is asked of the reader. He is not a mere passive listener; he is expected to bring into play his own imaginative and creative powers. He must fill in the gaps, must feel the emotions. Wordsworth could lecture: [11]

> Enough of science and of art,
>   Close up those barren leaves,
> Come forth and bring with you a heart
>   That watches and receives.

The modern poet is more likely to try to get us to feel whatever impulse he himself has experienced. Thus Auden writes: [12]

> Consider this our time
> As the hawk sees it or the helmeted airman. . . .
> Pass on, admire the view of the massif
> Through plate-glass windows of the Sport Hotel;
> Join there the insufficient units
> Dangerous, easy, in furs, in uniform
> And constellated at reserved tables

[11] Wordsworth, "The Tables Turned."
[12] W. H. Auden, "Consider This Our Time," *Poems* (New York, 1934). Reprinted by permission of Random House, Inc.

Supplied with feelings by an efficient band
Relayed elsewhere to farmers and their dogs
Sitting in kitchens in the stormy fens.

He does not tell us what conclusions to draw from this consideration although there are hints in such a line as, "Supplied with feelings by an efficient band." The whole picture is of course one of the surface life of the upper classes, a life Auden thinks barren and decadent. Some of the same theme appeared in his "Get there if you can, and see the land you were once proud to own." For as with many poets, one poem helps to explain another. That is one weakness of anthologies: we cannot see all sides of a poet's thought.

The condensed metaphor is characteristic of much recent verse. Prufrock's statement, "I have measured out my life with coffee spoons," is really a double image: one suggesting a life of afternoon teas; the other implying that Prufrock has only sipped life.

5. *Literary allusion.* Along with symbolism and implied meanings, modern poets often use literary allusion. Prufrock says: [13]

No! I am not Prince Hamlet, nor was meant to be;
Am an attendant lord, one that will do
To swell a progress, start a scene or two,
Advise the prince; no doubt an easy tool,
Deferential, glad to be of use,
Politic, cautious, and meticulous;
Full of high sentence, but a bit obtuse;
At times, indeed, almost ridiculous—
Almost, at times, the Fool.

[13] "The Love Song of J. Alfred Prufrock" from *Collected Poems of T. S. Eliot.* Copyright, 1936, by Harcourt, Brace and Company, Inc.

To get the full meaning of that, one must have some knowledge of Shakespearean plays, the parts played by the attendant lords and fools. Back of these lines are Rosencrantz and Guildenstern, Polonius, Osric —possibly the Fool in *King Lear*. "Full of high sentence" echoes Chaucer's description of the Clerk of Oxford. Eliot is especially rich in literary allusion, often to little known works. His own notes are necessary to an understanding of such a poem as *The Waste Land*.

MacNeice in a stanza of his own, uses the line: "We are dying, Egypt, dying." [14] This is an echo of Anthony's words in Shakespeare's play. Remembering the context of the original line, we realize that Mac-Neice wants us to recall the dying Anthony saying farewell to Cleopatra, and to transfer something of the same mood to the situation in his own poem.

A more subtle use of literary sources is to take a stanza form with definite connotations. Thus Wordsworth in writing about Robert Burns, used Burns's characteristic form, the rhyme couee, and Shelley wrote his elegy on Keats in the Spenserian stanza that Keats himself had loved, and sometimes used. We have seen how Auden, writing an attack on the society of his day, used the form of Tennyson's "Locksley Hall," a poem of social criticism.

Or the poet may use a form for its ironic contrast with the material. C. Day Lewis thus takes Marlowe's

[14] Louis MacNeice, "Song: The Sunlight on the Garden," *Poems 1925–1940* (New York, 1940). Reprinted by permission of Random House, Inc.

idyllic pastoral, "The Passionate Shepherd to His Love" for: [15]

> Come live with me and be my love
> And we will all the pleasures prove
> Of peace and plenty, bed and board
> That chance employment may afford.
>
> I'll handle dainties on the docks
> And thou shalt read of summer frocks:
> At evening by the sour canals
> We'll hope to hear some madrigals.

And he takes a Christmas carol as his model for: [16]

> Oh hush thee, my baby,
> Thy cradle's in pawn:
> No blankets to cover thee
> Cold and forlorn.
>
> The stars in the bright sky
> Look down and are dumb
> At the heir of the ages
> Asleep in a slum.

There are other reminiscences here too: "the heir of the ages," comes from Tennyson, who was describing the fortunate English child as contrasted with the benighted children of the tropics. The method is a form of parody, but the purpose is not to make fun of the

[15] C. Day Lewis, "Come Live with Me," *Collected Poems: 1929–1933* (New York, 1935). Reprinted by permission of Random House, Inc.

[16] C. Day Lewis, "Oh Hush Thee My Baby," *Collected Poems: 1929–1933* (New York, 1935). Reprinted by permission of Random House, Inc.

original; instead the poet is ironically showing how different his own time is from the happier world (he thinks) of the older poet. Unless one gets the literary allusion, he will miss some of the meaning.

It is probably unfortunate that so many modern poets rely so much upon books rather than upon life for their images. Of course poets have always used the literature of the past: *Beowulf* contains many references to other Germanic tales; Spenser and Milton are filled with classical allusions; for that matter most traditional poetry uses them freely along with references to Biblical stories and famous earlier literary works. This causes little difficulty because these things are a part of the knowledge of most educated persons. Even writers like Shakespeare, who never went to college, knew these stories and legends. The trouble with modern poetry is that the allusions are too esoteric, that is, known to only a limited group, sometimes as with Eliot, only to the poet himself. But admitting this as a serious limitation, we must recognize some of these obscure poets as able artists who have something important to say. One cannot fully understand the 1920's without some knowledge of Eliot's *The Waste Land,* nor of England of the 1930's without reading Day Lewis, Auden, Spender, and MacNeice. Even people who do not like their work, find it important. One may not like *Das Kapital* or *Mein Kampf,* but no educated person dare be ignorant of them.

6. *Revolt against grammar.* A further cause of obscurity is the tendency to depart from standard grammatical forms and sentence patterns. Browning sometimes did this, but Gerard Manley Hopkins carried it

still further. Here is a fragment giving us the mood
aroused in him by storm winds: [17]

> Strike, churl; hurl cheerless wind, then; heltering hail
> May's beauty massacre and wisped wild clouds grow
> Out of the giant air; tell Summer No,
> Bid joy back, have at the harvest, keep Hope pale.

In order to gain vigor Hopkins has dispensed with
articles and prepositions. It might have been clearer
had he written:

> The wind like a churl, comes
> Bringing cheerless days and heltering hail,
> Destroying the beauty of May flowers.
> The wild clouds grow out of the air,
> Which like a giant holds back the summer and its joys,
> And injures the growing grain:
> Man feels hopeless.

That is only an approximate translation. It may be
clearer, but it is vastly less forceful than the original,
and it carries less emotional content. The original read
with a little imagination, proves to be less difficult than
it seems at first.

Wyndham Lewis explains the reason for this technique: [18]

> I sabotage the sentence! With me is the naked word.
> I spike the verb—all parts of speech are pushed over on
>   their backs,

[17] "Fragment: Strike Churl" from *Poems of Gerard Manley
Hopkins* (New York, 1931), p. 88. By permission of Oxford University Press.

[18] Wyndham Lewis, "The Song of the Militant Romance," *One
Way Song* (London, Faber and Faber, Ltd. Publishers, 1933).

I am the master of all that is half-uttered and imperfectly
   heard.
Return with me where I am crying out with the gorilla and
   the bird.

Day Lewis uses the technique to condemn the upper
class: [19]

> Getters not begetters; gainers not beginners;
> Whiners, no winners; no triers, betrayers;
> Who steer by no star, whose moon means nothing.
> Daily denying, unable to dig;
> At bay in villas from blood relations,
> Counters of spoons and content with cushions
> They pray for peace, they hand down disaster.

Like Hopkins' verse this has vigor. Probably it is a
technique useful for special purposes, but unsuited to
quiet themes; it lacks variety. The reader gets tired
of being shouted at.

Values and Dangers in These Methods

Many of the methods we have been considering
have been attacked by critics. Max Eastman, for instance, calls this "the cult of unintelligibility." Other
able critics admire and defend such poetry. In this
connection, one point of view must be mentioned, that
summed up in MacLeish's line: "A poem should not
mean but be." The theory is probably allied to George
Moore's doctrine of "pure poetry": the theory that too
much intellectual content destroys the emotional force
of a poem. It is held that a poem can communicate

[19] C. Day Lewis, "Getters Not Begetters," *Collected Poems: 1929–
1933* (New York, 1935). Reprinted by permission of Random
House, Inc.

emotion without being completely understood. There is at least some truth in this; a drowning man shouting for help may not enunciate clearly, but people usually understand what he means. Of course the shouting bather may only have lost his pants. Thus some recent poems communicate the poet's discomfort without making it quite clear whether he is drowning or has been merely nipped by a crab.

The reader, however, must be careful not to dismiss all difficult poetry as unintelligible. A knowledge of the methods and aims of the writers will do much to clear up obscure meanings. Very often the difficulty is present because the poet is dealing with complex ideas and emotions—in other words with very important matters. It would be a foolish psychologist who would study only simple emotion and uncomplicated behavior. A person who reads only easy verse is missing a lot which goes on.

V

Prose Style

To lump everything that is not poetry into a category called prose is unfortunately like the British habit of calling all non-Britons "natives," or our American one of calling all other peoples "foreigners." Yet the difference between an educated Chinese and an Australian bushman is scarcely greater than that between the King James translation of the Bible and, say, Bruce Barton's religious writing, or between the "Gettysburg Address" and a speech by Boss Hague. Furthermore, as was shown in the preceding chapter, the dividing line between prose and poetry is not always clear-cut. Certain kinds of prose have marked poetic qualities such as music and vivid imagery. In fact the difference between poetry and prose is often not of kind but of degree. Thus many of the things we ask for in first-rate poetry are required also of prose.

The Function of Prose

Perhaps the element which most often sets off the two is that of function. Coleridge believed that the first aim of poetry was pleasure rather than truth. It might present truth, the same truth as other sorts of writing, but that was not its primary aim. If that is true, then we might say that prose has for its primary object the presentation of truth, or more simply, the communication of ideas. Its first appeal is to the intellect rather than to the emotions. Thus both a poet and an essayist might write on the evils of war, but we would expect the poet to create an emotional effect: horror, perhaps, or loathing, or sympathy. He should cause us to experience something of his own emotional understanding of what war is. The essayist might do all this too, but we should expect him first of all to give us some factual material—anything from an example to statistics—material which can be grasped by the mind and reasoned about.

Differs from poetry. Both the poet and the prose writer may tell the same story. For instance, the Arthurian romances have been presented in both styles. But the poet is more likely to dwell on the emotional and aesthetic content of the story; the prose writer on what took place. Note, by the way, that some tales in verse are not poetry in the modern, limited sense of term, and therefore more closely resemble prose in their emphasis on fact and event. The medieval verse narrative, *Havelok the Dane,* is no more poetic than the prose tales of Malory. The difference in emphasis between poetry and prose can be illustrated by comparing Malory's story of Arthur's last battle with the same story by Tennyson: [1]

And thus they fought all the long day, and never stinted till the noble knights were laid to the cold earth; and ever they fought still till it was near night, and by that time was there an hundred thousand laid dead upon the down.

[1] Sir Thomas Malory, *Morte d'Arthur,* Chap. IV.

Then was Arthur wood wroth out of measure, when he saw his people so slain from him. Then the king looked about him, and then was he ware, of all his host and of all his good knights, were left no more on live but two knights; that one was Sir Lucan the Butler, and his brother Sir Bedivere, and they were full sore wounded. "Jesu mercy," said the king, "where are all my noble knights become? Alas that ever I should see this doleful day, for now," said Arthur, "I am come to mine end. But would to God that I wist where that traitor Sir Modred, that hath caused all this mischief." Then was King Arthur ware where Sir Modred leaned upon his sword among a great heap of dead men. "Now give me my spear," said Arthur unto Sir Lucan, "for yonder I have espied the traitor that all this woe hath wrought."

After some discussion with Sir Lucan, Arthur seizes his spear and fights Sir Modred, wounding him mortally. But Modred has strength for one more blow:

And right so he smote his father Arthur, with his sword holden in both his hands, on the side of the head, that the sword pierced the helmet and the brain-pan, and therewithal Sir Modred fell stark dead to earth; and the noble Arthur fell in a swoon to the earth, and there he swooned ofttimes. And Sir Lucan the Butler, and Sir Bedivere, ofttimes heaved him up. And so weakly they led him betwixt them both, to a little chapel not far from the seaside. And when the king was there, he thought him well eased. Then heard they the people cry in the field.

Malory's prose is straightforward and rapid. Certainly he could not be called long-winded. Yet note how Tennyson has made the story more compact: [2]

So all day long the noise of battle rolled
Among the mountains by the winter sea;

[2] Tennyson, "Morte d'Arthur."

Until King Arthur's table, man by man,
Had fallen in Lyonesse about their Lord,
King Arthur; then because his wound was deep,
The bold Sir Bedivere uplifted him,
Sir Bedivere, the last of all his knights,
And bore him to a chapel nigh the field,
A broken chancel with a broken cross,
That stood on a dark strait of barren land.
On one side lay the Ocean, and on one
Lay a great water, and the moon was full.

Then spake King Arthur to Sir Bedivere:
"The sequel of to-day unsoldiers all
The goodliest fellowship of famous knights
Whereof this world holds record. Such a sleep
They sleep—the men I loved. I think that we
Shall never more, at any future time,
Delight our souls with talk of knightly deeds,
Walking about the gardens and the halls
Of Camelot, as in the days that were."

Obviously this tells us less of what happened than
did Malory. It contains more description, and the emotional content, the sorrow over departed happiness,
is heightened. The details of the scene: "a broken
chancel with a broken cross," "a dark strait of barren
land," are keyed to the mood of Arthur's speech. The
poet strove for a unified effect. The prose writer also
can strive for a unified effect, a blend of scene and
mood, but he is likely to do so only secondarily. In so
far as Malory does these things, he uses them to reinforce his tale; Tennyson uses the tale as a framework
for the mood and emotion he wishes to create.

So marked a difference in purpose is by no means
always found. Poe's prose tales are often little more

than frames upon which he builds his emotional and descriptive effects. But whenever a prose writer strives chiefly for an aesthetic effect, he takes over many of the materials of the poet, such as rhythm, vivid imagery, compact diction, and words rich in emotional connotation.

When, like Malory, the prose writer is chiefly concerned with conveying information, his work has a strong factual content. Thus Malory tells us about Sir Lucan the Butler because he was a part of the original story; whereas Tennyson, in the interests of effectiveness, leaves him out. Malory is careful to tell the exact way in which Arthur was wounded—through the helmet and the brain-pan; Tennyson does not. In other words the poet uses the principle of selection to a much greater extent than does the prose writer.

Historical Development

More important for our purposes than the often subtle differences between poetry and prose is a study of some of the elements of good prose, and of the differences between prose styles.

1. *Anglo-Saxon.* Appearing much later than poetry as a literary form, prose was much later in reaching a high degree of development. The prose of Shakespeare's day, for instance, is far below the quality of Elizabethan poetry. The structure of Malory's prose is typical not only of its own time, but of undeveloped prose in all ages. Note the large number of compound sentences. One idea is added to another by means of *and* or simply by being placed next to the preceding

one. The Anglo-Saxons used the same method. Here
is a passage from the *Chronicle:*

877. In this year came the army into Exeter from Ware-
ham, and the ship army sailed around the west, and
then they met a storm at sea, and there perished 120
ships at Swanick; and the king Alfred after providing
the army with horses, rode with the warriors as far
as Exeter, and could not overtake them from behind
before they were at their fort where no man was able
to reach them, and they yielded him their hostages
as many as he would have, and swore many oaths
and then kept good peace, and then at harvest time
the army fared to Mercian land, and some yielded
to Ceolwulf, and some separated from it.

2. *Elizabethan.* That sounds not unlike a school-boy
composition or even a freshman theme. Its weakness
lies not only in its monotony, but in a lack of clarity;
pronouns and clauses are not always clear in their ref-
erence. The problem became more acute after English
dropped most of its inflectional endings. When a noun
has the same form for nominative, dative, or accusa-
tive, the writer must place it carefully so as to make
clear its meaning. Because of the monotony of the
earlier prose, the Elizabethans tried to develop more
elevated and literary style. To do this they added ornaments: alliteration, elaborate figures of speech, and unusual words. To give it a structure they tried balance
and antithesis. Here, for example, is a passage from
Lyly's *Euphues,* a book which set a literary fashion:

This queen being deceased, Elizabeth, being at the age
of twenty-two years, of more beauty than honor, and yet

of more honor than any earthly creature, was called from a prisoner to be a prince, from the castle to the crown, from the fear of losing her head, to be supreme head. . . .

This is she that, resembling the noble queen of Navarre, useth the marigold for her flower, which at the rising of the sun openeth her leaves, and at the setting shutteth them, referring all her actions and endeavors to him that ruleth the sun. This is that Caesar, that first bound the crocodile to the palm tree, bridling those that sought to rein her. This is that good pelican, that to feed her people spareth not to rend her own person. This is that mighty eagle, that hath thrown dust into the eyes of the hart that went about to work destruction to her subjects, into whose wings although the blind beetle would have crept, and so being carried into her vest, destroyed her young ones, yet hath she with the virtue of her feathers, consumed that fly in his own fraud. She hath exiled the swallow that sought to spoil the grasshopper, and given bitter almonds to the ravenous wolves that endeavored to devour the silly lambs, burning even with the breath of her mouth like the princely stag, the serpents that were engendered by the breath of the huge elephant, so that now all her enemies are as whist as the bird Attagen, who never singeth any tune after she is taken, nor they being so overtaken.

This is the fashion Shakespeare satirized by causing the dotard Polonius to talk so. And like Queen Gertrude, the reader demands "more matter and less art." Obviously the far-fetched metaphors drawn from the zoölogical misinformation of the time were designed more to impress Queen Elizabeth than to convey information.

3. *Seventeenth century.* The writers of the next century abandoned the absurdities of the Euphuistic style, but they too tried to give prose a greater dignity than everyday speech. In place of native words they used

sonorous Latin derivitives, and instead of the short,
simple statements of conversation, they wrote elaborate and involved sentences. They strove for rhythm
and music more stately than that of daily use. Bacon,
Jeremy Taylor, Sir Thomas Browne, and Milton all
wrote this noble and sonorous prose, as in Browne's
Hydriotaphia, Urn-Burial:

Pyramids, arches, obelisks, were but the irregularities
of vain-glory, and wild enormities of ancient magnanim-
ity. But the most magnanimous resolution rests in the
Christian religion, which trampleth upon pride, and sits
on the neck of ambition, humbly pursuing that infallible
perpetuity unto which all others must diminish their
diameters, and be poorly seen in angles of contingency.

Pious spirits who passed their days in raptures of fu-
turity, made little more of this world than the world that
was before it, while they lay obscure in the chaos of pre-
ordination, and night of their fore-beings. And if any have
been so happy as truly to understand Christian annihila-
tion, ecstasies, exolution, liquefaction, transformation, the
kiss of the Spouse, gustation of God, and ingression into
the divine shadow, they have already had an handsome
anticipation of heaven; the glory of the world is surely
over, and the earth in ashes unto them.

Even those who have not shared Browne's mystic
experience can get an emotional effect from his music. It is like listening to a Latin mass. But such prose
is unsuited to the rough and tumble of business and
politics. It requires leisure to savor it on the tongue.
Its appeal is limited to men of learning. Even some
college students cannot understand it.

4. *Eighteenth century.* Thus in the eighteenth century, with the development of newspapers and jour-

nals designed for more general circulation, a simpler prose developed. Some critics call this the beginning of modern prose. Certainly Defoe's style has gone a long way toward that of today. In proposing an academy for women, he wrote: [3]

I have often thought it one of the most barbarous customs in the world, considering us as a civilized and a Christian country, that we deny the advantages of learning to women. We reproach the sex every day with folly and impertinence; while I am confident, had they the advantages of education equal to us, they would be guilty of less than ourselves.

One would wonder, indeed, how it should happen that women are conversible at all, since they are only beholding to natural parts for all their knowledge. Their youth is spent to teach them to stitch and sew or make baubles. They are taught to read, indeed, and perhaps to write their names or so, and that is the height of woman's education. And I would but ask any who slight the sex for their understanding what is a man (a gentleman, I mean) good for that, is taught no more?

Defoe, however, was not a university man, and he was accustomed to writing for the middle-class reader. More fashionable writers like Addison, while not preserving the more extreme qualities of seventeenth-century style, did not adopt the colloquial diction and informal sentence structure of Defoe. Note, for instance, such phrases as "stitch and sew" and "good for," and the use of parenthetical remarks as in conversation. There is none of this in Addison's discussion of taste: [4]

[3] Daniel Defoe, *The Education of Women* from *An Essay on Projects.*
[4] Joseph Addison, *The Spectator,* No. 409.

Gratian very often recommends fine taste as the utmost perfection of an accomplished man. As this word arises very often in conversation, I shall endeavor to give some account of it, and to lay down rules how we may know whether we are possessed of it, and how we may acquire that fine taste of writing which is so much talked of among the polite world.

Most languages make use of this metaphor, to express that faculty of mind which distinguishes all the most concealed faults and nicest perfections in writing. We may be sure that this metaphor would not have been so general in all tongues, had there not been a very great conformity between that mental taste, which is the subject of this paper, and that sensitive taste which gives us a relish of every flavor that affects the palate. Accordingly we find there are as many degrees of refinement in the intellectual faculty as in the sense which is marked out by this common denomination.

Here there are few concrete words. Literary phrases like "endeavor to give some account" are substituted for the ordinary "try and tell"; "denomination" for "name." Yet despite the formality and lack of vividness there is an ease and especially, a clarity which caused this style to remain current for a hundred and fifty years. Written prose set the pattern for conversation instead of following it. Thus Dr. Johnson, a great admirer of Addison, not only patterned his essays upon the *Spectator*, but tried to talk like it. He once remarked that a play, *The Rehearsal*, "had not wit enough to keep it sweet"; then fearful of being quoted in such colloquial speech, changed it to "has not vitality enough to preserve it from corruption."

Johnson, with a Boswell to take down his remarks, felt the necessity of making his conversation memorable. Most men have talked more naturally. And as Bonamy Dobrée has shown, it is this conversational style which has become the basis for modern prose. Here, for instance, is a fairly typical passage from Arnold's *Culture and Anarchy,* and another from his letters:

And religion, the greatest and most important of the efforts by which the human race has manifested its impulse to perfect itself,—religion, that voice of the deepest human experience,—does not only enjoin and sanction the aim which is the great aim of culture, the aim of setting ourselves to ascertain what perfection is and to make it prevail; but also, in determining generally in what human perfection consists, religion comes to a conclusion identical with that which culture,—culture seeking the determination of this question through *all* the voices of human experience which have been heard upon it, of art, science, poetry, philosophy, history, as well as of religion, in order to give a greater fulness and certainty to its solution,— likewise reaches.

That is all one sentence. Such a sentence requires careful planning and revision. In sentence structure and diction it is not far different from one of Addison's: note for instance such words as "manifested" and "ascertain" where one would say "shown" and "find out." Then turn to Arnold's letter written about the same time:

My dearest Mother—I don't think this will go to-night, but I will write it, to make sure of its reaching you before you leave Fox How. . . .
I shall see dear old Budge, who perhaps will come home on Saturday to stay Sunday. I think I told you he had, at my instigation, buckled to and got a *Bene* for his syntax,

in which, as it was quite new to him, he had been finding great difficulty. The merit of Budge is, though he is an idle dog, that he can, and will, answer to a call. He says he likes school very much better now, and that he is getting on very well. . . .

I have been bothered composing a letter to Sainte Beuve, who has sent me the new edition of his poems. Every one is more sensitive about his poems than about his other works, and it is not on Sainte Beuve's poems that his fame will rest; indeed, except in songs, I do not see that French verse *can* be truly satisfactory. I myself think even Molière's verse plays inferior to his prose ones.

Not only are the sentences shorter here, but there is a complete difference in word choice, even slang of the day like "buckled to" and "idle dog." Even in the discussion of literature the words are simple. "Been bothered" is a thoroughly colloquial and straightforward phrase. This, however, was not the official literary prose of the time.

It is one of the mysteries of literature that prose writers were so slow in following the lead of the poets. As far back as 1800, Wordsworth had argued for a natural word order and a "language really used by men." Arnold himself, in one of his most famous poems wrote: [5]

> Strew on her roses, roses,
>   And never a spray of yew!
> In quiet she reposes;
>   Ah! would that I did too!
>
> Her mirth the world required;
>   She bathed it in smiles of glee.
> But her heart was tired, tired,
>   And now they let her be.

[5] Matthew Arnold, "Requiesat."

Her life was turning, turning,
   In mazes of heat and sound.
But for peace her soul was yearning,
   And now peace laps her round.

Her cabined, ample spirit,
   It fluttered and failed for breath.
To-night it doth inherit
   The vasty hall of death.

I am afraid that in prose he might have written something like:

After a fashionable existence devoted, despite her inclinations to the contrary, to mundane affairs and to the vivacity of her immediate circle, her magnanimous spirit, unable longer to endure its mortal habitation, has sought ampler realms.

Modern Prose

Since Arnold's day at least two things have happened to prose. To a large extent, the more informal, conversational style, such as Arnold himself used in letters, has become more common; and second, there has been a tendency toward the concrete and the specific. Thus Stuart Chase begins an essay on trends in population: [6]

There are more than a million empty desks in the elementary schools of America this year. In 1930 the total enrollment was 21,300,000; in 1938 it had fallen to about 20,000,000. Consider what these empty desks signify in terms of jobs for teachers, school building programmes,

[6] Stuart Chase, "Population Going Down," *The Atlantic Monthly,* February, 1939.

textbook sales, schoolbudgets, taxes, public finances. This is only the beginning.

And in an article in *Fortune* on "Youth in College" we find a characteristic paragraph beginning: [7]

In all this discussion of college social attitudes it should be kept in mind that nothing has gone so deep as to kill old prejudices. The "thing to do" is often more important than any real issues. For instance, at Yale, Walter Millis's *Road to War* is a popular book. It has helped to create an anti-foreign-entanglement feeling. Yet influential undergraduates refused to turn out for the Peace Strike simply because the demonstration was run by the "black men." This brings us to the question of snobbery. It still prevails at Yale, Harvard, and Princeton, though the girls' colleges no longer feel strongly about social prestige on the campus. At the wealthier men's liberal-arts colleges the campus is divided into the "white men" and the "black men." The black men are known as "drips" and "meatballs." (Ten years ago the word was "wet smack"; twenty years ago, the "unwashed.")

Note that this is a discussion of social groups in relation to a nation's culture—a similar problem considered by Arnold in *Culture and Anarchy*. This is no mere change of surface fashion; it represents a change in ways of thinking. The greater informality may be little more than a reflection of current manners—in other words a contemporary convention. Pomposity has come to be identified with stuffed shirts. But beneath the surface are two of the great forces of our time: empiricism and democracy.

[7] "Youth in College," *Fortune*, June, 1936.

Influence of empiricism. Empiricism is the method of thinking which seeks knowledge by observation and experiment—the method of science. It is the reverse of the type of philosophy which starts from general beliefs and principles. Addison said that he was going to lay down the rules of taste; Arnold stated that religion was the most important of the efforts made by the human race in trying to perfect itself. Both statements run counter to the empirical methods. Addison is going to lay down general principles; Arnold does lay down one. This leads to what Dobrée calls the "door banged" prose style, ". . . it consists not of thoughts closely followed, not of ideas suggested, but of utterances, of pronouncements . . . we feel as though we were on parade receiving orders."

Chase, on the other hand, starts out with the specific facts from which he is going to draw conclusions. The *Fortune* article, it is true, states a generalization, but a generalization immediately supported by specific facts such as the effect of Millis' book at Yale. Like many another recent magazine article, this one was based upon a survey—the application of the empirical method to social phenomena. The effect upon prose style has been immense. The most marked change has been the greater concreteness and specificness. Thus in discussing university education, Newman wrote sentences like this: [8]

It is a great point then to enlarge the range of studies which a University professes, even for the sake of the students; and, though they cannot pursue every subject which is open to them, they will be the gainers by living

[8] John Henry, Cardinal Newman, *The Idea of a University.*

among those and under those who represent the whole circle.

The *Fortune* article discussing a similar point reads: [9]

It was student curiosity that led to the widespread inflation of sociology, history, and economics departments. But the increases in the number of instructors in the social sciences has not been sufficient to assuage the inquisitiveness of the thinking 5 or 10 per cent of the undergraduates. In many colleges—North Carolina, Minnesota, Princeton, Yale, and Dartmouth, to pick random examples—the cerebrating 5 to 10 per cent has, on its own initiative, invited guest speakers such as General Hugh S. Johnson, Harold Laski, Westbrook Pegler, Norman Thomas, Arthur Krock, Raymond Moley, George Soule, Jr., Fiorello La Guardia, Edmund Wilson and Jouett Shouse.

Specificness cannot go much further than that. It is similar to Walt Whitman's technique in such a poem as "I Hear America Singing." Writers today are less likely to discuss "literature" or "classics" than to write: [10]

A great book deals with these problems and is as good today as it was yesterday. It is a book that is contemporary in any age and in any place. [So far pretty general and pretty trite.] What are the best sellers? *Uncle Tom's Cabin? Horatio Alger? Peck's Bad Boy? Gone with the Wind?* Not compared with the Bible, *The Divine Comedy, Don Quixote, Hamlet,* or *Paradise Lost.* These books have been read by millions in every language. It may be estimated, so conservatively as to raise no dispute, that the

[9] "Youth in College," *op. cit.*
[10] Milton Mayer, "Socrates Crosses the Delaware," *Harper's Magazine,* June, 1939.

Iliad had been read over the last 3,000 years by 25,000,000 people. Last year's best sellers are forgotten or out of print.

This is not cited as particularly good prose, but as writing characteristic of our time. In addition to its specific quality, it has the short, elliptical sentences of conversation. But it is the use of specific terms which gives this not very original idea its effectiveness.

Influence of democracy. In addition to empiricism as a force in modern prose, there is another which is probably a phase of democracy. Prose is no longer addressed as in Addison's time, or even Arnold's, to gentlemen with a classical education. Nor is that the background of many of the writers. We ask of our novelists that they write of their experience with all sorts of human beings, and of our social critics that they know life as well as books. As a result the doings and ideas of the common man have become an increasingly vital part of literature. This is part of the realistic method which Chaucer used, and Mark Twain, but which did not become characteristic of American literature until the work of Dreiser, Sherwood Anderson, and Sinclair Lewis. Its most important effect upon prose style has been in language. More than at any time since Chaucer, the writers are using the actual language of men.

This can be seen in the passage quoted from *Fortune* where the current slang terms play an important part. Mark Twain in a celebrated essay on James Fenimore Cooper wrote in this fashion: [11]

[11] Mark Twain, "Fenimore Cooper's Literary Offenses," *A Defense of Harriet Shelley and Other Essays* (New York, Harper & Brothers, 1918).

We must be a little wary when Brander Matthews tells us that Cooper's books "reveal an extraordinary fulness of invention." As a rule I am quite willing to accept Brander Matthews literary judgments and applaud his lucid and graceful phrasing of them; but that particular statement needs to be taken with a few tons of salt. Bless your heart, Cooper hadn't any more invention than a horse; and I don't mean a high class horse, either; I mean a clothes horse.

Phrases like "taken with a few tons of salt," "bless your heart," and "clothes horse" come directly from the speech of the people. Twain's style was not then the accepted one for literary criticism. But today we find Max Eastman writing of "a literary style . . . of wearing false hair on the chest," and Mencken calling Robert Frost "a Whittier without the whiskers."

The important thing about such remarks is not their satirical quality, for that can be found in all sorts of prose, but rather that they are in the style of the "wisecrack"—in other words the phraseology of the common man.

This change of fashion demonstrates a growing belief that the common man's language has a vitality and freshness not found in more literary phraseology. It is a doctrine which has the scholarly support of books like Mencken's *The American Language* and Robertson's *The Development of Modern English.*

This belief that the vigor of a language comes from the people and not from the dictionary is especially characteristic of writers of fiction. Here, for instance, is Stephen Vincent Benét's description of a New Hampshire farmer: [12]

There was a man named Jabez Stone, lived at Cross Corners, New Hampshire. He wasn't a bad man to start with, but he was an unlucky man. If he planted corn, he got borers; if he planted potatoes, he got blight. He had good enough land, but it didn't prosper him; he had a decent wife and children, but the more children he had, the less there was to feed them. If stones cropped up in his neighbor's field, boulders boiled up in his; if he had a horse with the spavins, he'd trade it for one with the staggers and give something extra. There's some folks bound to be like that, apparently. But one day Jabez Stone got sick of the whole business.

That, as Benét intended it, might be much as a New Hampshireman would tell a story. It is a language full of concrete images: borers, potatoes, boulders, and spavined horses. The rhythms are those of conversation. Story tellers have always tended to use concrete images but not quite in the same way. Scott described the Saxon serf, Wamba, thus: [13]

Beside the swineherd, for such was Gurth's occupation, was seated, upon one of the fallen Druidical monuments, a person about ten years younger in appearance, and whose dress, though resembling his companion's in form, was of better materials, and of a more fantastic description. His jacket had been stained of a bright purple hue, upon which there had been some attempt to paint grotesque ornaments in different colors. To the jacket he added a short cloak, which scarcely reached half-way

[12] "The Devil and Daniel Webster" from *Thirteen O'Clock*, published by Farrar & Rinehart, Inc. Copyright, 1926, by Stephen Vincent Benét.

[13] Sir Walter Scott, *Ivanhoe*.

down his thigh; it was of crimson cloth, though a good deal soiled, lined with bright yellow; and he could transfer it from one shoulder to the other, or at his pleasure draw it all around him, its width, contrasted with its want of longitude, formed a fantastic piece of drapery.

That is thoroughly concrete and filled with images, but the phraseology—"resembling his companion's," "fantastic description," "want of longitude," "piece of drapery"—is that of books rather than of conversation. So too are the rhythms, more stately and formal than those used by Benét. The contrast of the two styles is another indication of the steady progress of prose since the Renaissance toward a flexible and vivid medium based upon the actual living speech.

Qualities of Prose

1. Vivid diction. This does not mean that all good prose belongs to modern times. Throughout the various changes of fashion there have appeared certain enduring qualities, qualities of good prose in all ages. Take the matter of vivid diction. It is common knowledge that the prose of the King James translation of the Bible has had immense influence on English style. Professor Lowes, in his study of the nature of this prose, speaks of the Biblical vocabulary as "compact of the primal stuff of our common humanity—of its universal emotional, sensory experiences." But Martin Luther, talking of the same thing, says, "Paul's words are alive, they have hands and feet; if you cut them they bleed." Luther is not only talking about concrete diction; he is using it. He is much closer to the Biblical style than is Lowes. For as Lowes demonstrates, the Hebrew writers "instead of merely naming an emotion . . . reproduce the physical sensation that attends it."

O God, thou art my God; . . . my soul thirsteth for thee, my flesh longeth for thee, in a dry and thirsty land where no water is; . . .[14] As the hart panteth after the water brooks, so panteth my soul after thee.[15]

The abstraction *faith* in God becomes: [16]

The Lord is my shepherd; I shall not want. He maketh me to lie down in green pastures; he leadeth me beside the still waters.

And the generality *spring*: [17]

For, lo, the winter is past, the rain is over and gone; the flowers appear on the earth; the time of the singing of birds is come, and the voice of the turtle is heard in our land; the fig tree putteth forth her green figs, and the vines with the tender grape give a good smell.

That is all but poetry. It has vivid imagery, words rich in connotation, music, intensity, and emotional power. In fact it is the prose translation of a poem. Thus we see that the best prose has many of the qualities of the best poetry. Good writing of all kinds has much in common. Lincoln, for instance, could take this Biblical prose style and use it in a political speech: [18]

[14] Psalms XLII:1.
[15] Psalms LXIII:1.
[16] Psalms XXIII:1.
[17] The Song of Solomon II:11–13.
[18] Abraham Lincoln, "Second Inaugural Address," March 4, 1865.

With malice toward none; with charity for all; with firmness in the right, as God gives us to see the right, let us strive on to finish the work we are in; to bind up the nation's wounds; to care for him who shall have borne the battle, and for his widow, and his orphan—to do all which may achieve and cherish a just and lasting peace among ourselves, and with all nations.

In addition to concrete words rich in emotional suggestion such as "nation's wounds," "widow," "orphan," there are abstract words like "malice," "charity," "right," "peace." But they are abstractions so familiar and so definite in meaning that they too have emotional coloring. Compare with that the typical phraseology of the scholar, for instance of John Dewey: [19]

The alpha and omega of this preparation is realization that no matter what our sentiments and our preferences, or our loyalties, to the causes which we believe are at stake in the European war, our primary obligation and all-controlling responsibility and loyalty are to the freedom and objectivity of inquiry and communication for which the universities are supposed to stand; and to which we, as constituents of the universities, are morally committed.

Like Lincoln's Second Inaugural address, that too is an appeal to hold fast to an ideal in time of crisis. But "all-controlling responsibility" and "objectivity of inquiry" are not moving words.

2. *Music.* Lincoln's prose has another quality which Dewey's lacks—music. The music of prose is more difficult to analyze than that of poetry. It does not, as a

[19] John Dewey, "Higher Learning and the War," *Bulletin,* American Association of University Professors, October, 1939.

rule, fall into recognized patterns like iambic or anapestic; it does not depend upon rhyme or alliteration;
it has not stanzaic form. In fact prose patterns which
are too regular are not regarded as the finest. The
music of prose should be varied and subtle, and above
all should bear a relation to the meaning. Strongly
marked rhythm belongs to writing with strong emotional content rather than to intellectual analysis.
Sonorous polysyllables are more suited to stately occasions than to humble matters. Contrast the musical
effects of the two following passages. In the first the
widowed Ruth is speaking to her husband's mother: [20]

And Ruth said, Intreat me not to leave thee, or to return from following after thee: for whither thou goest, I
will go; and where thou lodgest, I will lodge: thy people
shall be my people, and thy God my God: Where thou
diest, will I die, and there will I be buried: the Lord do so
to me, and more also, if ought but death part thee and me.

In the second John Milton is petitioning Parliament
for freedom of press: [21]

Methinks I see in my mind a noble and puissant nation,
rousing herself like a strong man after sleep, and shaking
her invincible locks. Methinks I see her as an eagle mew-
ing her mighty youth, and kindling her undazzled eyes at
the full midday beam; purging and unscaling her long-
abused sight at the fountain itself of heavenly radiance;
while the whole noise of timorous and flocking birds, with
those also that love the twilight, flutter about, amazed at
what she means, and in their envious gabble would prog-
nosticate a year of sects and schisms.

[20] Ruth I:16–17.
[21] Milton, *Areopagitica.*

Here is all the difference between a folk song and a triumphal march—yet each is suited to the idea and the emotion presented. Ruth speaks in quiet, mournful rhythms; Milton in oratorical crescendos. The diction of both is filled with images, but Milton's is more sonorous because of the greater number of polysyllables.

Then contrast the subtle and varied music of those two passages with Robert Ingersoll's remarks on Napoleon: [22]

I saw him walking upon the banks of the Seine contemplating suicide. I saw him at Toulon; I saw him putting down the mob in the streets of Paris; I saw him at the head of the army in Italy; I saw him conquer the Alps and mingle at Ulm, and Austerlitz; I saw him in Russia where the infantry of the snow and the cavalry of the wild blast scattered his legions like winter's withered leaves; I saw him at Leipsic in defeat and disaster—driven by a million bayonets back upon Paris—clutched like a wild beast— banished to Elba. I saw him escape and retake an empire by the force of his genius. I saw him upon the frightful field of Waterloo, where Chance and Fortune combined to wreck the fortunes of their former king, and I saw him at St. Helena, with his hands crossed behind him, gazing out upon the sad and solemn sea.

I thought of the orphans and widows he had made, of the tears that had been shed for his glory, and of the only woman he ever loved, pushed from his heart by the cold hand of ambition; and I said I would rather have been a French peasant and have lived in a hut with a vine growing in the rays of the autumn sun; I would rather have been that poor peasant with my loving wife by my side, knitting as the day died out of the sky, with my children

[22] Robert Ingersoll, *Lectures* (Philadelphia, David McKay Company, 1935).

about my knee and their arms about me; I would rather have been that man and gone down to the tongueless silence of the dreamless dust than have been that imperial personification of force and murder.

It was this sort of thing which led Edgar Lee Masters to speak of "the rhinestone rhythms of Ingersoll." At first glance or to the untutored eye they give the effect of real jewels. Let us see why they are not. Notice the repetition of the same devices: "I saw," "I would rather"; the parallel prepositional and participial phrases. Scene is piled upon scene. Figures of speech are elaborate: "infantry of the snow and the cavalry of the wild blast"; alliteration is frequent; and almost every noun is qualified with an adjective: "withered leaves," "frightful field," "sad and solemn sea," "loving wife," "tongueless silence," "dreamless dust." Few of those adjectives add anything to the meaning; they are there for effect. That is the real trouble with the passage—a too obvious striving for effect by means of certain musical and rhetorical devices. The ideas are subordinated to the elaborate style. For after all Ingersoll is simply trying to tell us that he would have preferred to be a French peasant than Napoleon. Or perhaps he was more interested in trying to tell us that Robert Ingersoll was a great orator.

3. *Clarity.* If so, he was violating the basic principle of all good prose. For however valuable are such things as imagery and music, they are not the most important qualities of prose. They are chiefly valuable in so far as they reinforce the one essential—clarity. For the first purpose of prose should be the conveying of ideas, the presentation of truth. This is the best rea-

son for the concrete, specific word instead of the vague
abstraction; the distinct image rather than the foggy
one. Even music and rhythm can reinforce an idea
with the complementary emotion. Lincoln is easier to
understand than John Dewey because he uses a simpler diction and the rhythm of his prose is one natural
to the eye and ear.

Good rhythm has a physiological basis. Photographs
of eye movements show that the skilful reader moves
his eyes with a regular rhythm across the page, taking
in three or four words at a glance. It is quite possible
that the ear too follows speech with a certain rhythmic
pattern. Certainly the speaker's rhythm is governed by
the rhythm of breathing. Notice how difficult it is to
grasp Dewey's long periods: "our primary obligation
and all-controlling responsibility and loyalty"; "to the
freedom and objectivity of inquiry and communication for which the universities are supposed to stand."
How much easier to grasp or to speak Lincoln's
phrases: "with malice toward none"; "with charity for
all"; "with firmness in the right, as God gives us to see
the right."

4. *Faulty diction.* Lack of clarity most often comes
from faulty diction. Compared to vague or inaccurate
use of words, grammatical errors are a minor sin. Sam
Goldwyn's statement, "Include me out," is vastly better than Hoover's description of prohibition as "an
experiment noble in purpose" or Coolidge's "I do not
choose to run." What Hoover seems to have meant was
that the purpose of prohibition was noble, but that
the result was not, and Coolidge is thought to have
meant that he would not seek the nomination, but

would accept it. The fact that the real meaning of both statements was hotly debated for a long time is proof of their lack of clarity. Both probably belong to the class Theodore Roosevelt called "weasel words"—words that sneak instead of coming out into the open. They may be good politics, but they are not good prose.

5. *Abstractions*. Abstractions, even learned abstractions, are another source of fogginess. Thus an essayist starts off: [23]

The conflict between the traditionalists or, as they have recently begun to be described, the essentialists, and the progressives in education is more than the batracho-myomachis which it appears to be to the laymen and to a large part of the profession of teachers. It is a conflict between idealism in one form or another and pragmatism, between classicism and romanticism, between those who believe that the experience of the race has something to contribute to the enlightenment of the individual in the modern world and those who stress the primacy of immediate experiencing by the individual in and through the environment in which he lives.

I defy anyone to interpret that unless he already has some knowledge of the row between the two groups of pedagogues. *Idealism,* whatever that means, and *pragmatism* are certainly not in conflict; the men who hold those theories may be. Abstractions can fight no battles. Even as far back as 1360 the author of *Piers Plowman* realized this and turned the abstraction "covetousness" into a cheating merchant, and "gluttony" into the town drunkard. Worse still, many of

[23] I. L. Kandel, "Prejudice the Garden Toward Roses," *The American Scholar*, Winter, 1938–1939.

these words have numerous meanings. At the start of
a course on romantic poetry, I find it necessary to
spend an hour or two explaining the various meanings
of *romanticism,* and trying as best I can to tell what I
mean by it. What the writer of that paragraph means
by the word I have no idea.

The passage shows another common fault of scholarly diction, a use of technical jargon. When a scientist
developed the word "hormone" from a Greek verb,
he did so because he needed a new word to name a
new discovery. Terms like "fluid" or "secretion" had
too many shades of meaning for his purpose. But
"primacy of immediate experience by the individual
in and through the environment in which he lives
[where else could one live but in his environment?]"
is more long-winded and less definite than the words
for which it substitutes. It means "learning from life
rather than from books." The old proverb states it
clearly enough: "Experience is a dear school, but fools
will learn in no other."

This sort of diction was used by Wilkins Micawber
who told David Copperfield that "the twins have
ceased to derive their sustenance from the maternal
fount" when he meant they were weaned. In like
fashion the professors of education say "optimal
methodology" for "best methods," "quintile" for
"fifth," "orientation course" for "beginners' course";
economists, "submarginal saturation point" for "contented with little," "increments of satisfaction" for
"better pleased"; and English teachers, "corpus" for
"body" (of literature), and "passim" for "here and
there." Barbers, however, have largely given up the

term "tonsorial parlor," and undertakers less frequently advertise themselves as "morticians."

6. *Sentence patterns.* This kind of pig Latin, because it has no relation to the spoken language, usually leads to a sentence pattern equally foreign to natural speech. The weak passive is common: "attention is accorded" instead of "we study" and "is affected by" for "gives" or "offers." Statements are loaded with elaborate qualifying phrases—the sort of thing which Van Wyck Brooks calls "the Indian giver style," which takes back everything it grants. Brooks rightly accuses James Russell Lowell of writing in this manner: [24]

> It was, perhaps, this very sensibility to the surrounding atmosphere of feeling and speculation, which make Rousseau more directly influential on contemporary thought (or perhaps we should say sentiment) than any writer of his time. And this is rarely consistent with enduring greatness in literature. It forces us to remember, against our will, the oratorical character of his works. . . . Rousseau was in many respects—as great pleaders always are—a man of the day, who must needs become a mere name to posterity, yet he had in him some not inconsiderable share of that principle by which man eternizes himself.

Lowell was both a Yankee and a scholar so that grudging affirmatives like "not inconsiderable" and the cautious "perhapses" came natural to him. I almost wrote "may have come natural." A hardened scholar would have written "may have to some extent been a part of his heritage, and of course of his training, as they were for so many men whose backgrounds were to some extent not unlike his."

[24] James Russell Lowell, "Rousseau," *Literary Essays.*

There are many other kinds of bad prose: the mosaic style, made up of phrases from literature:

It is in the month of April, said "learned Chaucer" in the *Canterbury Tales,* that folk long to go on pilgrimages and to seek strange strands.

The writer is merely getting around to the fact that he likes to go hiking in the spring. But he tries to make the statement impressive by the use of Chaucerian phrases and "learned Chaucer" from Basse's verse on Shakespeare. As we would expect, the same writer talks of dawn as "the eyelids of the day" [Milton] and when it is hot, thinks "on the frosty Caucasus" [Shakespeare]. Good prose does not read like a page of Bartlett's *Quotations.*

7. *Derivative style.* Related to this, a sort of poor relation which didn't get to college, is the style filled with trite phraseology, usually derived from the newspapers. "Along this line," "colorful ceremony," "limped into port," "informed sources," "marking the occasion," "major factor"—the whole colorless collection of the freshman theme writer and college journalist.

Or a style may be derived from some one writer: Hemingway, James Joyce, Thomas Wolfe—a few years ago it was Cabell or Mencken. It is a moot question whether any highly mannered style is a good one, but there is no disagreement upon the point that imitative styles are bad. For one thing the imitative writer usually imitates the ideas as well as the style of his model. It could hardly be otherwise, for if a writer has created a style to suit a certain mood or idea, that style cannot usually be transferred to other moods or ideas. Thus Hemingway's brutal, hard-hitting phrases do not fit Pollyanna themes; nor would Wolfe's Niagara of words do in a book like *The Late George Apley.*

8. *Timelessness of good prose.* All prose, as we have seen, develops in part out of the time in which it was written, out of the manners and thoughts of that time. The elaborate styles of decoration and behavior of Elizabethan times are mirrored in Lyly's Euphuism; the hard-boiled post-war period in Hemingway's hard-bitten sentences. But really good prose so well expresses its meaning that it transcends its time; it speaks clearly to all men. Thus Hemingway found in the stately and rhythmic seventeenth-century prose of John Donne an idea so vividly stated that he took it as the keynote of his book *For Whom the Bell Tolls:* [25]

No man is an iland, intire of it selfe; every man is a piece of the *Continent,* a part of the *maine;* if a clod bee washed away by the *sea, Europe* is the lesse, as well as if a *Promentorie* were, . . . any man's *death* diminishes *me* because I am involved in *Mankinde;* and therefore never send to know for whom the *bell* tolls; It tolls for *thee.*

That is clear, vivid, and musical. So too is the unlettered appeal of Vanzetti before he was condemned to die: [26]

Well, I have already say that I am not guilty of these two crimes, but I never commit a crime in my life,—I have never steal and I have never kill and I have never spilt

[25] John Donne, "XVII Meditation," *Devotions upon Emergent Occasions.*

[26] From *The Letters of Sacco and Vanzetti* edited by Marion Edman Frankfurter and Gardner Jackson. Copyright, 1928, by the Viking Press, Inc., New York.

blood, and I have fought against the crimes, and I have
fought and I have sacrificed myself to eliminate the crimes
that the law and the church legitimate and sanctify.

This is what I say: I would not wish to a dog or to a
snake, to the most low and misfortunate creature of the
earth—I would not wish to any of them what I have had
to suffer for things that I am not guilty of. I am suffering
because I am a radical and indeed I am a radical; I have
suffered because I am an Italian, and indeed I am an
Italian; I have suffered more for my family and for my
beloved than for myself; but I am so convinced to be right
that if you could execute me two times, and if I could be
reborn two other times, I would live again to do what I
have done already.

The value of such writing grows out of its sincerity;
it accomplishes the chief purpose of prose, to convey
an idea. So too does Lincoln's letter in reply to Horace
Greeley's ranting editorials in the New York *Tribune*.

My paramount object in this struggle is to save the
Union, and is not either to save or destroy slavery. If I
could save the Union without freeing any slave, I would
do it; and if I could save it by freeing all the slaves, I
would do it; and if I could save it by freeing some and
leaving others alone, I would also do that . . . I have
here stated my purpose according to my view of official
duty, and I intend no modification of my oft-expressed
personal wish that all men, everywhere, could be free.

There are no weasel words there; no rhinestone oratory, no borrowed jewelry. It has style, the emphatic
style of an earnest man speaking his mind. Like the
best prose in all ages, it left no doubt of its meaning,
and a nation understood that meaning.

In our own time another President also spoke clearly to a troubled nation: [27]

I must tell you tonight in plain language what this undertaking means to you—to your daily life.

Whether you are in the armed services; whether you are a steel worker or a stevedore; a machinist or a housewife; a farmer or a banker; a storekeeper or manufacturer —to all of you it will mean sacrifice in behalf of country and your liberties.

You will feel the impact of this gigantic effort in your daily lives. You will feel it in a way which will cause many inconveniences.

You will have to be content with lower profits from business because obviously your taxes will be higher.

You will have to work longer at your bench, or your plow, or your machine.

Let me make it clear that the nation is calling for the sacrifice of some privileges but not for the sacrifice of fundamental rights. Most of us will do that willingly.

That kind of sacrifice is for the common national protection and welfare; for our defense against the most ruthless brutality in history; for the ultimate victory of a way of life now so violently menaced.

A half-hearted effort on our part will lead to failure. This is no part-time job. The concepts of "business as usual" and "normalcy" must be forgotten until the task is finished. This is an all-out effort—nothing short of all-out effort will win.

[27] Address by President Franklin D. Roosevelt, December 16, 1941.

VI

Fiction

Story-telling is as old as mankind, but prose fiction as an art is of comparatively recent date. As we have seen in the discussion of poetry, our ancestors tended to put their best stories into verse such as ballads and epics. The novel in anything like modern form did not appear in England until the eighteenth century. The development of the short story came in the nineteenth. Prose fiction existed before 1700, of course: the Arthurian romances of Malory; the Italian novella like Boccaccio's *Decameron;* the long and incredible French romances mentioned by Alexander Pope; the Spanish tales of rogues and vagabonds and their counterpart in Elizabethan England. But for various reasons, too complex to discuss here, none of these became very important. They bear much the same relation to modern fiction as the miracle plays and interludes bear to the drama: pioneering work which did not develop into an important art form.

One reason for this was the lack of a reading public. Most people were illiterate. Ballads and epics because of their verse form could be committed to memory and handed down from generation to generation. It therefore became the custom to think of literature and poetry as synonymous, so that writers of Chaucer's day quite naturally put their tales, even bar-room stories, into verse. Probably similar causes had led to the creation of poetic drama.

By the beginning of the eighteenth century many of the middle-class could read; the writers had a potential market. Whether or not Defoe is to be called the first novelist, he was the first to cash in on this market. Not realizing, perhaps, that people would accept fiction as such, he pretended that *Robinson Crusoe,* (1719) *Moll Flanders,* (1722) and *Roxana,* (1724) were factual narratives. Then in 1740, Samuel Richardson, a middle-aged printer, wrote *Pamela,* a work many critics regard as the first genuine novel. The book was designed to furnish instruction in female letter writing and morals. The letters by the heroine, a servant girl named Pamela, tell of her successful resistance to seduction by her employer, and her eventual reward—marriage to the same employer. Despite this unpromising material the book has many of the qualities we shall later take up as elements of good fiction. Defoe had given chiefly an extremely realistic account of a series of incidents happening to a character; Richardson had a plot, and he went much further than Defoe in character portrayal.

But both Defoe and Richardson gave the novel a direction it has never lost. Dr. Johnson in 1750 described it thus: [1]

The works of fiction, with which the present generation seems more particularly delighted, are such as exhibit life in its true state, diversified only by accidents that daily

[1] Samuel Johnson, "The Modern Novel," *The Rambler,* No. 4.

happen in the world, and influenced by passions and qualities which are really to be found in conversing with mankind. . . . Its province is to bring about natural events by easy means, and to keep up curiosity without the help of wonder: it is therefore precluded from the machines and expedients of heroic romance, and can neither employ giants to snatch away a lady from the nuptial rites, nor knights to bring her back from captivity; it can neither bewilder its personages in deserts, nor lodge them in imaginary castles.

There have been exceptions to this, of course, but the prevailing current throughout the two hundred years since Richardson has been that described by Dr. Johnson.

The short story has also followed this current. Many attempts have been made to define the difference between the short story and novel, but none of them is quite satisfactory. Both are prose fiction; both deal with the same sort of people, places, and happenings. It is customary to think of the short story as one built upon a single incident or situation; whereas the novel may have a number. However Conrad's *Typhoon* and Hemingway's *For Whom the Bell Tolls* are novels each dealing with a single situation, and Katherine Brush's short story "Night Club" introduces a half-dozen plots. Perhaps the definition of the bewildered student is as good as any: "A short story is a story that's short."

We shall not here be concerned with the short story and the novel as separate types. At best there is a very shadowy boundary line between a long short story like Mark Twain's "The Man That Corrupted Hadleyburg" and a brief novel like Edith Wharton's *Ethan Frome* or Steinbeck's *The Moon Is Down*. Sometimes the term *novelette* is used to describe this sort of work, but its definition, too, boils down to a question of comparative length. Our job, therefore, will be to seek those elements common to short story, novelette, and novel. We shall be concerned with the qualities which make up first-rate fiction—with fiction as an art form.

Purpose of Fiction

The primary purpose of fiction is entertainment. There may be additional aims, and in some stories one of these aims may be paramount, but taken as a whole, fiction is first of all entertainment. Richardson could have written essays on female virtue instead of a novel; Harriet Beecher Stowe could have done magazine articles on slavery, and Hemingway could have written a factual study of the Spanish Civil War. They chose instead to create characters, to construct a plot, to use suspense and dialogue—all artistic devices designed to please and entertain the reader. A story often contains much factual material; some modern novels are based upon years of research, but the writer in attempting to embody his material in an art form is thereby attempting to give his audience a kind of pleasure which does not come from mere presentation of fact.

There are, however, many different levels of entertainment. The story of "Goldilocks and the Three Bears" does not give the same sort of pleasure as does *War and Peace*. As children grow up, they demand increasingly complex stories about more interesting people than Jack the Giant-Killer and Chicken Little.

As adults mature intellectually, they demand more of a tale than exotic scenery, an ingenious plot, and a happy ending. The Cinderella theme still keeps appearing in the women's magazines, but not in the collections of good short stories. The reader must learn not to be taken in by luscious illustrations, a slick style, and a Hollywood stage set. Poor girls do sometimes crash expensive parties and meet and marry men who are wealthy, handsome, and young, but not often enough to make it a good risk to leave Lebanon, Pennsylvania with that end in view. In other words stories of that sort are designed for readers who prefer a dream world to an honest portrayal of life.

The Test of Fiction

What then is the test of a good work of fiction? Katherine Fullerton Gerould suggests that "a story should carry more than its own weight." Certainly most first-rate fiction does that. This more-than-its-own-weight may consist in giving us a deeper understanding of human nature. That is the particular excellence of a book like *Vanity Fair*. We see therein the forces that mold personality, the motives that cause people to act as they do. Or the writer may study the workings of the mind and the emotions from within as Virginia Woolf does. Novelists can give us an understanding of other times and other places in the way that Scott recreated the Middle Ages or Pearl Buck has given us an understanding of China and its people. Today this more-than-its-own-weight frequently takes the form of social criticism. This is not new:

Dickens did it constantly; Mrs. Stowe did it in *Uncle Tom's Cabin,* but since about 1920 it has become one of the dominant elements in fiction.

Both Poe's "The Pit and the Pendulum" and Faulkner's "A Rose for Emily" are horror stories. In both the suspense and the atmosphere are skilfully built up. Poe's story, however, is essentially sterile; we are no wiser or kindlier for having read it. Faulkner's, on the other hand, reveals in the horrible, twisted character of Emily the effects of a social system. Behind the tragedy there is the overweening pride in family, the tyranny of a strong-willed father supported by social custom, the decadent small town with few eligible men, the cult of respectability. "A Rose for Emily" is first of all a good horror story, and as such is entertainment, but it is also a social document. A work of art is not economics or sociology or psychology, but it may shed light on any or all of these.

Arrowsmith and a radio serial soap opera both can show the struggles of a young physician, but *Arrowsmith* also shows us some of the forces in American life which commercialize science and learning. We understand our own time better for having read it. Hemingway's *For Whom the Bell Tolls* has a very simple plot—the efforts of a Loyalist soldier to blow up a bridge at the right moment. In the telling of this, Hemingway gives us the panorama of a nation at war: the hates and heroisms, the cruelties and sacrifices, the taste and smell and feel of that experience.

Fictional truth. This brings us to the problem of truth in fiction. From Dr. Johnson on down, literary critics have demanded in the representation of people and events a fidelity to those principles we see in life itself. From daily observation we know that evil men seldom become good over night. On the basis of many feminine reports on the subject, Dorothy Dix assures her readers that the magic of a wedding ceremony does not change a rake into a tame husband. We know, usually from personal experience, that Pallas Athene does not step down from Olympus to get us out of the messes we create for ourselves, whatever she may have done in Homer's day. Nowadays we cannot count on the Red Sea to conveniently open for our armies and drown those of our enemies. It has even become rare for long forgotten uncles to arrive from China in the nick of time to save the family homestead from the sheriff. Long lost relatives are much more likely to turn up broke and with an appetite for whiskey. It is chiefly in the women's magazines that hard-working widows with five children, still beautiful and witty at forty-five, are wooed by both the wealthy business man and the humorous, pipe-smoking college professor who loves dogs and children.

There are, however, various kinds of truth. There is observed fact, the material of the newspaper and the court of law. A great deal of modern fiction is a reworking of this kind of material. This was the basis of Defoe's novels. Few writers since have equalled his use of factual detail: the names of actual streets and alleys, the shillings and pence in business dealings and robberies; the specific articles rescued from a ship, or the number of people who died in a plague. Material of this sort has an important place in fiction, especially in modern work designed for an audience materialistic in temper and used to the careful detail of movie sets.

There is also another sort of truth, not easily defined. It is the sort of truth one finds in Shakespeare's plays. For instance, we need not believe in ghosts to accept the appearance of Banquo's spectre at the banquet and to see therein a true portrayal of Macbeth's sense of guilt. In Stephen Vincent Benét's famous short story, "The Devil and Daniel Webster," we meet not only Satan himself, but an entire jury brought back from Hell for the trial of Jabez Stone. No one in our day believes that any of this could happen, but readers have recognized in the story some profound truths about the American ideals. Perhaps no factual biography of Daniel Webster has so successfully caught those qualities of the man which made him a legend in his own time.

Probably no one believes that such a place as Shangri-La exists, but in *Lost Horizon,* James Hilton, like the creators of all the fictional utopias before him, used the imaginary setting as a means for social criticism and constructive thinking. Sir Thomas More's *Utopia* never existed nor did those of Plato and Francis Bacon, and William Morris, and Edward Bellamy and Frederick Tappan Wright; yet all of these men in their fictional worlds have told us a great deal about our real one.

Imaginative truth. We might call this sort of thing *imaginative truth* as opposed to factual truth. Whatever its name, it has been and is an extremely important element in fiction, whether prose or verse, dramatic or narrative. Take out of our literature *Hamlet,*

Paradise Lost, The Ancient Mariner, "The Christmas
Carol," "Rip Van Winkle," "Dr. Jekyll and Mr. Hyde,"
Our Town along with all the works we have just been
discussing, and we realize how much knowledge of
human nature and the nature of the world itself we
should lose.

This does not mean that any ghost-story or tall tale
presents a profound truth. Far from it. The exploits
of Tarzan and Superman are sterile adventure yarns,
giving only a temporary escape from the world of fact.
To this class, too, belong many more pretentious
works: the Gothic novels of the eighteenth century;
the cloak and sword romances of Dumas and Stanley
Weyman and Sabatini; the thrillers of E. Phillips Oppenheim, or for that matter the pseudo-realistic romances of the pulp magazines. As a class the murder
mysteries belong to this literature of escape. This is
not to condemn them as unfit for human consumption;
it is merely to warn against accepting synthetic sweets
as nourishing food. Both candy and detective stories
are very pleasant additions to the diet, but indulged
in to excess produce excess fat of body and mind.

Nor is it enough for a story to be true, either factu-
ally or imaginatively. It must also be a work of art.
It must seem true. Wordsworth's "Idiot Boy," based
on an actual happening, seems more incredible than
Coleridge's *Ancient Mariner.* In the daily papers we
constantly read of incidents whose news value lies in
their unlikelihood—the believe-it-or-not sort of story.
There is the jobless man who finds ten thousand dollars in an old mattress in time to pay for his wife's
operation; the long separated twin brothers who meet

on the park bench; the laborer who inherits a duke-
dom; the chance discovery of a miracle drug. Such
things do happen. To that extent they are true. To
children they are no more incredible or unlikely than
the pot of gold at the end of the rainbow. But the sad
experience of adults is that they are not a normal part
of life. The very element that makes them newsworthy
makes them as a rule unsuitable for literature which
tries to picture life honestly.

Chance and coincidence do play a part in life, and
therefore have their uses in fiction. A chance meeting
or an accident can set in motion a series of events
which make a story. Those things happen often enough
in life to be a normal part of it. But the chance meeting or accident which solves a problem is much less
normal. Like the bridge hand with thirteen spades, it
is not to be counted on when one is losing. In drama
this is called the *deus ex machina,* the god from the
machine who was let down by pulleys to solve the
difficulties of the mortals on the stage. It is an infallible mark of a poor story.

Laws and conventions. A story is a work of art; not
merely a piece of reporting. And as in all the arts, that
of fiction has certain conventions. The writer consciously or unconsciously must abide by certain rules
of the game. As is pointed out in the chapter on this
subject, conventions in literature change from one
age to another, but this one against the solution of
problems by accident has remained fairly constant
throughout the centuries. In fact with our contemporary emphasis on fact and realism, the convention is
stronger than ever. The writer today must work out

his story in accord with laws almost as rigid as those for the solution of a problem in mathematics or the analysis of a chemical compound. He may not look up the answer in the back of the book.

These laws are not something that literary critics have dreamed up. They are those of economics, sociology, and psychology—especially psychology. That is why a character may not suddenly change his nature; it is opposed to the normal psychological processes. That is why in "Kneel to the Rising Sun" the half-starved sharecropper, Lonnie, betrays the Negro, Clem, to the lynching party. The forces of poverty, ignorance, and social pressure (economics and sociology) have made Lonnie a certain kind of person. In his case those forces are far too strong for him to overcome; the solution is inevitable.

Even imaginative stories must follow their own logic. In "The Devil and Daniel Webster" it would be unthinkable for Webster to refuse to plead a case before the devil himself, or to refuse a drink of applejack at the end. Daniel Webster was a certain kind of person and we feel that he would remain so in heaven or hell. It is possible, especially in a novel, to show a character changing from one kind of person to another, but this must happen logically through forces which produce the same sort of thing in life. Becky Sharp becomes more unscrupulous as she goes on; whereas her husband, Rawdon Crawley, ceases to be a rake because of his affection for Becky and for his son—and because he gets older. A person can go down hill under a series of misfortunes and follies as does Henchard in *The Mayor of Casterbridge*, or can develop and grow in a new and more favorable environment as does Strether in Henry James's *The Ambassadors*.

Elements of Fiction

Truth alone, whether factual or imaginative, does not make a work of fiction; it may only make a news item. To be a work of art a story must have additional elements. Traditionally there are *plot, setting,* and *character*. To these should be added *theme* and *style*.

1. *Plot*. Plot is not as important as it once was. It is usually thought of as a plan involving an exposition (who, when, where), an inciting force to set the action going; a rising action during which the reader is kept in suspense; a climax or turning point; and a dénouement or final unravelling. A short story tends to have a single action and a single climax; a novel often has several climaxes before the final one, and may have one or more sub-plots. But because real events do not follow so recognizable a pattern, some writers have discarded it in favor of the *cross-section-of-life* method. Here the writer may leave the action unfinished, the problem unsolved. Only as much of the story is told as will create the effect or develop the idea. In "Night Club" Katherine Brush gives us a glimpse of several actions, but does not show their conclusion. In this story, however, the reader can usually fill in for himself. In fact that is true of many stories of this sort; the perceptive reader can see where the action will lead.

The typical O. Henry story with its ingenious plot and surprise end is now outmoded. One reason is that

the writer too often had to falsify his material to produce the surprise. O. Henry's "The Cop and the Anthem" is typical. A tramp, in order to get into a warm
jail for the winter, breaks a store window, eats a meal
he cannot pay for, and so forth, but fails to achieve his
goal. Then listening to a church choir he decides to
reform, only to be run in for vagrancy. There is nothing inevitable about the action; it is purely a matter
of accident. The author simply set out to work a series
of surprises on the reader. Compare that with his much
better story, "A Municipal Report." There a murder
takes place for reasons which become obvious as the
story goes on. We do not expect the murder, but when
it comes we realize that given the characters and situation, it was a very probable result.

Many stories fall somewhere between the O. Henry
and cross-section-of-life patterns. They have a plot
which comes to a definite conclusion, but not a smash-
ing climax or surprise end. Such a story is Sherwood
Anderson's "I'm a Fool" or Hemingway's "The End
of Something." In both stories the action has come
to a final, irrevocable conclusion, but in neither case
has anything startling or unusual happened.

The basis of a plot of whatever nature is an unstable
situation. It may be caused by a character's falling in
love, losing his job, being in physical danger, or being
psychologically maladjusted. The reader is kept in suspense until the difficulty is solved in one way or another: losing the girl, getting married and living happily ever after; getting killed, or saving his life; going
crazy or getting over his maladjustment. Whatever
the result, at the end of a "plot" story the reader has

been told or led to imagine the outcome. Other things may afterwards happen to the characters, but that particular problem has been solved happily or unhappily for the persons involved.

2. *Setting.* Plot alone cannot make a good story. This is verified by the common experience of having someone tell the plot of a movie he has seen or a story he has read. No matter how good the original, the retelling is usually intolerably dull. One reason is that it lacks the accompanying details which give life and reality. That part of the detail which tells us when and where the story takes place is called setting. It may be given at the start or worked in as the plot unfolds. There is no best method.[2]

I got another barber that comes over from Carterville and helps me out Saturdays, but the rest of the time I can get along all right alone. You can see for yourself this ain't no New York City and besides that, the most of the boys work all day and don't have no leisure to drop in here and get themselves prettied up.

Thus begins Ring Lardner's famous story, "Haircut." In those few sentences we get the atmosphere of a small town barbershop, the background against which the story is developed. In the second paragraph of "The Sire de Maletroit's Door" Stevenson writes: [3]

It was September, 1429; the weather had fallen sharp; a flighty piping wind, laden with showers, beat about the township; and the dead leaves ran riot in the streets. Here

[2] Ring Lardner, "Haircut," *The Love Nest and Other Stories* (New York, Charles Scribner's Sons, 1926).

[3] Robert Lewis Stevenson, "The Sire de Maletroit's Door," *New Arabian Nights* (New York, Charles Scribner's Sons, 1882).

and there a window was already lighted up; and the voice of men-at-arms making merry over supper within, came forth in fits and was swallowed up and carried away by the wind. The night fell swiftly; the flag of England, fluttering on the spiretop, grew ever fainter and fainter against the flying clouds—a black speck like a swallow in the tumultuous, leaden chaos of the sky. As night fell the wind rose and began to hoot under archways and roar amid the tree-tops in the valley below the town.

Not only does this give us the setting, it creates the mood of the story. "A fine night for a murder," or at least for exciting adventure—that is what the reader is expected to feel.

The importance of setting varies. Take away the elaborate bizarre atmosphere of Poe's "Masque of the Red Death" and there is no story left. On the other hand Hemingway's "Twenty Grand" uses almost no scenery. In some stories the setting plays an important part in the action. Willa Cather's "Paul's Case" shows in detail the drab home which Paul hates and the artificial glitter of the theaters and hotels he longs for. These are the springs of his theft of money which leads to the final tragedy. One type of fiction, the "local color" story, of necessity gives much attention to setting. Skilfully drawn settings are an important element in good fiction. This involves accurately observed and vividly represented detail.

3. *Character.* More important in fiction as a whole than either plot or setting is characterization. It is usually by their people that the great novels live on from generation to generation. Fielding's *Joseph Andrews* has a rambling plot, marred by unrelated incidents and the use of chance and coincidence, but it

gives us the unforgettable Parson Adams. A list of great novels in English gives us a list of memorable people: there is Matthew Bramble in *Humphrey Clinker;* Uncle Toby in *Tristram Shandy;* the Bennet family in *Pride and Prejudice;* Becky Sharp in *Vanity Fair;* Dickens has a host of literary faults but he lives because of Sam Weller, Mr. Pickwick, Aunt Betsy Trotwood, Mr. Micawber, Uriah Heep, Grandfather Smalwee—a whole gallery of portraits. In America we have had Tom Sawyer, Huckleberry Finn, Colonel Sellers, Captain Ahab, Penrod, George F. Babbitt, Elmer Gantry, Scarlett O'Hara.

The short story is less likely to contain memorable characters. We more commonly find the portrayal of a single element in a person's nature, or see him at a single stage of his life. However even here there are some memorable persons: Jim Kendall in "Haircut," Susan in Ruth Sukow's "Susan and the Doctor," Paul in "Paul's Case," the boy in "I'm a Fool." Brief as is our sojourn with these people we feel that we know all about them, how they would act in a given situation.

Some characters, however, are merely types: the brave young knight, the Walter Scott heroine, the nagging wife, the rich man, and the radical. Denis de Beaulieu is this sort of character; he could be transferred into any adventure story, and would act in the same way. He is simply a reworking of the chivalrous young knight of medieval romance. Rhett Butler in *Gone with the Wind* is the clever and romantic scoundrel of a hundred novels and movies. He may be a pirate or a gypsy or a knight, but in whatever dress we find him he is always Clark Gable. A generation ago he was Douglas Fairbanks. This question is discussed further in the chapter on "Convention and Originality." The important thing is that a truly first-rate character portrayal should individualize the person. The reader should feel that he knows him in the way he knows the qualities and quirks of an intimate friend.

4. *Symbolic characters.* There is of course the character who is a symbol rather than an individual. Scrooge is not individualized to the same extent as Mr. Micawber. Stories like "Dr. Jekyll and Mr. Hyde," "Rip Van Winkle," "The Great Stone Face," "The Man Who Missed the Bus" are not dealing with human beings as we know them, but with the personification of qualities like miserliness or the evil and good in a single nature. When they are well done, such stories present imaginative rather than factual truth.

This matter of characterization is more than merely successful photography. A well-handled portrait is all to the good, but the finest literature does more than that; it shows us the mind and nature of the character. As we noted with *Hamlet,* Shakespeare by showing us the workings of Hamlet's mind and emotions, has revealed to us more about ourselves. In a different way Dickens showed to the men and women of his age, the twisted souls like Uriah Heep and the Murdstones produced by the Victorian cults of respectability and ostentatious piety. In George F. Babbitt, Sinclair Lewis showed a later age the shallowness resulting from a set of false values. Novelists like D. H. Lawrence and Sherwood Anderson have showed us the frustrations produced by sex and society. In fact many of our ablest modern novelists have been preoccupied with the fundamental problems of man's adjustment to his world. In the sufferings and strivings of their characters the writers of fiction have revealed our own struggle and strife. It is not only individuals who sit for their portraits, but mankind.

For as it seems to happen at times in society, the individual exists not as a unit, but as part of an organism. Thus the writer often tries to show us *Le Comédie Humaine* (perhaps best translated as "the human drama"). In France we find this in the work of men like Balzac (from whom we get the term), Romains, and Du Gard. In America Dos Passos is a good example of this. In *U.S.A.* his individuals are seen and understood as part of society as a whole.

5. *Theme.* This brings us to another element in fiction—theme. The term borrows part of its connotation from its use in music where it means the leading melody in a composition. In a story it means the dominant idea or emotion. It is one of the things which differentiates the telling of a mere series of events from a story. Amateur stories often lack it. For instance a student sometimes writes a narrative about a motor trip followed by a camping expedition in which someone nearly drowns or suffers some other mishap. There is no relation other than that of sequence between the various parts of the account. It is like a medley containing a waltz, a rhumba, and a hymn. On the other hand a novel like *Don Quixote* contains many unrelated adventures, but the theme is so clearly marked that it has given us the term *quixotic*. All the adventures show Don Quixote's unrealistic devotion to an

ideal. *Vanity Fair* tells the lives of a number of people besides Becky Sharp, but throughout all of them we get the recurrent theme which gives the book its name. *Main Street* is another novel whose title gives us the theme.

The theme of a story may be as simple as a song by Robert Burns: friendship, love won or lost, the tragedy of old age, humor, fear, or hate. In some stories, especially long novels, several minor themes may be introduced, but if they are skilfully handled they support and enrich the major theme. Thus though *Pride and Prejudice* is primarily the story of Elizabeth Bennet, the love affairs of two of her sisters show all the more clearly what sort of person Elizabeth is. Jane's namby-pamby nature and Lydia's flightiness throw into relief Elizabeth's vigor and good sense.

Some novelists use a counterpoint technique. In fact Aldous Huxley calls attention to this in his novel *Point Counterpoint* in which one set of events contrasts, yet blends with another set. A simple and familiar example of the method is found in Shakespeare's *The Merchant of Venice* where the love affair of Nerissa and Gratiano repeats in minor key that of Portia and Bassanio.

The important thing is that a work of fiction should at the end leave a dominant impression. *David Copperfield* for all its variety, leaves us with the sense that people are essentially kindly; that life despite its troubles is essentially good. The novel *Tobacco Road* had as its theme the evils of the share-cropper system. When the book was made into a play, the theme was confused by being partially turned into farce. It had the lack of unity of effect that might be produced by running *Esquire* cartoons of the mountain boys in a page of the *New Republic*.

6. *Point of view*. Thus theme is closely related to point of view. The point of view is the author's way of looking at his subject. The same theme can be treated in various ways. For instance the theme of business success is handled very differently in *The Saturday Evening Post* and in the novel *Babbitt*. Puppy love may be regarded as humorous or pathetic; jealousy as comic or tragic. Amateur writers often try to write a serious story with a sudden humorous twist at the end, thus confusing the theme by a shift of point of view. Only the most skilful writer is capable of presenting a theme from more than one point of view as Dickens often shows life as at once humorous and pathetic. In Thurber's short story "The Secret Life of Walter Mitty," we see the same thing. In *The Cream of the Jest* Cabell gives us the novelist, John Chartris, as a rather unpleasant person in daily life, but also John Chartris as a dreamer and artist, and then as a human being with tragic overtones.

7. *Treatment of theme*. It is perhaps here that many of the novels of "social significance" so often fall down; the theme is not sufficiently varied and enriched. For all its variety of scene and incident, Dos Passos' *U.S.A.* never for a moment varies the theme of the social and economic maladjustment of the times. Whether the characters work, get drunk, or make love; whatever their relations to one another, they do it as members of a class, as units of an industrial society. As a picture of certain phases of that society the book is excellent,

but as a picture of the U.S.A. it falls far short. The optimism and vision that made our industrial empire, the humor that our soldiers do not lose in the jungles of the East nor on the sands of Africa; the courage revealed in time of war—all of these are missing. There is no hint that the America of 1919–1932 could become the producing and fighting nation of 1942. Of a less pretentious book we should ask less, but the theme as announced is the United States of America. No one artist can catch the whole thing, but it is a theme which cannot be composed from one melody, nor played exclusively by the brass section.

To sum up then, a work of fiction requires a theme presented either from a single point of view or from well-integrated points of view; and the presentation must be adequate to the theme. Thackeray, for instance, realizing that his style and method were not suited to portraying war scenes, wisely let the Battle of Waterloo happen off stage. Walter Scott in praising the novels of Jane Austen said, "the big bow-wow strain I can do myself like anyone now going; but the exquisite touch, which renders ordinary commonplace things and characters interesting, from the truth of the description and sentiment, is denied me." In other words Scott recognized that different themes require different methods of treatment.

8. *Style.* Method of treatment is really another name for style. There is no such thing as a best style. It must however suit the story. Ring Lardner's extremely colloquial style is ideally suited to his stories of baseball players and travelling salesmen and barbers. Benét's "The Devil and Daniel Webster" has the

diction and sentence patterns of New Hampshire where the scene is laid. Thomas Wolfe's gushing eloquence reflects the emotional richness and vigor of his people. Katherine Mansfield, writing usually about persons of wealth and fashion, is restrained and highly polished.

A story may have too obvious or too mannered a style—too much striving for effect. Many critics find fault with Poe for this reason. Here, for instance, is a passage from his "Eleonora":

Suddenly these manifestations—they ceased; and the world grew dark before mine eyes; and I stood aghast at the burning thoughts which possessed, at the terrible temptations which beset me; for there came from some far, far distant and unknown land, into the gay court of the king I served, a maiden at whose beauty my whole recreant heart yielded at once—at whose footstool I bowed down without a struggle in the most ardent, in the most abject worship of love. What, indeed, was my passion for the young girl of the valley in comparison with the fervor, and the delirium, and the spirit-lifting ecstasy of adoration, with which I poured out my whole soul in tears at the feet of the ethereal Ermengarde? Oh, bright was the seraph Ermengarde! And in that knowledge I had room for none other. Oh, divine was the angel Ermengarde! And as I looked down into the depths of her memorial eyes, I thought only of them—and of her.

Note the pseudo-Biblical rhythms; the poetic phrases such as "mine eyes," "none other"; the inversions "bright was," "divine was"; the Hollywood use of superlatives: "burning thoughts," "terrible temptation," "most ardent," "most abject," "fervor and de-

lirium," "ethereal Ermengarde." Good style avoids
such obvious attempts to impress. That is one reason
James Branch Cabell has lost his vogue; his style is too
mannered, too obviously musical.

9. *Dialogue.* The question of style in general is
discussed in the chapter on prose. Two elements especially characteristic of modern fiction should, however, be mentioned here: dialogue and vividness. Dialogue in stories is not new; witness its use in many
children's tales of ancient vintage. However in recent
years it plays an increasingly important part in narrative. Such stories as Hemingway's "The Killers" and
"Twenty Grand" are told almost exclusively in dialogue. The effect is to make the reader feel he sees the
action happening; it is the technique of drama adapted
to the short story and novel.

There are a number of requirements of good dialogue. First of all it must sound like real conversation.
The bookish, stilted sentences of the Rover Boys sound
little like the talk of real boys. Whether anyone but
Dr. Johnson ever talked in the elevated style of characters in an eighteenth-century novel is impossible to
tell—probably not in everyday affairs. But however
people talked in the past, today they speak in sentence
fragments and elliptical phrases. They repeat themselves; they leave thoughts half finished. With the contemporary emphasis on realism, the writer of fiction
tries to reflect all this in his stories. In stories by
Dorothy Parker, Ring Lardner or Sinclair Lewis, note
how the writer catches the phrases, the actual rhythms
of American speech.

Dialogue should also characterize the speakers. Here, for instance, is George Milburn's picture of a dean talking to a freshman about low grades: [4]

"What's the trouble, Wingate? Tell me!"

"I don't know, sir, except I work at night and—"

"Oh, I see it here on your enrollment card now. Where do you work?"

"I work nights for Nick Pappas, down at the Wigwam."

"How many hours a night do you work?"

"Ten hours, sir. From nine till seven. The Wigwam stays open all night. I eat and go to eight o'clock class when I get off."

"Very interesting, Wingate. But don't you suppose that it would be advisable to cut down a bit on this outside work and attend a little more closely to your college work? After all, that's what you're here for, primarily—to go to college, not work in a cafe."

"I couldn't work fewer hours and stay in school, sir. I just barely get by as it is. I get my board at the Wigwam, and I pay my room rent, and I've been paying out on a suit of clothes. That leaves only about a dollar a week for all the other things I have to have."

". . . Well there's this about it, Wingate. The University is here supported by the taxpayers of this state, for the purpose of giving the young men and women of this state educational opportunities. The University is not here for the purpose of training young men to be waiters in all-night restaurants. And, so far as I can see, that's about all you are deriving from your University career. So it occurs to me that you should make a choice: either find some way to devote more attention to your college work or drop out of school altogether."

Note that we need no stage directions: "Wingate said," or "the dean replied." The boy's hesitant, oc-

[4] "A Student in Economics" from *No More Trumpets* by George Milburn. Copyright, 1933, by Harcourt, Brace and Company, Inc.

casional slangy speech contrasts with the pompous phrases of the dean. We can almost hear the tones of the voices: Wingate's polite pleading, and the dean's professional heartiness. Even in the few speeches here quoted we realize that Wingate is an earnest youngster and the dean a stuffed shirt, cold and insincere.

At the same time this dialogue carries on the action of the story, and it gives us information about the situation. For in modern stories the tendency is to give us the exposition as we go along instead of in a lump at the beginning. It is again the method of the drama, to show characters in action. Not all stories, of course, depend so heavily upon dialogue. Some writers represent the thoughts and feelings of their characters, but here too, usually in the words and phrases in which the character thinks. Nearly always we are shown the thoughts, the speech, the action, not merely told about them.

10. Vividness. To further give the reader this sense of seeing or participating in the events of a story, the contemporary writer often tries to reproduce the physical sensations of his characters. The descriptions are at times as vivid and detailed as those in poetry. Here is Thomas Wolfe's account of a boy looking in a store window: [5]

And now, indeed, he was caught, held suspended. A waft of air, warm chocolate-laden, filled his nostrils. He tried to pass the white front of the little eight-foot shop; he paused, struggling with conscience; he could not go on. It was the little candy shop run by old Crocker and his wife. And Grover could not pass.

[5] Thomas Wolfe, "Lost Boy," *Beyond the Hills* (New York, Harper & Brothers, 1942).

"Old stingy Crockers!" he thought scornfully. "I'll not go there any more. But—" as the maddening fragrance of rich cooking chocolate touched him once again—"I'll just look in the window and see what they've got." He paused a moment, looking with his dark and quiet eyes into the window of the little candy shop. The window, spotlessly clean, was filled with trays of fresh-made candy. His eyes rested on a tray of chocolate drops. Unconsciously he licked his lips. Put one of them upon your tongue and it just melted there, like honeydew. . . .

The reader becomes the boy, smelling the candy and licking his lips. And we are not merely told that Mrs. Crocker weighs out the candy with great care; we are there, watching her do it: [6]

. . . A customer had gone in and made a purchase, and as Grover looked he saw Mrs. Crocker, with her little wrenny face, her pinched features, lean over and peer primly at the scales. She had a piece of fudge in her clean, bony, little fingers, and as Grover looked, she broke it primly, in her little bony hands. She dropped a morsel down into the scales. They weighted down alarmingly, and her thin lips tightened. She snatched the piece of fudge out of the scales and broke it carefully once again. This time the scales wavered, went down very slowly, and came back again. Mrs. Crocker carefully put the reclaimed piece of fudge back in the tray, dumped the remainder in a paper bag, folded it and gave it to the customer, counted the money carefully and doled it out into the till, the pennies in one place, the nickels in another.

And here is part of George Anthony Weller's account of foot-ball practice: [7]

[6] *Ibid.*

[7] George Anthony Weller, *Not to Eat, Not for Love* (New York, 1938). Reprinted by permission of Random House, Inc.

. . . Epes found that a low direct block, a shoulder hitting the hip, sufficiently delayed the sophomore. Forward passes followed one another, scantily varied on the two models they had learned. Again and again the sophomore's big hands clubbed down on Epes' head and Epes checked for half a second the upward churn of the heavy knees. He listened no more to the signals and found himself growing simpler at this simple work.

Then he began to hear an irregular noise from the sideline. He did not dare turn his head. Between plays he forgot to look for it. Then he heard it again in the pause between the first and second series of signals.

"No fancy breaking through, remember," the line coach reminded the line. "That will come later," he added easily.

Of course. You're engaged for the season.

"Just take two quick steps and hold 'em out."

He heard the sound again. It came from each side of the field, but separately, in soft intermittent thuds, as though someone were striking the wooden fence from the outside.

After about ten plays the silence following the whistle's squeal was entered by the words of the coach, serene and clear: "That's all."

There was a small red sunset behind the black trees, compact and thrifty like a winter hearth.

He went toward the bench to get a blanket and saw other blackshirts getting up from their places, like old men, letting slip their blankets, and walking stiffly across the field with cold dry faces.

The sophomore's name was Tannin. He turned his helmet once in his hands, then tossed it away. The blue dusk chilled his sweatdamp ears. One of the managerial candidates, in baseball cap and soiled flannels, picked up his helmet. He noticed, then, what the light thudding sound had been. On both sides of the cooling field the managers were picking up the helmets scattered around the red equipment wagons and throwing them in.

The reader sees and feels that as Epes Todd sees and feels it. His attention, like Todd's is absorbed by the sophomore before him. Only with the coach's whistle does the tension relax: other sights come into focus; the sophomore becomes a man named Tannin; the faint thuds in the periphery of consciousness are for a moment noted consciously. The reader has himself been on that field, absorbed in the game.

Thus more than ever, good fiction becomes not an escape from life, but an extension of life. Our understanding of people and events is widened; our experiences are more varied; the limitations of our own lives are swept away.

Schools of Fiction

Before we leave the subject of fiction, we should perhaps have some knowledge of the various modes of writing. This discussion deals with matters of a more technical nature than the qualities of good writing in general. As the problem is primarily the concern of the critic and the literary scholar, it will not be presented in detail, but because many of the terms occur in book reviews and literary discussion, even the reader who is not a literary specialist needs to know something of their meaning. Furthermore, if we realize what sort of writing an author is trying to do, the better able we are to judge its effectiveness. It would be silly to complain of *Ivanhoe* because it is not written like *For Whom the Bell Tolls*.

1. *The romantic. Ivanhoe* is in the style usually called *romantic*. By that is meant that it deals not with

the present or with everday affairs, but with far-away
places or times; that it shows the heroic and glamorous
side of the life it pictures. In fiction the romantic style
easily leads to a literature of escape—the picture of
life more interesting and more noble than reality. On
the whole, romantic fiction has been less important
than romantic poetry. It need not be basically unreal:
it can, like Shakespeare's romantic plays, give us imaginative truth. At his best Scott does this. In *Ivanhoe,*
for instance, he dramatized effectively the conflicting
ideals of Norman and Saxon. Kingsley did a similar
thing in *Westward Ho!* and *Hereward the Wake;* the
first showing the Elizabethan conflict between England and Spain; the second dealing with the Norman
Conquest. Perhaps the most important function of the
romantic novel has been to make history come alive;
its weakness has been its tendency to show the past
chiefly in its more glamorous aspects.

2. *The sentimental.* Another style of writing, one
especially characteristic of the late eighteenth and
early nineteenth centuries, is the *sentimental.* Here the
feelings and emotions of the characters are empha-
sized. The material is likely to be home life or polite
society. For all its tears, and faintings, and transports
of joy, this type of novel has been important. *Pamela,
The Vicar of Wakefield,* and *Tristram Shandy* belong
to this school. The writers showed that the doings of
ordinary people could be interesting or even tragic;
that stories need not be laid in medieval castles or remote places; that sieges and battles and murders were
not necessary for drama. They paved the way for Jane
Austen and Trollope, perhaps for Steinbeck and Saro-

yan. Dickens and Thackeray show the influence of this school.

3. *The realistic.* On the whole, however, Dickens and Thackeray represent the type of writing called *realistic*. Defoe and Fielding had laid the groundwork for this. In fact, perhaps this has been the prevailing mode of the novel in English. Dr. Johnson's definition of the novel, quoted at the beginning of this chapter, is primarily a definition of the realistic novel.

4. *Realism and naturalism.* Just what the critic means by *realistic* can perhaps be made clearer by comparing the term with a somewhat similar one, *naturalistic*. Naturalism is a further development of realism. An analogy of the difference between the two methods would be the difference between a portrait and a photograph. The portrait painter, like the realistic writer, represents actual life, but he selects; he heightens certain details and omits others. The background details may be entirely left out. The naturalist tries to give a cross section of life; he tries to represent his material as exactly as possible. If, as in life, a certain event leads nowhere, the realist might omit it; the naturalist would include it. Sinclair Lewis is essentially a realist; Dreiser a naturalist. Both picture the American scene in considerable detail; both use incidents and situations from daily life. But Lewis at times caricatures people or events (a form of heightening), and he selects from a character's life those incidents which are important to the theme of a novel. Dreiser shows us as far as he can the person as he is, the minor, unimportant events as well as the others.

Lewis belongs to the tradition of Dickens; Dreiser to that of Zola.

At first glance it might seem that the naturalist is more truthful than the realist. That is his intention— to show life exactly as it is; to show every wart and wrinkle of his subjects. But it is a question whether the camera portrait is more truthful than the painter's. And even the most careful naturalist is not a precision instrument; try as he will, he cannot entirely keep out his point of view, his emotions. In the end the differ- ence between realism and naturalism is one of degree rather than of kind.

5. *Stream of consciousness.* Experimentation is as characteristic of modern literature as it is of other con- temporary arts. Not only have writers attempted an exact representation of the world around them, but also of the workings of the mind. Anyone who analyzes a few moments of his own mental processes will real- ize that he does not think in complete sentences nor in the patterns of formal logic. Ordinarily, especially in reverie, one thought or picture leads to another not necessarily logically related; they follow some acci- dental association. Often we are conscious of more than one thing at a time, as Epes Todd watching the sophomore in front of him, also heard in the back- ground the soft thud of helmets pitched into a cart. The attempt to represent this flow of ideas and images through the mind is called the *stream-of-consciousness* method. Its inventor is a matter of dispute; perhaps it was Henry James. In recent years Virginia Woolf and James Joyce have used it. Here, for instance, is

Virginia Woolf's picture of a girl thinking about a book: [8]

At ten o'clock in the morning, in a room which she shared with a school teacher, Fanny Elmer read *Tom Jones*—that mystic book. For this dull stuff (Fanny thought) about people with odd names is what Jacob likes. Good people like it. Dowdy women who don't mind how they cross their legs read *Tom Jones*—a mystic book; for there is something, Fanny thought, about books which if I had been educated I could have liked—much better than ear-rings and flowers, she sighed, thinking of the corridors at Slade and the fancy-dress dance next week. She had nothing to wear.

They are real, thought Fanny Elmer, setting her feet on the mantel-piece. Some people are. Nick perhaps, only he was so stupid. And women never—except Miss Sargent, but she went off at lunch-time and gave herself airs. There they sat quietly of a night, reading, she thought. Not going to music-halls; not looking in at shop windows; not wearing each other's clothes, like Robertson who had worn her shawl, and she had worn his waistcoat, which Jacob could only do very awkwardly; for he liked *Tom Jones*.

That is perhaps typical of the sort of things that go through anyone's mind, but it is also individual; Fanny Elmer's lack of education, her interest in Jacob, her tastes and friendships—all play a part in her thinking. To that extent Virginia Woolf has given us a portrait not of a person's exterior, but of the mind and character.

James Joyce, who uses the stream-of-consciousness technique even more extensively, does not always use

[8] From *Jacob's Room* by Virginia Woolf. Copyright, 1923, by Harcourt, Brace and Company, Inc.

it in exactly the same way. Virginia Woolf's people
tend to associate a series of pictures, Joyce's often associate sounds. It is a trick of the mind we can notice
in a child talking to itself. Many of the words may
have no meaning at all—or at least no meaning to
anyone but the child itself. Joyce obviously believed
this a normal characteristic of all minds in reverie, but
it may well be that for him association through sound
was more natural than for most of us. It is possible
that pictorial association is more usual. Certainly it is
easier to represent successfully. Like the child's private gibberish, the language of parts of *Ulysses* and
much of *Finnegans Wake* carries little meaning to the
reader. Perhaps it even carries different meanings to
different readers. The mental associations related to
a sunset or a motor car are more likely to be similar
for many readers than those connected with some particular sound.

Here are the impressions and thoughts of a man
going to a funeral as Joyce represents them: [9]

As they turned into Berkley street a streetorgan near
the Basin sent over and after them a rollicking rattling
song of the halls. Has anybody here seen Kelly? Kay ee
double ell wy. Dead march from *Saul*. He's as bad as old
Antonio. He left me on my ownio. Pirouette! The *Mater
Misericordiae*. Eccles street. My own house down there.
Big place. Ward for incurables there. Very encouraging.
Our Lady's Hospice for the dying. Dead house handy
underneath. Where old Mrs. Riordan died. They look
terrible the women. Her feeding cup and rubbing her
mouth with the spoon. Then the screen round her bed for

[9] James Joyce, *Ulysses* (New York, 1918). Reprinted by permission of Random House, Inc.

her to die. Nice young student that was dressed that bite the bee gave me. He's gone over to the lying-in hospital they told me. From one extreme to the other.

And here is Mr. Bloom in a restaurant: [10]

Mild fire of wine kindled in his veins. I wanted that badly. Felt so off colour . . . Lobsters boiled alive. Do ptake some ptarmigan. Wouldn't mind being a waiter in a swell hotel. Tips, evening, dress, halfnaked ladies. May I tempt you to a little more filleted lemonsole, Miss Dubedat? Yes, do bedad. And she did, bedad. Huguenot name I expect that. A Miss Dubedat lived in Killiney I remember. *Du, de la,* French. Still it's the same fish, perhaps money, hand over fist, finger in fishe's gills, can't write his name think he was painting the landscape with his mouth twisted. Mooikill A Aitcha Ha. Ingnorant as a kish of brogues, worth fifty thousand pounds.

There are all sorts of mental associations represented here: the spelling of "ptarmigan" suggests the word "ptake"; the name "Dubedat" has resemblances to the Irish "bedad" and the French "du," but it also suggests the idea of Huguenot ancestry. And the filleted sole brings memories of the uneducated fishmonger who twisted his mouth when he signed a check. In the same book the reveries of Stephen Dedalus are often more difficult because he is a more complex character with a mind stored with literary and ecclesiastical phrases.

Whether or not writing of this sort is completely successful, it is another example of the attempt to represent psychological processes. Like modern poetry, it is often difficult reading, but also like modern poetry it

[10] *Ibid.*

can heighten our perceptions, can take us beyond the obvious surfaces of life.

6. *Fantasy*. This attempt to go beneath the observed surfaces of life takes other forms. In the chapter on drama this is discussed under the term *expressionism*. In prose fiction there is no single name for it. Some of the works of this type are those mentioned in the discussion of imaginative truth. One form of the thing is *fantasy*—the creation of a dream-world where characters and events follow a logic of their own. *Alice in Wonderland* is perhaps the most famous example of this. Robert Nathan frequently uses the method. His people have the surface characteristics of everyday people, but they are not bound by the limitations of everyday life. The most brilliant contemporary artist using fantasy works not in the medium of prose fiction, but in the movies is Walt Disney.

The literature of fantasy is difficult to classify. Often it is humorous in intent as it is in the comic strips from Krazy Kat to Popeye and Barnaby. On the other hand, it may have an underlying serious purpose, especially when it takes the form of satire. *Gulliver's Travels* is fantasy, but it is one of the most brilliant satirical criticisms of life ever written. Possibly because it is difficult to preserve the mood in long works, fantasy is often used in the short story or the novelette. The stories of A. E. Coppard are usually fantasy. They are not so obviously satirical as Gulliver, but they too, give us new perspectives. Beneath the surface there is a serious purpose, a criticism of life. Stella Benson's "The Man Who Missed the Bus" is fantasy, but the chief character, Mr. Robinson, represents a way of thinking, a self-centered preoccupation with his own points of view, that we have all met in daily life.

Demands upon the Reader

It is futile to argue that one way of writing is the best method. Important works of fiction have been written in each one of these techniques. And although one or another form may be more fashionable in a particular period, techniques do not become obsolete like the model T Ford. The extremely realistic *Moll Flanders* is contemporary with the fantasy, *Gulliver's Travels;* Virginia Woolf with A. E. Coppard and Sinclair Lewis. Steinbeck's *Of Mice and Men* combines elements of the sentimentalists and the most hard-boiled realists. In the 1930's, the best seller was *Gone with the Wind,* a novel in the style of Walter Scott.

The important thing about recognizing the technique of a work of fiction is that we may then judge it by the proper standards. It would be silly to condemn *Gulliver's Travels* because Lilliputians do not exist or to bemoan the lack of romantic action in *Main Street.* Virginia Woolf was not trying to tell the same sort of story as was Walter Scott. He was interested in the panorama of history, she in the inner panorama of moods and feelings. What we do ask is that each writer accomplish the thing he sets out to do. If he tries to give a cross section of life, then we have a right to object to high romance or fantasy in the same novel. The love story in *For Whom the Bell Tolls* may attract the cash customers, but it is out of keeping with the hard-boiled realism of the rest of the book. On the other hand, the tragic love story of the Norwegian girl and the German soldier in William Wood's *The Edge of Darkness* is completely in accord with the style and theme of the whole work.

Whatever the method, there is one respect in which a contemporary story is likely to differ from an older one: it is likely to demand more of the reader. In this respect modern fiction resembles modern poetry. There is an attempt to stimulate the thought and imagination. Even the exposition is likely to be given in hints as the story progresses instead of in a lump at the beginning. In works of fantasy like "The Man Who Missed the Bus" or the stories of A. E. Coppard we are often left guessing the real meaning. As has been noted, the cross-section-of-life technique of the naturalists tends to leave actions incomplete, problems unsolved as in life. Thoughtful, imaginative readers find this more stimulating than the older way of tying up all the threads at the ends, and perhaps stating the moral or conclusion in precise terms. The writer, as it were, asks us to experience life with him.

The real value of fiction, however, lies not in its style or technique, but in those other qualities we have discussed such as theme and characterization. Does the story carry more than its own weight? Does it work out the theme skilfully and vividly? Does it extend the boundaries of our thoughts and feelings? Do we understand the world and its men and women better for having read it? These are some of the things we ask of first-rate fiction.

VII

Drama

Drama is a form of literature not primarily designed for reading. The word *drama* comes from a Greek word meaning "to do" or "to perform." The reading of a play, therefore, can only give us part of what its author intended. We must learn to read printed drama as a kind of skeleton of the complete form. Thus when in the opening scene of *Hamlet* Bernardo says, "Who's there?" we must, unless we have seen the play, supply for ourselves his tone and actions. This we cannot do properly until we know more about the situation, until we have read further and learned that on the two preceding nights the sentries have seen a ghost, and that they are nervously alert. Knowing that, we can supply in our imaginations the nervous tension in Bernardo's voice.

Sometimes the editors help us by adding stage directions, and some modern dramatists have included rather elaborate directions in the printed editions of their plays. In older plays these editorial additions are usually very brief, so that the reader must visualize most of the action for himself, and must try to imagine the tones of the voice of each speaker. These things are much easier for the person who has seen a number of plays. Anyone who has seen a few Shakesperian plays knows the way a courtier bows or the antics of a court fool. A person who has seen Falstaff well-acted has little difficulty in imagining Sir Toby Belch in *Twelfth Night* when he meets him in print. It is therefore most important to see as many plays as possible if one is to read the drama intelligently.

Another requirement is intelligent rereading. Until one knows something about a character, it is impossible to imagine clearly his actions and way of talking. This does not necessarily mean rereading a whole play. Often it requires only that after a character has revealed his real nature, the reader go back over the preceding scene to understand the nature and purpose of this character's lines. For instance, on meeting Hamlet, Osric says, "Your lordship is right welcome back to Denmark." So far Osric might be any gentleman of the court. But we do not need to read very far before we find that Osric is a fop and a fool. We know then that his opening line was spoken in an affected manner and that he bowed too deeply, that he swept the floor with his plumed hat. On the stage we should have seen that at once. We would have been ready for Hamlet's contemptuous mockery.

Furthermore each type of drama has developed certain conventions for its presentation. If we know something about these, we get a better idea of how a play would appear on the stage. It is helpful to know that romantic, poetic drama such as Shakespeare's serious plays, is acted in a rather stately manner; that fluttering fans, snuff boxes, deep bows and hand kissing are characteristic of the comedy of manners such as Congreve's *The Way of the World* or Sheridan's *The School for Scandal*. A modern farce like *Three Men on a Horse* usually has much exaggerated action, hands clapped to the brow, people falling back into chairs to show astonishment—all the comic devices which we have seen both on the stage and in the movies. Reading a farce like *The Taming of the Shrew* we can be sure that the actors will heighten their lines by the same tricks—they will go in for "mugging," exaggerated facial contortions. On the other hand, drawing-room comedy is usually presented with much more restraint. The actors try to create the illusion of everyday life both in their gestures and the tones of their voices.

Types of Drama

It is helpful, therefore, to know something about the different types of drama. There is no need here of hair-splitting distinctions such as Polonius makes: "tragedy, comedy, history, pastoral, pastoral-comical, historical-pastoral, tragical-historical, tragical-comical-histor-ical-pastoral, scene individual, or poem unlimited." We must recognize, however, that the category called *comedy* can include anything from the cheerful non-sense of *A Midsummer Night's Dream* to the serious social criticism of Maxwell Anderson. The one needful element is that comedy shall have a happy ending. Obviously the term is too broad to be very useful in defining the nature of a play. We therefore distinguish *farce*, which is a kind of rough and tumble comedy us-ing far-fetched situations. *The Comedy of Errors, Charley's Aunt,* and *Three Men on a Horse* are farces. Then there is the comedy of manners, usually a satirical portrait of high society, presented chiefly by means of witty dialogue—such plays as *Sir Fopling Flutter*, *The Rivals*, and *The Importance of Being Earnest*. The modern variety is often called drawing-room comedy—plays like S. N. Behrman's *Biography* or Robert Sherwood's *Reunion in Vienna*. This type of play demands subtle action and cultivated voices.

1. *Romantic drama.* Throughout the history of English drama there is one distinction which must be recognized: the difference between romantic and realistic drama. Comedy and tragedy may be of either type, although comedy is more frequently realistic. By romantic drama we mean, not necessarily a love story, but an imaginative rather than a literal presentation of life. Most of Shakespeare's dramas are romantic: characters speak in poetry; the action can take place in never-never lands like the forest of Arden or the seacoast of Bohemia; ghosts or elves like Ariel can appear. In modern times Maxwell Anderson has written romantic poetic drama, as have a number of Irish playwrights like Yeats, Singe and Shean O'Casey. Such plays are usually presented today with beautiful scenery and with more grace of action and speech than we find in daily life. The writer's purpose is akin to that of other poets, to intensify experience, to heighten the emotional qualities of life. Therefore romantic drama is likely to give us villains like Iago or tragic figures like Lear; to tell love stories like that of Romeo and Juliet or Tristram and Iseult. Both characters and emotions are shown in heroic proportions like the sculpture on a temple or the music of a symphony.

2. *Realism.* This kind of drama has never entirely

gone out of fashion, but since Ibsen's time the tendency has been to portray life in more realistic terms. This realistic or naturalistic drama shows everyday people facing the sort of situations we meet in contemporary life: economic problems, narrow prejudices, political corruption, domestic maladjustments. Galsworthy wrote about labor troubles, about race prejudice, about conditions in prisons; Eugene O'Neill showed us the life of common sailors or on New England farms; Elmer Rice and Clifford Odets wrote of people in offices and cheap dwellings.

3. *Expressionism.* Some writers, however, felt that this kind of drama was too literal, that it represented what O'Neill called "the banality of surfaces." As a revolt against realism then, we have *expressionism*, an attempt to get below the surface, and represent thoughts, feelings, the unseen forces of the universe. In some aspects this kind of drama is like romantic drama: it can portray personifications like death or show characters speaking their thoughts as they do in *Strange Interlude.* Scenes can be laid in imaginary lands. Maxwell Anderson, for instance, in *The Time Machine* has characters go back to their youth and start over, so that he can contrast the ruthless pursuit of success with true happiness. The same characters try both roads, and we see the results. Thus Anderson seeks to present truth by other means than a realistic picture of life.

The reader, therefore, must learn to accept romantic drama for its poetic and imaginative qualities, and expressionistic drama for its inner meaning; he must not judge them by the standards of everyday fact. He

must learn to look for the purpose of any play. *Hamlet,*
for all its references to Denmark, is not to be taken as a
historical document. We study it as a revelation of
certain elements in human nature. Likewise a farce
falls to pieces if we say "nobody would be fooled by a
young man disguised as someone's aunt from Australia." *Charley's Aunt* is pretty far-fetched even for
farce, but audiences have long accepted that sort of
fooling. The critic is justified, however, in asking for
dialogue with some wit.

Universal Elements

Whether a play is realistic, expressionistic, or romantic; tragedy or farce, there are certain elements we
look for in all successful drama. First of all we expect
movement. Drama is by definition the performing of
some action in the form of a scene or play. This does
not necessarily mean violent action. The scene in
which Hamlet watches his uncle praying is intensely
dramatic, for Hamlet draws his rapier and then pauses.
Finally he puts it back in its sheath. Even without
Hamlet's words that shows in action the thoughts running through Hamlet's mind.

Contrast that with the scene in Browning's *Pippa
Passes* where the painter Jules is talking to Phene after
having been tricked into marrying her. After a long
monologue on his artistic theories, he tells Phene he is
going to take the money he had saved for travel, and
go in search of Lutwyche and the others who had
tricked him. He plans to kill them. Then Pippa sings
outside the window, and her song leads him to speak
as follows:

What name was that the little girl sang forth?
Kate? The Cornaro, doubtless, who renounced
The crown of Cyprus to be lady here
At Asolo, where her memory stays,
And peasants sing how once a certain page
Pined for the grace of her so far above
His power of doing good to, "Kate the Queen—
She never could be wronged, be poor," he sighed.
"Need him to help her!"

                      Yes, a bitter thing
To see our lady above all need of us;
Yet so we look ere we will love; not I,
But the world looks so. If whoever loves
Must be, in some sort, god or worshipper,
The blessing or the blessed one, queen or page,
Why should we always choose the page's part?
Here is a woman with utter need of me,—
I find myself queen here, it seems!

                        How strange!
Look at the woman here with the new soul,
Like my own Psyche,—fresh upon her lips
Alit, the visionary butterfly
Waiting my word to enter and make bright,
Or flutter off and leave all blank as first.
This body had no soul before, but slept
Or stirred, was beauteous or ungainly, free
From taint or foul with stain, as outward things
Fastened their image on its passiveness;
Now, it will wake, feel, live—or die again!
Shall to produce form out of unshaped stuff
Be Art—and further, to evoke a soul
From form be nothing? This new soul is mine!

Now, to kill Lutwyche, what would that do?—save
A wretched dauber, men will hoot to death
Without me, from their hooting. Oh, to hear

God's voice plain as I heard at first, before
They broke in with their laughter! I heard them
Henceforth, not God.

This is only about two-thirds of what Jules says on
this occasion. What he has said so far, in case you are
not quite clear about it, is that he is going to keep
Phene and not kill Lutwyche. We learn this not
through action, but by following Jules' somewhat involved reasoning. Browning's method is more like that
of the novelist than of the playwright. Jules has remembered the story of Queen Kate and her page; he
has philosophized about love—one must either worship or be worshipped, he thinks; and he has thought
about his own statue of Psyche and the butterfly sym-
bolizing the soul. He will give Phene a soul as the
sculptor brings to life the marble with which he works.
All that is in his mind; we do not see it happen. It is for
this reason that Browning with all his insight into character, could not write successful stage drama.

1. Conflict. The essence of a dramatic situation is
conflict, but we must see the conflict. Browning's situation is dramatic enough; Jules has two difficult decisions to make. One of them relates to Phene, who is
beside him. She has done some talking, but the problem is not resolved by means of a give and take between them. There is no genuine dialogue, merely a
series of monologues. Compare the scene in which
Hamlet lectures to his mother for marrying Claudius.
Hamlet does a lot of talking, but the scene moves. First
the Queen pleads with him to speak no more. But he
is excited and becomes more violent. Then the ghost

appears and Hamlet speaks to it. The Queen says, "Alas, he's mad!" And at once the scene has taken a new turn. Hamlet must then try to persuade her that he is sane.[1]

QUEEN. To whom do you speak this?
HAMLET.   Do you see noth-
   ing there?
QUEEN. Nothing at all; yet all that is I see.
HAMLET.   Nor did you
   nothing hear?
QUEEN. No, nothing but ourselves.
HAMLET. Why, look you there! look, how it steals away!
   My father, in his habit as he lived! Look, where he goes,
   even now out of the portal!
QUEEN. This is the very coinage of your brain:
            This bodiless creation ecstasy
            Is very cunning in.
HAMLET.   Ecstasy?
   My pulse, as yours, doth temperately keep time,
   And makes as healthful music: it is not madness
   That I have uttered. . . .

And so it goes, the give and take as in real conversation. And with the conversation goes the movement: Hamlet starting up to watch the ghost; the Queen's shrinking, in fear of his supposed madness; Hamlet's pointing after the disappearing ghost, and then turning back to defend his sanity. In Browning's scene there was little for Jules to do but stand and talk. For only the ham actor will declaim long speeches with wild gestures and stridings up and down.

Hamlet, it is true, soliloquizes, but remember that before he begins, Polonius and the king have just hid-

[1] *Hamlet*, Act III, Sc. 4.

den themselves to spy upon him, and his thoughts are interrupted by his discovery of Ophelia. The audience knows she is there. The scene, therefore, is no more static than a baited and set trap is static. The audience is kept in suspense throughout the scene.

This need for the presenting of a conflict in visual terms is one reason Shakespeare causes Banquo's ghost to appear to Macbeth at the banquet. It makes visible Macbeth's sense of guilt. In like fashion several modern playwrights have personified death on the stage. The realistic dramatist cannot use such devices, but he can represent conflicts by conflicts between persons. A novelist can show a man thinking out the problem of whether or not to become a Communist; the playwright must present the problem in visual terms. And a long debate between two characters on the topic soon becomes tiresome. A character must be presented with a choice of action—for instance, he might have to decide whether or not to hide a Communist from the police.

Of course there have been successful exceptions to this principle of dramatic presentation. Many of Bernard Shaw's plays are filled with scenes in which the characters sit around and talk. But Shaw's talk is so brilliant and his ideas so interesting that most playgoers have been willing to pardon the lack of action. Likewise in Congreve's comedies the play of wit largely takes the place of action. However a wit combat is also a conflict, and as such can make good theater. So far in the history of English drama only Irishmen have been sufficiently witty to let clever dialogue alone carry a play.

2. *Dialogue*. Dialogue, the conversation of the characters, is a most important part of any play. A story writer can use description and can tell us what goes on in his characters' minds; the playwright must use only action and the spoken word. And as we saw in *Pippa Passes*, a monologue will not serve the purpose. A play must not sound like a class in public speaking.

First of all, good dramatic dialogue must carry on the action of the play. Even in Shaw's plays some of the long expositions of a character's views on social and economic questions become very tiresome. In the hands of lesser writers such expositions are fatal. A character can give us his views on life, but he cannot successfully do so in monologue, and his speaking must have some relation to the action taking place. Thus Hamlet's pessimistic remarks about life grow directly out of the situation confronting him, and even more important, they help to create the suspense. His doubts and questionings make it seem that he is going to fail in carrying out the revenge. They bear upon the action he is about to take or to fail to take. In Anderson's *Winterset*, the elderly and persecuted Esdras tells us his philosophy of life: [2]

. . . There's no guilt under heaven,
just as there's no heaven, till men believe it—
no earth, till men have seen it, and have a word
to say this is the earth.
GARTH. Well, I say there's an earth
    and I say I'm guilty on it, guilty as hell.

[2] Maxwell Anderson, *Winterset*, Act I (Washington, Anderson House, 1935).

ESDRAS. Yet till it's known you bear no guilt at all—
   unless you wish. The days go by like film, like a long
   written scroll, a figured veil
   unrolling out of darkness into fire
   and utterly consumed. And on this veil,
   running in sounds and symbols of men's minds
   reflected back, life flickers and is shadow
   going toward flame. Only what men can see
   exists in that shadow. Why must you rise and cry out:
   That was I, there in the ravelled tapestry,
   there, in that pistol flash, when the man was killed.
   I was there, and was one, and was bloodstained!
   Let the wind
   and fire take that hour to ashes out of time
   and out of mind! This thing that men call justice,
   this blind snake that strikes men down in the dark,
   mindless with fury, keep your hand back from it,
   pass by in silence—let it be forgotten, forgotten!—
   Oh, my son, my son—have pity!

That is not in the play simply as a Platonistic discussion of the unreality of appearance; it bears directly on the action. Esdras is persuading himself that Garth need not confess his crime, nor be turned over to the police. This is one of the steps in the working out of the plot. Furthermore, it is a superb revelation of Esdras' character.

Perhaps a better and more typical way of handling such material is used by Galsworthy in *Strife*. Here is part of a scene at a meeting of the directors of a tin plate works. A strike is in progress and the board is discussing the problem. John Anthony, a man of seventy-six, is chairman of the board. His character and point of view emerge as the scene progresses. His son Edgar says sharply: "My father says: 'Do what we ought—and let things rip.' " [3]

WILDER. Tcha!

SCANTLEBURY. (*Throwing up his hands*) The chairman's a Stoic—I always said the chairman was a Stoic.

WILDER. Much good that'll do us.

WANKLIN. (*Suavely*) Seriously, Chairman, are you going to let the ship sink under you, for the sake of—a principle?

ANTHONY. She won't sink.

SCANTLEBURY. (*With alarm*) Not while I'm on the Board, I hope.

ANTHONY. (*With a twinkle*) Better rat, Scantlebury.

SCANTLEBURY. What a man!

ANTHONY. I've always fought them; I've never been beaten yet.

WANKLIN. We're with you in theory, Chairman. But we're not all made of cast-iron.

ANTHONY. We've only to hold on.

WILDER. (*Rising and going to the fire*) And go to the devil as fast as we can!

ANTHONY. Better go to the devil than give in.

That scene, of course, shows only part of Anthony's philosophy. More of it comes out when his daughter Enid says: "It's because you can't bear to give way. It's so—"

ANTHONY. Well?

ENID. So unnecessary.

ANTHONY. What do *you* know about necessity? Read your novels, play your music, talk your talk, but don't try and tell *me* what's at the bottom of a struggle like this.

ENID. I live down here and see it.

[3] John Galsworthy, *Strife*, Act I, in *Plays* (New York, Charles Scribner's Sons, 1936).

ANTHONY. What d'you imagine stands between you and
your class and these men that you're sorry for?
ENID. (*Coldly*) I don't know what you mean, Father.
ANTHONY. In a few years you and your children would be
down in the condition they're in, but for those who
have the eyes to see things as they are and the back-
bone to stand up for themselves.

Thus in the course of the play John Anthony reveals
himself as the spokesman of a class and point of view;
a strong, honest, fearless man, but an extreme reac-
tionary. He does it in the course of his conflicts with
the Board, with his family, and with the men. That is
the way the playwright must work. Galsworthy's dialogue is not brilliant, but it does two things good
dialogue must do: it reveals the characters of the
speakers, and it carries on the action. In the course of
the play various viewpoints about labor and capital
are presented, but they are not allowed to stop the action, nor become orations. Each remark bears upon the
action. Anthony talks to the Board, not primarily to
show his point of view, but to keep them from voting a
compromise settlement. His argument with Enid leads
her to revolt against his authority.

Another quality of good dialogue is that it should fit
the situation. The skilful dramatist ordinarily does not
have one character tell another what the latter already
knows. Probably no modern playwright would give us
such a speech as this from Goldsmith's *She Stoops to
Conquer*. Squire Hardcastle is speaking to his servants:

You, Diggory, whom I have taken from the barn, are
to make a show at the side-table; and you Roger, whom I

have advanced from the plow, are to place yourself behind my chair.

Most dramatists would find some other way of letting
the audience know that Diggory was a stableman and
Roger a plowman.

In realistic drama there has been an increasing tendency to represent the actual speech of everyday life.
This can take the obvious form of causing low characters to use profanity and obscenities. It also includes
the use of the half-finished sentences of conversation,
of the characteristic rhythms of colloquial speech.
Even granting the greater formality of Victorian
speech, it is difficult to imagine a real person saying: [4]

"Still, it caused a separation and a division between us,
and I never see my brother, because he lives abroad. Of
course the Marquise de St. Maur is my mother, and I look
upon her with a sort of superstitious awe."

The sentence rhythm is too stately, the words too carefully chosen and placed.

Compare these bits of dialogue from the two plays
of a similar nature, both written in the 1890's. The first,
from Pinero's *The Second Mrs. Tanqueray*, represents
two gentlemen talking. They are intimate friends: [5]

DRUMMLE. How are you getting on?
AUBREY. My position doesn't grow less difficult. I told you,
  when I met you last week, of this feverish jealous attachment of Paula's for Ellean?
DRUMMLE. Yes. I hardly know why, but I came to the
  conclusion that you don't consider it an altogether fortunate attachment.

[4] T. W. Robertson, *Caste*, Act II.
[5] Sir Arthur Wing Pinero, *The Second Mrs. Tanqueray* (Boston,
W. H. Baker Company, 1894), Act II.

AUBREY. Ellean doesn't respond to it.

DRUMMLE. These are early days. Ellean will warm towards your wife by and by.

AUBREY. Ah, but there's the question, Cayley!

DRUMMLE. What question?

AUBREY. The question which positively distracts me. Ellean is so different from—most women; I don't believe a purer creature exists out of heaven. And I—I ask myself, am I doing right in exposing her to the influence of poor Paula's light, careless nature.

DRUMMLE. My dear Aubrey!

AUBREY. That shocks you! So it does me. I assure you I long to urge my girl to break down the reserve which keeps her apart from Paula, but somehow I can't do it—well I don't do it. How can I make you understand? But when you come to us, you'll understand quickly enough, Cayley. There's hardly a subject you can broach on which Paula hasn't some strange, out-of-the-way thought to give utterance to; some curious, warped notion. They are not mere worldly thoughts—unless, good God! they belong to the little hellish world which our blackguardism has created: no, her ideas have too little calculation in them to be called worldly. But it makes it the more dreadful that such thoughts should be ready, spontaneous; that expressing them has become a perfectly natural process; that her words, acts even, have almost lost their proper significance for her, and seem beyond her control. Ah, the pain of listening to it all from the woman one loves, the woman one hoped to make happy and contented, who is really and truly a good woman, as it were, maimed! Well, this is my burden, and I shouldn't speak to you of it, but for my anxiety about Ellean. Ellean! What is to be her future? It's in my hands; what am I to do? Cayley, when I remember how Ellean comes to me, from another world I always think,—when I realize the charge that's laid on me, I find myself wishing, in a sort of terror, that my child were safe under the ground!

The next is a conversation between ladies in the first act of Wilde's *Lady Windermere's Fan:*

DUCHESS OF B. Agatha, darling!

LADY A. Yes, mamma. (*Rises*)

DUCHESS OF B. Will you go and look over the photograph album that I see there!

LADY A. Yes, mamma. (*Goes to table L.*)

DUCHESS OF B. Dear girl! She is so fond of photographs of Switzerland. Such a pure taste, I think. But I really am so sorry for you, Margaret.

LADY W. (*Smiling*) Why, Duchess?

DUCHESS OF B. Oh, on account of that horrid woman. She dresses so well, too, which makes it much worse, sets a dreadful example. Augustus—you know my disreputable brother—such a trial to us all—well, Augustus is completely infatuated about her. It's quite scandalous, for she is absolutely inadmissible into society. Many a woman has a past, but I am told that she has at least a dozen, and that they all fit.

LADY W. Whom are you talking about, Duchess?

DUCHESS OF B. About Mrs. Erlynne.

LADY W. Mrs. Erlynne? I never heard of her, Duchess. And what has *she* to do with me?

DUCHESS OF B. My poor child! Agatha, darling!

LADY A. Yes, mamma.

DUCHESS OF B. Will you go out on the terrace and look at the sunset?

LADY A. Yes, mamma.

DUCHESS OF B. Sweet girl! So devoted to sunsets! Shows such a refinement of feeling, does it not? After all, there's nothing like nature, is there?

LADY B. But what is it, Duchess? Why do you talk to me about this person?

DUCHESS OF B. Don't you really know? I assure you we're all so distressed about it. Only last night at dear Lady Fransen's everyone was saying how extraordinary it was that, of all men in London, Windermere should behave in such a way.

LADY W. My husband—what has *he* to do with any woman of that kind?

DUCHESS OF B. Ah, what indeed, dear? That is the point. He goes to see her continually, and stops for hours at a time, and while he's there she is not at home to anyone. Not that many ladies call on her, dear, but she has a great many disreputable men friends—my own brother in particular, as I told you—and that is what makes it so dreadful about Windermere. We looked upon *him* as being such a model husband, but I'm afraid there's no doubt about it. My dear nieces—you know the Saville girls, don't you?—such nice domestic creatures—plain, dreadfully plain, but so good—well, they're always at the window doing fancy work, and making ugly things for the poor, which I think are so useful to them in these dreadful socialistic days, and this terrible woman has taken a house in Curzon Street, right opposite them —such a respectable street too. I don't know what we're coming to. And they tell me that Windermere goes there four and five times a week—they *see* him. They can't help it—and although they never talk scandal, they— well, of course—they remark on it to everyone. And the worst of it all is, . . .

So the Duchess runs on, talking like a human being and not like a tract. Her conversation is at once that of a member of a certain social class (note such phrases as, "horrid woman," "so distressed about it," "so devoted to sunsets," "dreadfully plain") and an individual. Reading the lines we can almost hear them spoken, for we know exactly how the Duchess would accent and emphasize certain words. Drummle and Aubrey, on the other hand, each speak exactly the same sort of prose; there is little to individualize them;

they might be any two educated gentlemen—granting of course that any educated gentleman could be so priggish as Aubrey. Here his priggishness is not meant to individualize him; his point of view is much that of the author. His phrases ("strange, out-of-the-way thought to give utterance to," "too little calculation in them to be called worldly," "lost their proper significance for her") are those of books, and second-rate books, at that. Note too that Pinero's characters speak complete grammatical constructions: "What is to be her future?," "It is in my hands," "What am I to do?" Wilde used the elliptical phrases of natural speech: "Sweet girl! So devoted to sunsets! Shows such refinement of feeling, does it not?" The Duchess interrupts herself, puts in side remarks, gets off the subject, all the things that most people do when they are spreading gossip.

3. *Characterization.* The weakness of Pinero's dialogue goes deeper than mere style. Aside from its unlikeness to natural speech, it represents a character thinking and acting less as a human being than as an illustration of a point of view. A good play, like a good novel or short story, must not be a mere piece of ventriloquism. The playwright has a more serious problem here than does the novelist, for the playwright cannot stop the action in order to expound his views in his own person. He can, of course, let one of the characters speak for him. The Greek dramatists did this by means of the chorus, a group of people who recited a commentary on the action. Later dramatists often use a device of Shakespeare's in *Antony and Cleopatra,* where Enobarbus, the plain-spoken old sol-

dier, makes comments which can be taken as those of
the author. Thornton Wilder in *Our Town* introduced
a narrator whose method was much like that of the
chorus in Greek drama, but this to a modern audience
seems rather artificial.

The dramatist may, then, tell us his point of view if
he does not do it too obtrusively. But if he is first-rate,
he will not make his characters mere puppets who
speak for the author. Enobarbus is not William Shakespeare dressed as a soldier; he is an old campaigner
with the shrewd common sense and cynicism of such a
man, but he entirely lacks the ability to understand the
high romance of the events around him. Shakespeare's
whole point of view comes out in the play itself, not
in the speech of any one character.

The ability to create individuals with their good
points and their weaknesses, with their own quirks of
thought and mannerisms is one of the marks of the able
playwright. It is this ability which perhaps more than
any other makes Shakespeare great. As most people
know, he nearly always took old plots and reworked
them, but he reworked them in terms of characters so
real and so human that generations of playgoers think
of Falstaff and Shylock and Lady Macbeth as real persons—as real as the historic figures, Prince Hal and
Brutus and Cleopatra. It is true that a skilful actor can
often individualize a character so that we feel he is
real and alive. This often accounts for the popularity
of plays which seem very second-rate today. Lionel
Barrymore, for instance, has often made second-rate
movie characterization seem like real persons.

The creation of real characters is achieved by a

blend of many elements, chief among them: dialogue, mannerisms, and above all, psychological insight. The Duchess in Wilde's play showed her flibbertigibbet mind in her rattle-brained conversation; Dogberry, the stupid constable in *Much Ado About Nothing* loves pompous phrases, which he gets mixed up, as does Mrs. Malaprop in Sheridan's *The Rivals*. In *Strife* Scantlebury reveals his fuddy-duddy character before he has spoken a dozen lines. At the Board meeting to consider the strike he fusses over not having a screen between him and the fire, and complains of his poor lunch at the hotel.

The problem of psychological insight is not one which can be treated generally; it must be studied with regard to each character we meet. Writers of comedy are likely to give us one-sided characters representing a certain trait or "humor." Sir Toby Belch is a much less complex character than Macbeth. In the older plays, the character's name is often a sign of his outstanding trait: Johnson's Volpone, meaning "fox," is a sly scoundrel; Sheridan's Lydia Languish thinks only of sentimental romance. Of course, the more skilful the playwright the more likely is he to round out his portraits. Falstaff is not merely a tavern loafer; he has wit, shrewdness, even pathos. The persons in Kaufman and Hart's *You Can't Take It with You* are largely types—humor characters such as Ben Jonson created. Each one has a single eccentricity, and the conflict of these produces the fun. In O'Neill's *Ah, Wilderness* the hard drinking newspaperman, Sid Davis, seems at first to be merely the comic drunkard of hundreds of other comedies. But as we go along we get glimpses of depths beneath the surface. He starts to urge his brother-in-law to be lenient with Richard: [6]

> If I didn't know you so well, I'd say don't be too hard on him. (*He smiles a little bitterly*) If you remember, I was always getting punished—and see what a lot of good it did me!

And with that remark we learn a lot about Sid; he is no longer merely the comic drunk, but a kindly, frustrated human being as well.

In tragic or serious drama we ask for considerably more rounded portraits than in comedy. *The Second Mrs. Tanqueray*, for all its lumbering dialogue, does give us a memorable study of the woman with a past, a woman who for all her desire for respectability, finds respectability dull. She is desperately anxious to win the affection of her stepdaughter Ellean; yet she cannot avoid overdoing her act and thus repelling the girl. We sympathize with Eva Tanqueray; yet we are exasperated with her crassness. She is something more than a mere type. John Anthony in *Strife* is not simply the pig-headed employer; in his talk with Enid, we found something of why he refused any compromise; he felt that he was defending a way of life. He was ruthless, and we deplore his cruelty; yet he was honest, and within his limitations, fond of his family. He too has something of the complexity of a real person. Shakespeare's Polonius is often a fool, but he is not always a fool. He has moments of shrewd insight, and can at times talk good common sense as in his famous advice

[6] Eugene O'Neill, *Ah, Wilderness* (New York, 1933), Act IV. Reprinted by permission of Random House, Inc.

to Laertes. He has been an advisor to kings, and knows the tricks and fine phrases of diplomacy, but he is approaching his dotage; he talks too ramblingly and his schemes no longer come off. Polonius is an excellent example of the many-sided quality of first-rate characterization. The complexities of Shakespeare's Hamlet, Lear, and Cleopatra place them among the greatest psychological studies in literature. Well-drawn characters are seldom all wise or complete fools, monsters or saints. As in all good writing, the playwright does not draw people in terms of black and white.

Nor as a rule is he content to give us mere types. That is one of the faults with nineteenth-century melodramas. There was the villain, the pure innocent girl, the fine young hero, the grasping skinflint who held the mortgage on the homestead—character after character who could be transplanted from one play to another. Today we often find the unfeeling employer, the wage slave, the clear-eyed young radical who falls in love with the brave, beautiful and brilliant daughter of the commonplace wage slave and his shrewish wife. Characters tend to inherit their qualities less from their parents than from their predecessors in other plays.

4. *Meaning.* Character drawing is not usually an end in itself. As with prose fiction a good play should have some meaning; it should carry more than its own weight. Thus *Antony and Cleopatra* is not merely a tragic love story; nor *Julius Caesar* a murder melodrama; both give us a sense of the forces that make rulers or destroy kingdoms. Maxwell Anderson, after studying the great plays of the past, came to the conclusion that great plays show man in conflict with the

great forces of the universe—with evil, or fate, or death, or with their own weaknesses. Obviously the dramatist who shows man in conflict with these forces in life must have some concept of their nature and the nature of man; in other words, he must have a philosophy of life. If he preaches this philosophy too obviously we have a tract rather than a play.

Today the playwright often shows man in conflict with more specific forces, economic or social. Elmer Rice's *The Adding Machine* shows a man enslaved by machine-age civilization, the theme also of O'Neill's *The Hairy Ape*, and Čapek's *R. U. R.* Anderson's *Winterset* was inspired by the Sacco-Vanzetti case. This trend was probably started by Ibsen, who dealt with contemporary problems of his day. Thus the modern playwright is in danger of becoming topical or propagandist. As this problem is discussed in another chapter, it need only be mentioned here. Suffice it to say that the greatest plays, whether comedy or tragedy, give us a deeper insight into human nature, into human institutions, and into the forces of life and death.

5. *Structure.* Structure is another very important element in good drama. The long-winded, sprawling methods of a novelist like Theodore Dreiser would be fatal to a play. For one thing, the playwright must say what he has to say in about two hours and a half. Some dramatists, notably Eugene O'Neill, have revolted against this necessity, but without changing the convention. Dinner time and train schedules limit the dramatist's freedom; it is hard to get an audience together before eighty-thirty, or hold them after eleven. Another limiting force is the problem of scene changes.

Modern stage lighting and mechanical devices make this easier than it was thirty years ago, but even today Shakespeare's plays are usually reorganized somewhat to permit fewer and longer scenes than were used in Elizabethan times when there was no scenery to shift. Nor can an act run too long. Audiences are accustomed to going out for a smoke after thirty or forty minutes; they get restless if they are kept sitting too long. On the other hand if there are too many acts, and an audience is given too many intermissions, they lose the mood of the play; there is too much confusion and dropping of handbags.

For some of these reasons the contemporary convention is that of the three-act play. Shakespeare's five-act plays designed for different theatrical conditions are often reworked into four acts for our stage. Within a single act there may of course be several scenes, but if these require scene shifting, their number is necessarily limited. Even such devices as the revolving stage cause momentary breaks in which the attention of the audience can wander. There are many exceptions, of course, and may be more as the mechanisms of scene shifting are further perfected. The movies have accustomed people to much more rapid changes of scene than have been common since Shakespeare's time. Thus Marc Connelly's *Green Pastures* has eighteen scenes divided into two groups instead of the traditional three. *Waiting for Lefty* by Clifford Odets is about the length of a single act, but it has seven scenes. This is made possible by the blacking out of one scene and turning the spotlight on the next.

The contemporary dramatist has more freedom of

structure, therefore, than his predecessors, but he must still work within much more rigid limits than the novelist. For one thing, whether he uses two acts or four, he must end each one on a high note; there must be a kind of climax before each curtain. This may take the form of a situation which seems to have reached an impasse. The audience is then left with a strong enough feeling of suspense to carry over the intermission. Thus at the end of Act I of *Winterset* we see the murder of Shadow. Carr says, "God, it's easy putting a fellow away," and warns Mio to get out of the neighborhood. Mio refuses. The curtain falls, leaving the audience with the knowledge that Mio's life is in great danger. At the end of Act II, Mio has just discovered that the man he has been seeking to bring to justice is the brother of the girl he loves. What will his choice be? The curtain leaves us wondering. What will happen to a character? How will he choose? Two basic situations exist for the creation of suspense.

Another means is to introduce some new twist to the story which gives it an entirely new meaning. In Elmer Rice's *The Adding Machine* we meet Mr. Zero, a kind of Caspar Milquetoast who has been a bookkeeper in one office for twenty-five years. He is fired from his job and comes home to meet the nagging of his wife. Suddenly a policeman comes in and seizes him. Zero announces calmly to his wife that he killed the boss that afternoon, and must go with the officer. The curtain falls, leaving the audience startled and bewildered. They had not expected anything like this; the whole story has taken a new turn.

Climax and surprise are by no means the whole of

structure, but in drama they play a much more important part than they do in prose fiction. To hold an audience, the dramatist must never relax the suspense.
For this reason drama is usually more intense than
prose fiction. And for the same reason the playwright
is under great temptation to use cheap or sensational
tricks: to have an apparently honest man suddenly
turn out a scoundrel; to use explosions and pistol shots;
to have long lost rich uncles turn up, or cause apparently healthy persons to die suddenly. Mr. Zero's an-
nouncement that he is a murderer comes very close to
such a trick. He had provocation, certainly, but timid
bookkeepers are not given to committing murders
when they are fired. We had no indication that Mr.
Zero was capable of such a thing.

6. *Motivation and foreshadowing.* That brings us to
two other important elements in good playwriting—
motivation and foreshadowing. By motivation we
mean those forces or motives which lead a character
to act. They may come from within, like love or hate,
or from without, like the loss of a job. The important
thing is that they fit the character and the action.
Three men fired from their jobs might, on the basis of
the same motivation, take three different courses: one
might punch the boss in the nose; another might complain to his wife; and the third might get drunk. If a
dramatist gives us any of these actions, he must make
them consistent with the character; the type of man
who complains to his wife is not likely to knock down
the boss.

Of course people do unexpected things; this is especially true of characters in a play. But these things

must not be so unexpected as to make the action seem incredible. For this reason dramatists use foreshadowing, small hints of possible future developments. In the same office with Mr. Zero is Daisy. In the course of the play Daisy commits suicide, but before she does so, the thought of gas and carbolic acid has been in her mind. We didn't know she would get up courage enough to take her own life; in fact it seemed unlikely that she would, but when she does, we realize that we had been warned. In Robert Sherwood's *Idiot's Delight* the audience does not expect Harry Van to return to the hotel after he leaves with his road show. But when he does, his act is in accord with the streak of chivalry we have been shown earlier in his character. Foreshadowing does not tell us what is going to happen, but what could happen. Often we are unaware of it until the event has occurred; then we realize that the dramatist has prepared us for it. That is good playwriting.

Special Problems

1. *Exposition.* There are a number of special problems connected with telling a story in dramatic form. These too are related to structure. One of these is the exposition: telling the audience what has gone before, and what the situation is as the curtain rises. In *Our Town* Thornton Wilder simply had the stage manager, like the prologue in pre-Shakespearian plays, come out and tell the audience what was going on. This device seems artificial to audiences used to the realistic technique. One old stand-by is to have two servants talk about affairs in the house. Shakespeare used this one a number of times. Sheridan opened *The Rivals*

this way. A modern variant is to have the servant answer the telephone and tell someone that Mr. Blank has just returned from Chicago, and that Blank Jr. is due home from Harvard for the holidays, and that Mrs. Blank is giving a dinner party that evening.

There are more skilful ways of handling exposition. *Hamlet* begins with the nervous challenge of the sentry and the tense conversation about the ghost. Thus Shakespeare not only gives us information, but the mood of the play as well. We are plunged into the midst of action instead of being merely told about it. *Romeo and Juliet* begins with a street fight between servants of the Montagues and Capulets. Before it is over, the audience has a good bit of information about the long enmity between the two families; the mood of the play has been set, and the tragic action begun. Clifford Odets begins *Awake and Sing!* with a family argument at the supper table. We learn that Ralph is fed up with the petty drudgery of a small job, and that his father Myron believes in plugging away. And as families will in the course of an argument, these people rake up old grievances. Thus the audience is informed about the past, is given the mood of the play, is introduced to the characters, and is plunged into a conflict which produces the action of the play.

2. *Clarifying the action.* Another of the dramatist's special problems is the difficulty of making the action clear to the audience. The reader of a story can turn back a few pages if he finds that he has overlooked some step in the plot; the theater-goer is likely to nudge his neighbor in the next seat and start a whispered conversation, thus causing others to miss some

of what is being said on the stage. Shakespeare, being an actor, knew all about this. According to Hamlet many members of an Elizabethan audience were far from bright. Therefore Shakespeare took no chances; frequently he told what was going to happen, then showed it happening, and afterward told what happened, just in case someone had missed it. Thus Hamlet says: [7]

> I'll have these players
> Play something like the murder of my father
> Before mine uncle; I'll observe his looks;
> I'll tent him to the quick; if he but blench,
> I'll know my course. The spirit that I have seen
> May be the devil: . . .

Later we see the scene acted out by the players as Hamlet had planned. And after the guilty king stumbles from the stage, Hamlet says: [8]

> O good Horatio! I'll take the ghost's word for a
> thousand pound. Dids't thou perceive?
> HORATIO. Very well, my lord.
> HAMLET. Upon the talk of poisoning?
> HORATIO. I did very well note him.

Not only has the audience no doubt of the king's guilt, but they are shown that Hamlet is thoroughly convinced; there is no longer any possibility that the ghost was a devil come to tempt Hamlet to a murder.

Dramatists writing for a more orderly audience than the Elizabethans have not usually felt it necessary to be quite so explicit, but the problem still exists. Turning back to Jules' speech in *Pippa Passes*, you will note

[7] *Hamlet*, Act II, Sc. 2.
[8] *Ibid.*, Act III, Sc. 2.

that it takes several readings to determine just what Jules is or is not going to do. And we do not see the acting out of the decision. That is one reason why *Pippa Passes,* though in dramatic form, is not suited to the stage. Audiences like to be surprised; they do not like to be confused.

3. *Theatrical conventions.* Audiences, however, are willing to take certain things for granted. Even today they do not demand complete realism. If they did, no drama would be possible, for the most necessary convention of all is that they accept the taking down of the fourth wall of a house so that they may see what goes on inside. They accept too the telescoping of time so that a series of actions which is presented in less than three hours may seem to cover days, or even years. Faustus' last speech takes perhaps five minutes on the stage. During it the clock strikes the quarter-hours between eleven and midnight. Nor is there likely to be any complaint when the playwright arranges action so that most of it takes place in one or two rooms. In life a scene started in the kitchen may be continued in the living room, or on the front lawn. Important business is usually conducted in an office. But to avoid the interruption of scene changing, the playwright usually chooses one or two places for his characters to congregate and work out the play.

Some of the older conventions, however, are seldom used. The aside and soliloquy of Shakespeare's time have largely disappeared in modern plays. One reason is that in a small theater with a stage jutting out into the audience, it seemed more natural for an actor to make low-voiced remarks which other actors pretended not to hear. But in a huge, modern playhouse with a stage set behind an arch, it seems rather absurd for an actor to say something heard in the balcony half a block away, but apparently inaudible to people on the stage. Conventions of the drama, therefore, often grow out of the physical nature of the theater itself.

Dramatic Truth

We do not ask then that the drama be exactly true to life; we accept the arrangement of the action into certain structural forms, and its presentation in a certain manner. But we do ask that the action *seem* true. In this respect the drama is much like other types of fiction. The characters must seem like real people, and the things which occur must have probability. It is necessary here to make a distinction between realistic plays on the one hand, and the romantic and expressionistic plays on the other. For the two latter types the audience must be willing to accept certain impossible things: ghosts, allegorical figures such as Death, scenes laid in heaven or hell, talk more poetical and more revealing than we hear in life. Thus in both *The Adding Machine* and *Our Town* we meet characters after they have died. In *Winterset* the people living in a slum talk in blank verse, and all the important persons in a long past murder case turn upon the same dead-end street in a different city. It is as if the playwright said, "If people could speak after death, this is what they would say," or "If all these characters happened to come to the same place, here is what would happen." Audiences and critics have been willing to accept such if's.

1. Probability. What the critics will not accept is an unlikely happening in a play designed to be a realistic picture of life. The accidental coming together of all the principals in a murder case long past would seem absurd in a realistic play. A character disguised so that none of his friends recognize him would be a far-fetched device in anything but a farce or in romantic drama where that is a convention. Once in a while, of course, a very skilful playwright can get an audience to accept something very unlikely. For instance, Molnar in *The Guardsman* got away with the disguise trick, but remember, the person wearing the disguise was playing the part of an actor and might therefore have been able to execute such a trick. Furthermore, a large part of the fun grows out of the possibility that the actor's wife sees through the disguise. In any case, *The Guardsman* is very close to farce, where probabilities are less requisite.

In anything but farce or melodrama, however, we demand a certain type of probability. A play must follow its own logic. Thus if characters speak in poetry, other characters must act as if that were a natural way of talking. If human beings see ghosts, the humans ought to behave in some appropriate way such as showing fear or surprise. No rules can be stated for such things, however. For characters, on the other hand, there is a very definite rule; they must act in accord with their own natures. Even a modern audience will accept the scene in which Brutus sees Caesar's ghost; they will accept the signs and portents and prophecies in the play, but no intelligent audience would accept a scene in which Brutus sold out his side for money or power. Brutus is presented throughout as a man of high character; he cannot be false to his own nature. It would be just as false to have Iago suddenly reform and go about doing good deeds. Yet many second-rate plays have shown villains doing just that. King Lear becomes penitent and kindly, but only after going through hell. Nothing less than persecution and madness could change such a man as he was at first. His is no sudden or unmotivated conversion; it fits the nature of the man.

2. *Coincidence.* This problem of probability brings up a fundamental convention in all good fiction. We expect the action to grow not primarily out of accident or coincidence, but out of character. In life, we know that a man hated by his wife may get run over, thus making it possible for her to marry her lover. A bank clerk may bet on the winning horse and pay back what he has stolen before he is caught. A cruel father may drop dead leaving a big life insurance policy which solves all his family's problems. People do get unexpected legacies from rich uncles in Australia. But none of these situations makes a good solution for a play. It is like looking up the answer to a puzzle instead of solving it. As noted before, the technical name for this device is *deus ex machina,* the god from the machine. In Greek and Latin plays, a god was sometimes let down by a pulley on to the stage, where he proceeded to untangle the problems of the characters. But gods on pulleys and rich uncles from Australia are devices of poor playwrights.

We accept sudden legacies or deaths as motivating forces to start off the action; but we do not like them as solutions to a problem. Once the problem is created we expect the dramatist to abide by the rules of the game, that is to show how the people he has created will work out their own solution according to their own natures. This is what Shakespeare meant when he said that a playwright holds the mirror up to nature— that is, human nature.

This requirement that a play follow certain rules for the solution of the plot is one of the oldest and soundest of dramatic conventions. It produces both entertainment and meaning. There would be little suspense if we knew that at any moment the playwright could solve all problems by trick or accident. No game is fun if rules may be set aside at will. We should not want to see a football game decided by the toss of a coin. We prefer to see the result worked out in terms of the forces involved, and are disappointed if some fluke brings victory.

It is more important that the meaning or value of a play grows out of this convention. An action becomes meaningless when it is stopped or solved by accident. If, for instance, Hamlet's uncle had been killed by a fall from a horse, the whole play would go to pieces. We would never know whether or not Hamlet would have carried out the revenge required of him. All his worries and plans would have had no part in bringing about the action. *The Second Mrs. Tanqueray* loses much of its effectiveness because Pinero used a coincidence to bring his plot to a conclusion. The man who wants to marry Ellean turns out to be a former lover of Mrs. Tanqueray's. Mrs. Tanqueray, feeling that the situation thus created is impossible, commits suicide. Thus the problem of the play is solved by a far-fetched accident.

3. *Stock situations.* Another temptation to which the playwright is especially liable is to use stock situations. The reader or playgoer who is familiar with many plays, soon learns to recognize them. One of the oldest is to have a character hide in a closet or behind a screen to avoid meeting someone else. The second character then makes remarks which he would not wish the hidden person to hear, or gives away damaging information. The host is much embarrassed, but must try to keep A and B apart. Or the hidden character may attempt to come out at an inopportune time. Ben Jonson used this sort of thing in *The Alchemist;* Shakespeare has Falstaff hidden in a basket of clothes in *The Merry Wives of Windsor,* and Sheridan has two hidden persons in Joseph Surface's room in *The Rivals.* The movies continue to use the device. There are many other such, and they are more prevalent in poor plays than in good ones. A clever dramatist like Sheridan can at times give them a new twist, but usually they produce staleness. They often appear along with the stock types of character we discussed earlier.

4. *Values.* Stock scenes and stock characters are objectionable not only because they have been used before, but also because they show that the playwright has nothing important to say. As stated before, a good play, like any other good work of fiction, should have some meaning. This does not mean obvious moralizing, nor even that the play deal with some important

social or economic question. Most certainly a good play does not have to be solemn. *Ah, Wilderness* is a pleasant domestic comedy. Yet seeing it, we feel that we better understand adolescence, and for a little while have experienced what life was like in the early 1900's. *The Merchant of Venice* is put together out of several rather far-fetched plots. No sensible person would pledge a pound of flesh, nor a woman marry the man who picked a certain box, nor be able to use disguise to get a ring away from her husband. The portrait of Shylock, and his punishment is partly an outgrowth of the Renaissance attitude toward Jews. Yet despite absurdities and the prejudice, there is much which is memorable and valid. We are likely to start thinking about legality and justice, and about the common humanity of all races. Shakespeare was not so blinded by the prejudices of his time that he made Shylock a monster like Barabas in Marlowe's rival play *The Jew of Malta*. In showing Shylock as a suffering and persecuted human being, Shakespeare gave us vastly more than a poetic reworking of an old story.

Since Ibsen started the trend, there has been a tendency for serious plays, even for comedies, to deal with political, social, and economic questions. Even a musical comedy like *Of Thee I Sing* satirizes the methods of American politics. In other words it has a core of serious purpose. As the problem of propaganda in art is discussed elsewhere, we need only mention here the point that a first-rate play is not a tract or a sermon, but a story acted out. And as we have seen, the characters must not be mere types: the capitalist, the worker, the woman with a past, the corrupt politician

—they must be real people. Robert Sherwood's *Idiot's Delight* is an anti-war play, but it is first of all a good story, full of original situations, and with a most unusual hero. Harry Van, the wise-cracking manager of a travelling girl show, is one of the most memorable characters in any recent play. Clifford Odets' *Awake and Sing!* is a play showing the effect of our economic system upon a working class family, but it is first of all a portrait of real people, each an individual: Jacob, the elderly radical, who takes out his revolution in talk; Bessie, the shrewd, practical mother, who on occasion can use cruel means to get what she thinks best for the family; Moe, the hard-boiled smart guy, bitter over the raw deal life has given him, but for all his cynicism, capable of falling completely in love. These people are not merely the proletariat, oppressed by a system; their fates are, in the end, the result of their own characters. The system merely provides the background against which their parts are played.

Both *Idiot's Delight* and *Awake and Sing!* show us people caught in the sweep of powerful currents: war and economic depression. Both center the interest on the people themselves, and both tell interesting stories. In other words, the interest is first of all on characters and plot. Both are plays—that is entertainment. But because in the course of that entertainment we get a fuller understanding of the way these great forces affect men's lives, both plays carry more than their own weight.

There have been three great periods of drama in English: the Elizabethan, the Restoration; and the modern which begins with Shaw. The first of these gave us great poetry and brilliant portraits of human emotion and psychology; the second gave us a witty and satiric picture of a social group; the present one, using the knowledge gained from psychology, economics, and sociology, is giving us an interpretation of a civilization. Each of these periods has had a theater sufficiently popular to attract first-rate writers. One necessary element in the development of any art form —poetry, music, fiction, or the drama—is that there be an appreciative audience. When people lose their taste for verse, writers turn to prose; when they prefer circuses and vaudeville to plays, we get few good plays. Today, first-rate writers are giving us good plays; it is up to us to provide an audience trained to appreciate them. If we learn to know a good play when we see one, we need have no fears for the drama.

VIII

Humor

George Meredith has said: "We know the degree of refinement in men by the matter they will laugh at." A child has no real sense of humor. It takes long training to develop one, and some people never achieve it. A sense of humor implies standards of judgment. We recognize absurdities because we have come to recognize certain things as logical and orderly, and to see absurdity in violations of this logic. A child may laugh to see an adult stand on his head, but he sees nothing strange in the performance. Nor would a grown-up see anything absurd in that action on the part of an acrobat. But were he to see a judge entertaining his granddaughter with acrobatic stunts, he would laugh. His standard of behavior for judges does not include tumbling.

Varieties of Humor

1. *Boorish humor.* The question resolves itself into one of standards. The ignorant man sets up his own behavior as a pattern, and finds all other patterns absurd. He laughs at the manners and dress of other nations, at the social usages of other groups and at the religion or beliefs of anyone who differs with him. American

tourists are accused of this type of boorishness. George Meredith has pictured in Sir Willoughby the classic example of this kind of stupidity. Sir Willoughby is entertaining Laetetia Dale with the following account of his European travels: [1]

I mentioned the Pope's parti-coloured body-guard just now. In my youth their singular attire impressed me. People tell me they have been re-uniformed: I am sorry. They remain one of my liveliest recollections of the Eternal City. They affected my sense of humour, always alert in me, as you are aware. We English have humour. It is the first thing struck in us when we land on the Continent: our risible faculties are generally active all through the tour. Humour, or the clash of sense with novel examples of the absurd, is our characteristic. I do not condescend to boisterous displays of it.

It is the same sort of "sense of humor" which leads Americans to laugh at the beef-eaters outside the tower of London or at a man wearing a monocle. Persons who, like Sir Willoughby, boast of their sense of humor usually have this kind.

Writers, short-story writers in particular, have not been above commercializing this instinct to laugh at anything they are not accustomed to. Magazines designed for mass circulation frequently use stories that show the absurd social usages of the four-hundred. And the sophisticated periodicals do the same thing with ash men, shop girls, and bookkeepers. The stories of Octavus Roy Cohen show the same method applied to a single racial group. Of recent years the mountaineer has replaced the farmer as the butt of this

[1] George Meredith, *The Egoist*.

kind of humor. Some writers have even had the bad taste to laugh at college students.

This sort of laughter arises largely from a sense of superiority. Thus the very stupid man becomes amusing. To appeal to slow-witted persons, the object of laughter must be made very stupid indeed. This explains the impossibly foolish characters so popular on the radio and in the movies. Shakespeare drew Launcelot Gobbo to delight the groundlings, those theater patrons, who, according to Hamlet, were "incapable of anything but inexplicable dumb shows and noise." Shakespeare no doubt arrived at this judgment by observing the kind of things laughed at by the vulgar. The things laughed at are some of the safest guides to the intelligence of a college class.

2. *The wise-crack.* Most freshmen laugh loudest at the "wise-crack." Furthermore, a whole body of so-called modern humor is built upon that foundation. The wise-crack is neither so modern nor so clever as many persons believe. It often takes the form of a catch phrase, frequently meaningless and usually impolite. Expressions like "baloney," "applesauce," "so what?" belong to this class. Shakespeare's tavern loafers had many similar words at their command. Authors have always put them into the mouths of low characters to give verisimilitude to their conversation.

The twisting of a serious remark is also common in Elizabethan plays. Like punning, this was at one time regarded as witty. High-school youngsters often twist an innocent remark to make it appear to have a risqué significance. Thirty years ago the mere mention of the word *spoon* would send the girls off into a gale of laughter; in more recent times the word *neck* has had a similar effect.

As in all kinds of humor there are different grades of wise-cracks. A really good one is funny because it strikes home or makes a point. When Coleridge, referring to his Unitarian ministry, asked Lamb, "Charles, did you ever hear me preach?" Lamb replied, "I never heard you do anything else." That is essentially a wise-crack; it twists the meaning of the word *preach*. It is fairly good because it caught Coleridge in a weak point, his tendency to spout. A much better one was the remark made by the painter Whistler to Oscar Wilde. In answer to some clever thing of Whistler's, Wilde said, "I wish I had said that." "Don't worry, Oscar. You will," was Whistler's reply—a reply that, like most wise-cracks, was clever at the expense of someone else and could apply to but a single situation. Thus it lacks the universality which makes for lasting humor.

3. *The pun.* Today this type of wise-crack is more in fashion than the pun. But, unlikely as it may seem, there have been good puns. *The Autocrat of the Breakfast Table* has a number of them; for instance: "Put not your trust in money, but put your money in trust." This, like the more famous one of Franklin's, "We must all hang together or we shall all hang separately," has more to it than a mere play on words. The play on words is a means to an end; it heightens the wit of the remark itself, making it easily remembered. Perhaps the worst feature of the usual pun is that it leads to another. The punster, like the professional funny

man, can never take it or leave it alone. Puns are more
habit-forming than alcohol.

4. *The epigram.* Both wise-cracks and puns are
alike in this: they can add spice to writing, but they
cannot make a satisfactory staple dish. A similar kind
of spice is provided by the epigram, a neat, witty saying, usually with a core of truth. Its effectiveness depends not only upon its wit, but upon its idea or point.
Franklin's pun is really an epigram as well. Oscar
Wilde was one of the greatest masters of this in English:

The nineteenth century dislike of Realism is the rage of
Caliban seeing his own face in a glass.

Even things that are true can be proved.

Men marry because they are tired; women because they
are curious; both are disappointed.

More than half of modern culture depends upon what
one shouldn't read.

One after another he poured them forth, but for most
readers there are too many; the dish is overspiced.
Good epigrams, however, are quoted generation after
generation; but most wise-cracks of our age will be
obsolete in the next.

5. *Nonsense humor.* Another type of humor is the
kind the Victorians would have called "amusing nonsense," and which today might be named "nut humor."
It is found in *Tristram Shandy*, and appears in the
nineteenth century with such things as Lewis Carroll's "Jabberwocky" and Edward Lear's "The Owl and
the Pussy Cat." A few years ago it was found in limer-

icks. "The Purple Cow" of Gelett Burgess is characteristic of the whole school: [2]

> I never saw a purple cow;
> I never hope to see one.
> But this I'll tell you anyhow,
> I'd rather see than be one.

Some writers like Hilaire Belloc have tried to ex-
cuse themselves by labeling their work "child rimes."
Here, for instance, is "The Gnu": [3]

G stands for Gnu, whose weapons of defence
Are long, sharp, curling horns and common sense.
To these he adds a name so short and strong
That even hardy Boers pronounce it wrong.
How often on a bright autumnal day
The pious people of Pretoria say
"Come let us hunt the—" then no more is heard
But sounds of strong men struggling for a word;
Meanwhile the distant Gnu with grateful eyes
Observes his opportunity and flies.

In England especially, these "child rimes" are particularly popular with adults. They probably belong to
the literature of escape.

In America certain comic strips belong to this tradition. Herriman's Krazy Kat and its descendant, Sullivan's Felix, are of this school. So too is Popeye; and
in the movies there are Walt Disney's "Silly Sym-
phonies."

Now, whereas there are many types of escape lit-

---

[2] "The Purple Cow" from Gelett Burgess, *The Burgess Nonsense
Book* (New York, Frederick A. Stokes & Co., 1901).

[3] "The Gnu." Reprinted from *Bad Child's Book of Beasts* by
Hillaire Belloc, by permission of and special arrangement with
Alfred A. Knopf, Inc. Copyright, 1931, by Hillaire Belloc.

erature, all these just mentioned have another element in common—fantasy. Like the Mad Hatter of *Alice in Wonderland*, Ignatz Mouse, Whimpy, Micky Mouse, and all the rest belong to never-never lands, each with a private logic of its own. This is not the place to discuss the social significance of the immense popularity of this sort of humor—a popularity that jumps the boundaries of language, creed, or political faith. Quite possibly such characters are the modern equivalents of those mischief-makers of old like Puck and Queen Mab. If so, they are another testimonial to mankind's instinctive notion that within an orderly universe there is a screw loose.

6. *The mock-heroic.* It is not practical here to try to analyze all the varieties of this nonsense humor. Often it derives its effect less from its material than from its manner. Thus Joe Cook's meaningless monologues gain their point from the completely plausible tone in which they are delivered. Here we have the incongruity between subject and style, which on another level becomes the mock-heroic as in "The Nun's Priest's Tale" and *The Rape of the Lock.* A modern variant is the scientific manner applied to a trivial subject. Here is one by Will Cuppy on the Nightingale: [4]

The Nightingale

The Nightingale is a familiar figure in poems beginning "O, Nightingale!" all based on other poems beginning "O, Nightingale!" The Nightingale is famous for

[4] Will Cuppy, "The Nightingale." Permission *The New Yorker.* Copyright the F-R. Publishing Corporation 1931.

singing all night as well as all day. He sings in the middle of hedgerows and spinneys, where nothing can hit him. He is much loved by persons who are slightly deaf. The Nightingale goes "Zo zo zo zo," "Ze ze ze ze," and sometimes "Jug jug jug jug tereu," like parts of Beethoven's "Pastoral Symphony." The Nightingale sings with the syrinx. The larynx isn't good enough. The psychology of the Nightingale has been much misunderstood. He does not sing to impress his wife, who remains in the nest with her ears tucked under her wings, trying to forget. He is training for the annual visit of the British Empire Naturalist's Association and his radio public. He is wound up and nothing can stop him except a charge of No. 10 shot.

This is really a blend of nonsense humor and the mock-heroic, and, like much other mock-heroic writing, has something of a satiric intent. Thus when Pope describes a card game as if it were a Homeric battle, and the cutting off of a lock of hair in the terms of a military campaign, he makes both situations ridiculous. One of the best ways to satirize overseriousness about trivial matters is to heighten the overseriousness so that the absurdity of the whole thing is revealed.

7. *Parody.* A related procedure is to burlesque or parody serious writing by overdoing its tricks of style. Here the purpose is often twofold—to ridicule a literary style and to make fun of the ideas of a writer. Thus Southey in all seriousness wrote: [5]

"You are old, Father William," the young man cried,
  "The few locks which are left you are gray;
You are hale, Father William, a hearty old man,—
  Now tell me the reason I pray."

[5] Robert Southey, "The Old Man's Comforts."

"In the days of my youth," Father William replied,
   "I remembered that youth could not last;
I thought of the future, whatever I did,
   That I never might grieve for the past."

This might seem silly enough as it is, but Lewis Carroll parodied it thus: [6]

"You are old, Father William," the young man said,
   "And your hair has become very white;
And yet you incessantly stand on your head—
   Do you think at your age it is right?"

"In my youth," Father William replied to his son,
   "I feared it might injure the brain;
But now I am perfectly sure I have none,
   Why I do it again and again."

You will note that Carroll has caricatured, but not beyond recognition, the sing-song style and the trite moralizing of the original. In a similar manner Charles Stuart Calverley parodied the imitators of the old ballads: [7]

The auld wife sat at her ivied door,
   (*Butter and eggs and a pound of cheese*)
A thing she had frequently done before;
   And her spectacles lay on her aproned knees. . . .

The farmer's daughter hath soft brown hair;
   (*Butter and eggs and a pound of cheese*)
And I met with a ballad, I can't say where,
   Which wholly consisted of lines like these.

To be good a parody must have a real resemblance to the original, and it must burlesque real faults of

---

[6] Lewis Carroll, *Alice in Wonderland.*
[7] Charles Stuart Calverley, "Ballad."

style or real absurdities of thought. What Calverley
no doubt had in mind were ballads such as Rossetti's
"Troy Town," which opens:

> Heavenborn Helen, Sparta's queen
>   (*O Troy Town!*)
> Had two breasts of heavenly sheen,
> The sun and moon of the heart's desire;
> All Love's lordship lay between.
>   (*O Troy's down,*
>   *Tall Troy's on fire!*)

Though this too may look like burlesque, Rossetti
seems not to have intended it as such.

Compare with Calverley's parody, the one Dr. Johnson wrote of the old ballads: [8]

> I put my hat upon my head,
>   And walked into the strand,
> And there I met another man
>   Whose hat was in his hand.

He was trying to show what he regarded as the trivial-
ity of subject matter and childishness of the verse form
of the ballads, but his stanza so little resembles them
that it has usually been regarded as showing only
Johnson's literary prejudices. At times Dr. Johnson had
a resemblance to Sir Willoughby.

8. *Satire.* Parody is only one form of satire—it ridicules chiefly literary forms. More often satire ridicules
human vices or folly. As we have seen with Sir Willoughby, it can backfire on the satirist if he ridicules
things he does not understand or with which he is
unfamiliar. Thus Byron in his youthful "English Bards

[8] Johnson, quoted in Wordsworth, Preface to *Lyrical Ballads.*

and Scotch Reviewers" made fun of a number of
his contemporaries about whom he knew little. For
instance, he pictured Scott as a mercenary writer.
Throughout his life Byron kept apologizing to one or
another person he had ignorantly misjudged. But
when he wrote of things he really knew about, like
the hypocrisy of high society and the foibles of human beings, Byron was one of the most excellent sati-
rists in the language. Here is his picture of aristocratic
education in his day: [9]

> The languages, especially the dead,
>   The sciences, and most of all the abstruse,
> The arts, at least all such as could be said
>   To be the most remote from common use,
> In all these he was much and deeply read:
>   But not a page of anything that's loose,
> Or hints continuation of the species,
> Was ever suffered, lest he should grow vicious. . . .
>
> Juan was taught from out the best edition
>   Expurgated by learned men, who place
> Judiciously, from out the schoolboy's vision,
>   The grosser parts; but, fearful to deface
> Too much their modest bard by this omission,
>   And pitying sore this mutilated case,
> They only add them all in an appendix,
> Which saves, in fact, the trouble of an index.

One of the elements which makes this particularly
effective is that Byron has picked out things worthy
of satire. Hypocrisy and stupidity, particularly the
stupidity of persons who should know better, are always fair game. A man's physical infirmities, on the

[9] Byron, *Don Juan*, Canto I.

other hand, are not—at least to people with a well-developed sense of fair play. Thus when Dryden laughs at Shaftesbury's physical deformity by saying he was "born a shapeless lump, like Anarchy," most readers are pained rather than amused. This form of wit is preserved by radio gag men, but it is not often a part of more sophisticated literature.

It is not particularly difficult to get a laugh at the expense of persons or institutions admittedly stupid. It took no great perspicacity on Byron's part to discover that Wordsworth's "The Idiot Boy" was a silly poem or for Pope to recognize that Colley Cibber was a fool. Nor is there anything particularly humorous in a fool doing foolish things. But when a normally intelligent man does a foolish thing there is a real violation of our sense of logic—as in the example of a judge doing handsprings for his granddaughter. The ability to notice and then caricature the follies of the successful and the intelligent is the real test of the satirist. Pope is at his best in his portrait of Addison, one of the three or four most brilliant literary men of his time: [10]

> Peace to all such! but were there one whose fires
> True Genius kindles, and fair Fame inspires,
> Bless'd with each talent and each art to please,
> And born to write, converse, and live with ease;
> Should such a man, too fond to rule alone,
> Bear, like the Turk, no brother near his throne;
> View him with scornful, yet with jealous eyes,
> And hate for arts that caus'd himself to rise;
> Damn with faint praise, assent with civil leer,

[10] Pope, "Epistle to Dr. Arbuthnot."

And without sneering teach the rest to sneer;
Willing to wound, and yet afraid to strike,
Just hint a fault, and hesitate dislike;
Alike reserv'd to blame or to commend,
A tim'rous foe, and a suspicious friend;
Dreading ev'n fools; by flatterers besieged,
And so obliging that he ne'er obliged;
Like Cato, give his little Senate laws
And sit attentive to his own applause: . . .

Pope has not made the mistake of attributing to Addison faults which he obviously had not, such as viciousness or dullness; instead he has skilfully picked out and heightened (but not beyond recognition) Addison's caution and his liking for the praise of lesser men. But when Wordsworth called Voltaire dull, he made only himself ridiculous. Furthermore, Pope has satirized not only his rival, Addison, but he has to some extent hit off all men with similar characteristics. "Damn with faint praise," and "so obliging that he ne'er obliged" have become part of the language because they so perfectly describe a certain kind of human frailty. Part of the force of all successful art derives from its universal quality. Pope in showing us Addison has shown us ourselves also.

9. *Irony.* Closely allied to satire in intent, but differing in method, is irony. The ironist satirizes in a back-handed manner; he pretends to say just the reverse of what he means. Much of the effectiveness of this form of writing and speaking grows out of the incongruity between what is said and what is meant. The victim, like the "fall guy" of the old-fashioned vaudeville, is lulled into a false sense of security. The

audience is kept in pleasurable suspense until the victim is flat on his back. Only the ironist uses intellectual rather than physical devices. In English literature Swift stands alone as the master of irony. No one else has so completely mastered the deacon-like solemnity combined with the quick and unexpected swing of the blackjack. Thus in his defense of Christianity: [11]

I readily own there hath been an old custom time out of mind, for people to assemble in the churches every Sunday, and that shops are still frequently shut, in order, as it is conceived, to preserve the memory of that ancient practice, but how this can prove a hindrance to business or pleasure is hard to imagine. What if the men of pleasure are forced one day in the week, to game at home instead of the chocolate-houses? Are not the taverns and coffee-houses open? Can there be a more convenient season for taking a dose of physic? Are fewer clops got upon Sunday than other days? Is not that the chief day for traders to sum up the accounts of the week, and for lawyers to prepare their briefs? But I would fain know how it can be pretended that the churches are misapplied? Where are more appointments and rendezvouzes of gallantry? Where more care to appear in the foremost box with greater advantage of dress? Where more meetings for business? Where more bargains driven of all sorts? And where so many conveniences or enticements to sleep?

Like Byron, Swift commonly chose the best possible objects for his satire: hypocrisy, cruelty, stupidity, and tyranny.

Of course irony can take the form of a single remark, and it may be blended with other kinds of writ-

[11] Jonathan Swift, *An Argument to Prove that the Abolishing of Christianity in England May . . . Be Attended with Some Inconveniences.*

ing either serious or humorous. Thus Burns in his story of Tam O'Shanter moralizes ironically on Tam's heedlessness of his wife's advice: [12]

> How many lengthened sage advices
> The husband frae the wife despises.

The single word, "lengthened," tips the reader off to the poet's real intention.

Nor are satire and irony always humorous. Siegfried Sassoon's picture of civilian callousness about wounded soldiers in "Does It Matter?" is far too biting to be amusing. And Swift's picture of the Yahoos in "A Voyage to the Houyhnhnms," satirizes the more loathsome qualities of the human species. There is little laughter in that fourth book of *Gulliver's Travels*.

There are times when humor is out of place, and it is a wise writer who recognizes this. Some of the most painful passages in all literature are those where a writer has tried to be funny at the wrong time. That is one of the many faults of "The Idiot Boy." Truly civilized people do not relish humor which grows out of the suffering of others. It is this fact which makes the practical joke particularly distasteful. One of the most loathsome characters in modern literature is the practical joker, Jim Kendal, in Ring Lardner's "Haircut." The whole story is a vivid illustration of the point mentioned earlier: what a man laughs at is a good indication of his intelligence. The barber-shop crowd who thought Jim Kendal amusing are made almost as loathsome as he.

"Haircut" is an example of that type of writing

---

[12] Robert Burns, "Tam O'Shanter."

wherein the characters satirize themselves; the author selects and heightens the things they say so that they reveal their own ignorance and folly. It is the device Swift used in his "Verses on the Death of Dr. Swift":

> My female friends, whose tender hearts
> Have better learned to act their parts,
> Receive the news in doleful dumps:
> "The Dean is dead (pray, what is trumps?)."
> "The Lord have mercy on his soul!
> (Ladies, I'll venture for the vole.)"
> "Six deans, they say, must bear the pall
> (I wish I knew what king to call)."
> "Madam, your husband will attend
> The funeral of so good a friend?"
> "No, madam, 'tis a shocking sight,
> And he's engaged to-morrow night:
> My Lady Club will take it ill
> If he should fail her at quadrille.
> He loved the Dean (I lead a heart),
> But dearest friends, they say, must part.
> His time was come; he ran his race;
> We hope he's in a better place."

10. Kindly humor. Biting satire and irony are not particularly prevalent in English and American literature, at least not before 1920. More characteristic is a kindly laughing at human foibles rather than an exposure of human depravity. The method is that of Chaucer, of Shakespeare, of Fielding, of Dickens and of Wodehouse, even of Sinclair Lewis. George Babbitt is in the end a character to be pitied rather than hated. This kind of humor is a satire touched with pity. Even the Pardoner, perhaps the most savagely portrayed of the Canterbury pilgrims, is not made dis-

tasteful to the reader. And at the end of his tale, we
suddenly realize that his bravado is a front; that he
has a streak of decency—that he is a sinner unhappy
in the rôle he has created. Finishing his cynical revelation of how he preaches for his own profit, he says: [13]

> —And lo, sires, thus I preche.
> And Jesu Christ, that is oure soules leche,
> So graunte you his pardon to receyve,
> For that is best; I wol you nat deceyve.

The next moment he steps back into the rôle of the
mountebank, but Chaucer has shown us a man and
not a devil.

Very often the writer uses the foibles to make the
character more human and more lovable. Goldsmith's
parson in "The Deserted Village" and Dickens' Pickwick, Micawber, and many another are made fun of
in the way we speak of a well-loved, eccentric member of the family. Swift had no affection for the ladies
he pictured at their card game. Contrast with them
the Wife of Bath: [14]

> A good Wif was ther of biside Bathe,
> But she was somdel deef, and that was scathe.
> Of clooth-making she hadde swich an haunt,
> She passed hem of Ypres and of Gaunt.
> In al the parisshe wif ne was ther noon
> That to the offrynge bifore hire sholde goon:
> And if ther dide, certeyn so wrooth was she,
> That she was out of alle charitee.
> Hir coverchiefs ful fyne weren of ground;
> I dorste swere they weyeden ten pound
> That on a Sonday weren upon hir heed.

[13] Chaucer, "The Pardoner's Tale," *The Canterbury Tales.*
[14] Chaucer, "The Wife of Bath," *The Canterbury Tales.*

Hir hosen weren of fyn scarlet reed,
Ful streite yteyd, and shoes ful moyste and newe.
Bold was hir face, and fair, and reed of hewe.
She was a worthy woman al hir lyve:
Housbondes at chirche dore she hadde fyve,
Withouten other compaignye in youthe,—
But thereof nedeth nat to speke as nowthe.
And thries hadde she been at Jerusalem;
She hadde passed many a straunge strem;
At Rome she hadde been, and at Boloigne,
In Galice at Seint Jame, and at Coloigne.
She koude muchel of wandrynge by the weye.
Gat-tothed was she, soothly for to seye.
Upon an amblere esily she sat,
Y-wympled wel, and on hir heed an hat
As brood as is a bokeler or a targe;
A foot-mantel aboute hir hipes large,
And on hir feet a paire of spores sharpe.
In felaweshipe wel koude she laughe and carpe.
Of remedies of love she knew per chauce,
For she koude of that art the olde daunce.

Certainly Chaucer bore this woman no ill-will. Yet she is a garrulous, boastful, bossy, lustful, middle-aged woman on the lookout for a sixth husband. She could easily have been made the butt of bitter satire. Instead we find her prologue revealing her wit, earthy common sense, and ability to laugh at herself. Most readers find her one of Chaucer's most delightful characters.

This kind of good-natured, even affectionate, satire has been called *humor* as distinguished from *wit* which implies a more intellectual quality, a sharper edge. Pope and Swift are notable for the quality of wit. Pope's couplet: [15]

---

[15] *The Rape of the Lock,* Canto III.

> Not louder shrieks to pitying Heaven are cast,
> When husbands, or when lapdogs breathe their last;

is clever and biting, but it has no kindliness. However it is not the purpose of the present chapter to analyze these rather fine-spun distinctions. For those who wish to study the matter further, there is the famous *Essay on Comedy* by George Meredith. The important thing is that this kindly humor is almost the exact reverse of the practical joke. Little Audrey, who just laughed and laughed because she knew the fat lady was sitting on a freshly painted bench, is far removed from Shakespeare's Falstaff. Scoundrel though he is, everyone who has known him can echo Pistol's speech: [16]

> Boy, bristle thy courage up; for Falstaff he is dead
> And we must yearn therefore.

To which Bardolph answers:

> Would I were with him, wheresome'er he is, either in
> heaven or in hell!

No one feels thus about the people in the plays of Terence and Plautus, nor about a character like John O'Hara's Pal Joey. This kindly humor, although most common in English literature, is not found only there. Don Quixote and Huckleberry Finn are a part of this great tradition. It is a tradition which has had no small part in civilizing mankind. Meredith in 1877 warned that a Germany, lacking in the comic spirit, was in danger of fanaticism.

11. *Laughing at oneself.* Max Eastman points out a

[16] *Henry V*, Act II, Sc. 3.

further development of humor, a development particularly characteristic of America. This is the trick of laughing at oneself instead of at others. The humorist tells of his own mishaps and mistakes, and in doing so he makes his audience a party to them; his misadventures are those of all of us. This is the method of Mark Twain's *The Innocents Abroad,* of Davy Crockett and Artemus Ward—and more recently of Will Rogers and James Thurber. Typical was Rogers' remark, "All I know is what I read in the papers." Lincoln, who nearly always adopted this manner, admired Artemus Ward so much that on Monday, September 22, 1862, when his cabinet was waiting tensely for him to read the Emancipation Proclamation, he first read this from a new book Ward had just sent:

High Handed Outrage at Utica

In the fall of 1856, I showed my show in Utiky, a trooly grate sitty in the State of New York.

The people gave me a cordyal recepshun. The press was loud in her praises.

1 day as I was givin a descripshun of my Beests and Snaiks in my usual floury stile what was my skorn & disgust to see a big burly feller walk up to the cage containin my wax figgers of the Lord's Last Supper, and cease Judas Iscarrot by the feet and drag him out on the ground. He then commenced fur to pound him as hard as he cood.

"What under the son are you about?" cried I.

Sez he, "What did you bring this purssylanermus cuss here fur?" & he hit the wax figger another tremenjus blow on the hed.

Sez I, "You egrejus ass, that air's a wax figger—a representashun of the false 'Postle."

Sez he, "That's all very well fur you to say, but I tell

you, old man, that Judas Iscarrot can't show hisself in Utiky with impunerty by a darn site!" with which observation he kaved in Jadassis hed. The young man belonged to 1 of the first famerlies in Utiky. I sood him, and the joory brawt in a verdict of Arson in the 3d degree.

The outrageous grammar and spelling are part of the game; they were designed to picture the writer as an ignorant and rather foolish person—the writer is the butt of his own humor.

James Russell Lowell used these devices in his *Biglow Papers;* they were part of the method of Mr. Dooley and Will Rogers. They are often a part of dialect humor. In fact the use of dialect for humorous purposes helps to give the audience a sense of superiority to the character who cannot speak good English. Dialect humor is at least as old as Shakespeare's Fluellen, but the American humorist tends to attribute it to himself, in other words to make himself ridiculous.

The effect of all this is to remove the cruelty from humor. In so far as satire is a part of it, it is satire on man in general, including the writer. The better writers have tended to get away from dialect and illiterate style. In recent years, James Thurber's accounts of his own misadventures are some of the most successful examples of this type of humor. It is a humor which makes for tolerance and pity. The humor of the child and the savage is cruel. That is why George Meredith can say, "An excellent test of the civilization of a country . . . I take to be the flourishing of the comic idea and of comedy." Perhaps it is not only a product, but one of the chief causes of that civilization.

12. American love of the absurd. In most American

humor, there is another characteristic element—a love of the wildly absurd. It may take the form of the exaggerated lie—the whopper; or it may be a sudden and extreme anti-climax; or it may be merely the juxtaposition of completely irreconcilable materials. Ever since Benjamin Franklin's account of whales climbing Niagara Falls to spawn, this sort of thing has completely baffled the British. It is quite different from Pope's use of anti-climax and juxtaposition of oddly assorted elements: [17]

> Some dire disaster, or by force or slight;
> But what, or where, the fates have wrapt in night.
> Whether the nymph shall break Diana's law,
> Or some frail China jar receive a flaw;
> Or stain her honor or her new brocade;
> Forget her pray'rs, or miss a masquerade;
> Or lose her heart, or necklace, at a ball;

Once you get the pattern, the anti-climaxes amuse but do not startle. All are related to the affairs and behavior of an eighteenth-century belle.

Compare that with Artemus Ward's sudden introduction of "arson in the third degree" or E. B. White's couplet: [18]

> Placing his lips against her brow
> He kissed her eyelids shut. And how.

O. Henry's similes belong to the same school. He describes cuspidors "so wide-mouthed that the crack pitcher of a lady baseball team should have been able

[17] *The Rape of the Lock*, Canto II.
[18] E. B. White, "How to Tell a Major Poet from a Minor Poet," *Quo Vadimus* (New York, Harper & Brothers, 1939).

to throw a ball into one of them at five paces distant,"
and a waiter "with a voice like butter cakes and an eye
like the cherry in a Manhattan cocktail." The tramp,
Soapy, thrown out of a restaurant, arises "joint by joint
as a carpenter's rule opens."

13. *Non-sequitur humor*. The extreme non-sequitur
humor of Will Cuppy and Robert Benchley is a more
recent development of this juxtaposition of things not
ordinarily thought of together. Note how Benchley
gets his effects by means of sudden surprises: [19]

In an article on How Authors Create, in which the writing methods of various masters of English prose like Conrad, Shaw, and Barrie are explained (with photographs
of them in knickerbockers plaguing dogs and pushing
against sun-dials), I discover that I have been doing the
whole thing wrong all these years. The interviewer in
this case hasn't got around to asking me yet—doubtless
because I have been up in my room with the door shut
and not answering the bell—but I am going to take a
chance anyway and tell him how I do my creative work
and just how much comes from inspiration and how much
from hashish and other perfumes. I may even loosen up
and tell him what my favorite hot weather dishes are.

Lasting Humor

It is quite probable that this humor of manner rather
than of matter will not be enduring. Most of Josh
Billings, one of the older practitioners of this school,
is now pretty boring stuff. In fact any literary convention which relies chiefly upon its style or manner is

[19] Robert Benchley, "How I Create," *No Poems, or Around the
World Backwards and Sideways* (New York, Harper & Brothers,
1932).

likely to become outmoded. On the contrary long after the style of Chaucer, Shakespeare, Dickens or Mark Twain has gone out of date, the Wife of Bath, Falstaff, Sam Weller, and Huckleberry Finn are alive and well. I suspect that Leonard Q. Ross's Hyman Kaplan will outlast the amusing didoes of Robert Benchley.

Just as satire endures if it satirizes enduring human failings, so humor endures if it deals with enduring human qualities. The greatest humor, like the greatest poetry, leads man to understand his own nature and the nature of the universe. The greatest irony is the irony of life itself. For whether in bitterness like Romeo's "I am fortune's fool" or in laughter like John Gay's epitaph: [20]

> Life is a jest; and all things show it,
> I thought so once; but now I know it.

man has in his wisest moments recognized that neither he nor the universe operates quite as human logic would expect.

[20] John Gay, "My Own Epitaph."

IX

Originality and Convention

In these days, especially in the United States, conventionality has become synonymous with dullness or even with hypocrisy. We strive for informality in manners and in prose style. Slang, even profanity, has become the rule in the most formal society and the most serious writing. In a serious essay upon literature Henry Seidel Canby uses such phrases as "hard-boiled books," "debunking," and "jazz intellect"; and H. L. Mencken discusses why poetry "should go on the rocks." It is often overlooked that informality has itself become a convention.

Some kind of convention there has always been whether in life or literature. For the American Indian, convention governed the proper way of torturing a captive and the form of his songs. When today a policeman stops you for driving too fast, he is likely to begin with the question, "Where's the fire?"—an opening that has become a convention. The greeting one student calls to another is almost invariably some phrase that is at the moment a campus convention.

The roots of convention lie deep in human nature. Man's desire to be accepted among his fellows leads him to act and speak as they do. The young, because of a greater feeling of insecurity, a sense of being on trial in the world, are especially given to following the social conventions of the moment. It is not so much a spirit of revolt which leads a young man to drink or to boast about his conquests; rather he does these things because of a belief that they are expected of a man.

The same tendency appears in literature. Student themes tend to imitate the style of *The Saturday Evening Post, Collier's,* Walter Winchell, Ernest Hemingway, or James T. Farrell, depending upon the individual's literary preferences. A sad commentary upon these is that most freshman verse is patterned after Robert Service or Eddie Guest.

All this is not meant to imply that conventions are foolish. It is a difficult thing to begin a poem or a conversation, and often the safest plan is to use some formula which has been accepted. All children's stories used to begin, "Once upon a time," and finish with, "And they lived happily ever after." Certain writers for the popular magazines are still using practically the same formula although children's stories have abandoned it. The old ballads, composed as they were by people with a limited literary horizon, were filled with conventional phrases and thought patterns. One of the most obvious is the question and answer method of telling a story. Many ballads use the same opening lines; they have the same phrases: "the red gold," "the milk white steed," "the blood red wine"; events tend to happen in threes. These things gave the untutored versifiers a pattern to follow when they made up new songs.

Some literary periods have been much more given to the use of conventions than others, but no period has been without them. They govern such things as the literary form, the attitude of the writer toward life, and the characters he draws. The student soon learns to recognize them when they appear in the literature of the past; he is usually unconscious of them in modern writing. This is one reason the older classics often seem to him artificial or unreal. If, however, he can learn to recognize a convention when he sees it, he will then be in a position to recognize also the quality of originality.

Conventional Forms

1. The dream-vision. Let us examine first some of the conventional literary forms. In the Middle Ages one of the most popular was the dream-vision. The poet or story-teller represented himself as going to sleep and dreaming the story that he afterwards told his readers. It is thus that *Piers Plowman* opens; it is the form of Chaucer's *Book of the Duchess* and *The Legend of Good Women.* Spring and summer seem to have been the most propitious seasons for these dreams, possibly because a nap in the meadow was then particularly pleasant, and outdoor sleeping was supposed to be especially productive of literary visions. The device was useful for allegorical tales to enable the author to explain a particularly fanciful story. Bunyan used the same device for *The Pilgrim's Progress.* More recently H. G. Wells in *Men Like Gods* has used the dream vision form for exactly the same reason. Students often represent particularly fanciful themes as dreams they have had. The convention therefore met a real problem: that of presenting a highly imaginative story.

Most conventions have appeared to meet some such problem. For instance, how would you go about paying a compliment to a girl? Very likely you would resort to slang: "Gee, you're swell!" or some such expression. At the moment there are few helpful conventions in the matter. That is one reason Americans are said to be poor at making love; they have never mastered the art of paying compliments. The American youth can only make expensive gestures: buying football tickets, paying taxi bills, or sending candy. The Elizabethans, who were notable, even notorious lovemakers, took over from the Italians a very neat and very inexpensive convention for this purpose— the sonnet.

2. *The sonnet.* There is no inherent reason why a sonnet should not be twelve lines or sixteen lines, but ever since Petrarch created the fourteen-line form, this length has been a convention. It is in fact a convenient size. A compliment, like a corsage, should not be too large or it becomes embarrassing. A lover who had poetic skill enough could send one often. The difficulty of fitting an idea exactly to a set number of lines and of working out the elaborate rhyme scheme gave the sonnet the quality of something very special, not just a trifle a man might send to any girl. The fact that it was, after all, a convention gave it also a useful ambiguous quality: a man can't be sued for breach of promise for paying a conventional compliment; yet he can always imply that he really means it. Some men

can say, "Your hair looks lovely tonight," in such a way that it sounds like a proposal of marriage. Lacking the convention of the sonnet, most of you will have to struggle along with the present convention of, "Gee, you're swell!"

There have been dozens of literary conventions in regard to form: the Elizabethan five-act play and the modern three-act play; the Popean couplet and free verse; the pastoral elegy such as "Lycidas" and the modern formal resolution passed by a club in honor of a deceased member; the leisurely Victorian novel and the fast-moving novel of today. Each of these has been in accord with a fashion of its own time. Twenty-five years ago most short-story writers followed the O. Henry formula of the surprise ending; many students still use it in their themes, usually to the complete destruction of all unity and probability. Conventions have their uses, but today we demand that they shall not be followed to the extent of falsifying the truth about life. Realism is the convention of the moment.

Conventional Attitudes

For conventions include not only literary forms, but also the artist's attitude toward life. During the Middle Ages writers had what is described as an "other worldly" view of life. This was especially true of the drama where both the miracle and morality plays were concerned with religious themes. Often considerable horse play and rough humor were introduced into the story, but convention required that every play should deal somewhat with religion. With the coming of the

Renaissance the writers discovered and followed the Greek and Roman fashion of writing plays about the doings of men, of focusing their attention upon this world. Such moral teaching as appears is implied rather than expressed. *Macbeth,* for instance, shows the evils of ambition, and *Othello* of jealousy; yet Shakespeare never spoils his art with obvious preaching.

1. *Elizabethan love poems.* In the Elizabethan period the love lyric followed a conventional pattern of ideas. Shakespeare's famous 116th sonnet shows the accepted theme of everlasting constancy:

> Let me not to the marriage of true minds
> Admit impediments. Love is not love
> Which alters when it alteration finds,
> Or bends with the remover to remove:
> O, no! it is an ever-fixed mark
> That looks on tempests and is never shaken;
> It is the star to every wandering bark,
> Whose worth's unknown, although his height be taken.
> Love's not Time's fool, though rosy lips and cheeks
> Within his bending sickle's compass come;
> Love alters not with his brief hours and weeks,
> But bears it out even to the edge of doom.
> If this be error and upon me proved,
> I never writ, nor no man ever loved.

This is only one of a host of sonnets and songs by Elizabethan poets who said much the same thing. Or if the lady was untrue, the sonneteer promised to die promptly. Always there was the insistence on the ideal of constancy, and the lover was ever the humble suitor. Thus for Spenser: [1]

[1] Spenser, *Amoretti,* 34.

Yet hope I well, that when this storm is past,
My Helice, the lodestar of my lyfe,
Will shine again, and looke on me at last,
With lovely light to cleane my cloudy grief.
Till then I wander carefull, comfortlesse,
In secret sorrow, and sad pensivenesse.

And Sir Philip Sidney says to his beloved: [2]

Stella, since thou so right a princess art
Of all the powers which life bestows on me; ...
                    dismiss from thee my wit!
Till it have wrought what thy own will attends ...

Ben Jonson's "Song to Celia" carries the same note of humble adoration:

Drink to me only with thine eyes,
    And I will pledge with mine;
Or leave a kiss but in the cup,
    And I'll not ask for wine.
The thirst that from the soul doth rise
    Doth ask a drink divine;
But might I of Jove's nectar sup,
    I would not ask for wine.

2. *The Jacobean.* Fashions in verse, like those in everything else, change after a time, usually when someone comes along with a style that seems clever or that suits new conditions. John Donne was the poet who did more than anyone else to overturn the Elizabethan lyric convention. His "Indifferent" will illustrate what happened:

I can love both fair and brown;
Her whom abundance melts, and her whom want betrays;

---

[2] Sir Philip Sidney, *Astrophel and Stella*, No. 107.

Her who loves loneness best, and her who masks and plays;
Her whom the country formed, and whom the town;
Her who believes, and her who tries;
Her who still weeps with spongy eyes,
And her who is dry cork and never cries.
I can love her, and her, and you, and you;
I can love any, so she be not true.

Almost at once Donne's cynicism became fashionable. George Wither asks: [3]

Shall I, wasting in despair,
Die, because a woman's fair?

Court poets like Sir John Suckling sang: [4]

Out upon it, I have loved
Three whole days together!
And am like to love three more,
If it prove fair weather.

It is doubtful if the men of the seventeenth century
were more inconstant in love than those of the six-
teenth, the century, by the way, of Henry VIII and
Mary, Queen of Scots. Each time was only following
a literary fashion.

3. *The Victorian.* We can see the same thing if we
compare the Victorian attitudes toward war or toward
women with those fashionable today. Both Tennyson
and Siegfried Sassoon have poems on stupid blunders
which cost the lives of hundreds of men. Tennyson is
rather bland about the whole thing: [5]

[3] George Wither, "Shall I Wasting in Despair."
[4] Sir John Suckling, "The Constant Lover."
[5] Tennyson, "Charge of the Light Brigade."

Forward the Light Brigade!
Was there a man dismayed?
Not though the soldier knew
    Someone had blundered.
Theirs not to make reply,
Theirs not to reason why,
Theirs but to do and die.
Into the valley of Death
    Rode the six hundred.

If there was any man dismayed, it was certainly not
Tennyson. Compare this with Sassoon's poems in
Counter-Attack. There the "glory" preached by the
politicians is translated into the mud, the decaying
corpses, the slow death in shell holes, the dud attack
paid for in human agony.

4. *The Modern.* If you think war was any pleasanter
in the nineteenth century, read Strachey's biography
of Florence Nightingale or the novel, *Gone with the
Wind.* Note, however, that both of these were written
after the World War, in other words after the theirs-
but-to-do-and-die attitude went out of fashion. Try
to find a first-rate book or poem on war, written since
1920, which pictures it as a glamorous adventure—
not just the World War, but any war. Even those who
believe that democracy is worth fighting for see war
as a dirty job that may have to be done. The point is
not that the present convention is wrong; certainly it
is a saner one than that Tennyson followed, but we
must recognize the modern attitude as a convention
also.

Strangely enough contemporary conventions which
govern the writer's attitude toward life are more frequently recognized by students than are modern fash-

ions in literary form or in the portrayal of character. Most students recognize the "debunking" biography for what it is—a literary fashion—as they recognize the hard-boiled school of fiction.

Conventional Characters

1. Medieval. Likewise it is fairly easy to spot conventional characters in the older literature. There was the Griselda type: the patient heroine who would undergo uncomplainingly the worst insults and indignities. She was a favorite in medieval literature; it is quite possible she was not often met with in the community. The brave, courteous, modest, and virtuous knight was another. Sir Gawains and Sir Galahads appear more frequently in literature than in history. More recently the Victorian heroine was in fashion, the clinging-vine maiden much given to tears and fainting.

2. Modern. Today we have a full quota of stock characters: the drawing-room-comedy hero, travelled, witty, kindly, and with a British accent; the woman's magazine heroine, well-read, clever, courageous, good at house-keeping but without dishpan hands; *The Saturday Evening Post* hero, athletic, intellectual, handsome, and a success in business. How many of them are in your class at college? Have you ever met a girl like this one? [6]

She was a stalk of ripe corn, but bound not as cereals are but as a rare first edition, with all the binder's art. She

[6] F. Scott Fitzgerald, "A Freeze-Out," *The Saturday Evening Post*, December 19, 1931.

was lovely and expensive, and about nineteen, and he had never seen her before. She looked at him for just an unnecessary moment too long, with so much self-confidence that he felt his own rush away to join hers.

Before our hero stalks out of the shop, he has heard her ask for a recording of an esoteric piece of music and an unusual book, either in French or in translation. As one would expect, she drives a roadster, "an enormous silver-colored roadster of English make and custom design." But of course she is not spoiled by all this beauty, learning, and wealth, nor is she tainted with the ill-gotten millions of her father's. As she says to the boy, "My standards are as high as yours, and I can't start out with my father's sins on my shoulders." (She has of course no such scruples about her father's millions.)

Later when her suitor leaves his home for her sake, she says: [7]

"I've been thinking of your leaving your house on account of me, and how you loved your family—the way I'd like to love mine—and I thought how terrible it was to spoil all that. Listen Forrest! Wait! I want you to go back. Yes, I do. We can wait. We haven't the right to cause all this pain."

Beautiful, wealthy, learned, wise, magnanimous—and only nineteen. Thus we find that the modern heroine, like her Victorian ancestor, is not subject to the laws of heredity and environment. She is about as real as the girls in a John La Gatta drawing.

Another school of writers, appearing in sophisti-

[7] *Ibid.*

cated periodicals like *The New Yorker*, are more likely to get their types from the drawings of Helen Hokinson. Here is Mrs. Twitchell from "An Account of Suburban Life, Rejected in Turn by *Good Housekeeping*, *Better Homes and Gardens*, and *The Ladies' Home Journal*":

Mrs. Twitchell looked up from her cream-cheese-pineapple-nuts-and-jelly sandwich. "Nothing like this," she said dully, "has ever happened in the manor before."

"Nothing," Mrs. Harbour agreed.

Mrs. Twitchell laughed briefly, almost bitterly. "I suppose it was really our fault," she said, "that we didn't suspect right at first that the Fritherbees were—well, that they—"

Mrs. Harbour minced no words. "That the Fritherbees were simply not the Manor Park Gardens type," she said.

3. *Real persons.* The Manor-Park-Gardens type may do fairly well for purposes of satire, but types are not the stuff from which great literature is made. If there is one thing above all for which conventions are unsuited, it is the portrayal of characters. The essence of character in fiction is individuality. Chaucer could take a type like the talkative middle-aged woman, and create an individual like the Wife of Bath. The "revenger," the man called upon to avenge a murder, was common enough in Elizabethan tragedy. That is what Hamlet was when Shakespeare found him in an old play; he left him one of the most complex personalities in all literature. Jane Austen, instead of following the accepted pattern of clinging-vine heroines, gave us Elizabeth Bennet, a witty, somewhat thorny person with a mind of her own. It is said

that she used herself as a model. That is one way.
Dickens found his people in the streets and shops of
London—not in books by other authors.

Literary Form

Neither Shakespeare nor Dickens was particularly
interested in creating a new literary form, as for instance was Donne. Not only did John Donne break
away from the theme of undying love; he discarded
the neat, polished verse style of the Elizabethan lyric,
such as Johnson's "Song to Celia." Here is a characteristic stanza from "The Canonization":

> For God's sake hold your tongue, and let me love;
>   Or chide my palsy, or my gout;
>   My five gray hairs, or ruined fortune flout;
> With wealth your state, your mind with arts improve;
>   Take you a course, get you a place,
>   Observe his Honor, or his Grace;
> Or the king's real, or his stamped face
>   Contemplate; what you will, approve,
>   So you will let me love.

Here, instead of the usual polish and smoothness, we
have vigor, even harshness. Words like "palsy" and
"gout" were not ordinarily used in love poetry. The
whole thing with its sharp, almost ill-natured impera-
tive statements is designed to create the effect of a
man driven to desperation by love. The original form,
then, has a real function; it is not used simply because
it is a new form.

Within old forms. When a man like Donne breaks
with the old fashion and sets a new one, we say he

has the quality of originality. Often, however, the writer continues or revives some existing convention, but gives it new life. Shakespeare used the standard five-act play of his day; he wrote in the customary blank verse; he followed a dozen other conventions of the drama of his time. Sometimes as he did in *Hamlet* he even took a story which had already been used in a play. Yet within the existing forms he created Falstaff and Macbeth; Juliet and Lady Macbeth. He took the old blood-and-thunder melodrama of *Hamlet* and, without changing the plot, left it a psychological study, a drama of ideas. Using the customary blank verse, he left line after line stamped with his image and superscription: all the superb combinations of words that have become a part of the vocabulary of all of us. When you say: "The play's the thing," "method in his madness," "tear a passion to tatters," "out-herods Herod," it is because you are quoting or misquoting Shakespeare. For part of his originality lay in his ability to put words together in unforgettable combinations.

Let us see what Milton did with the sonnet. We have already seen how the Elizabethans used it; in their hands it dealt almost exclusively with love. Now the style of a love song would not ordinarily appear to be suited to political discussion, much less to humor, nor to a diatribe against tyranny. Yet you can see the first of these in his sonnet, "On the New Forces of Conscience under the Long Parliament"; the second in the one, "On the Detraction Which Followed Upon My Writing Certain Treatises." And if these seem far removed from the Elizabethan sonnets to a lady's eyebrow, how about this one, "On the Late Massacre in Piedmont"?

> Avenge, O Lord, thy slaughtered Saints, whose bones
> Lie scattered on the Alpine mountains cold;
> Even them who kept thy truth so pure of old,
> When all our fathers worshipped stocks and stones,
> Forget not: in thy book record their groans
> Who were thy sheep, and in their ancient fold
> Slain by the bloody Piedmontese, that rolled
> Mother with infant down the rocks. Their moans
> The vales redoubled to the hills, and they
> To heaven. Their martyred blood and ashes sow
> O'er all the Italian fields, where still doth sway
> The triple tyrant that from these may grow
> A hundredfold, who, having learnt thy way,
> Early may fly the Babylonian woe.

Note that the diction, the somber music with its long vowel sounds, and the realistic descriptions of horrid scenes are all fused into one unit. In Milton's hands the sonnet ceases to be a billet doux and becomes an oratorical thunderbolt. This kind of thing is also the mark of an original genius.

On the other hand, William Cullen Bryant, once a very popular poet, is lacking in originality. Although he was a rather skilful poet, he was too often content to take traditional verse forms and use them for the same sort of ideas that had been often written about before. Here is the final stanza of "The Death of the Flowers":

And then I think of one who in her youthful beauty died,
The fair meek blossom that grew up and faded by my side.
In the cold moist earth we laid her, when the forest cast
    the leaf,

And we wept that one so lovely should have a life so brief:
Yet not unmeet it was that one like that young friend of
   ours,
So gentle and so beautiful, should perish with the flowers.

The whole theme of the poem, the sadness of the approach of autumn, is an old one in poetry. The comparison of a girl to a flower has been a convention since the Middle Ages. The theme of sorrow over the untimely death of a beautiful young girl is hardly original. In fact nearly all of Bryant's poetry is in the Wordsworthian tradition of writing of the beauties of nature. This convention had supplanted the pseudo-classic one of writing witty, satiric poems about fashionable society.

Whitman needs a new form. By the mid-nineteenth century the Wordsworthian convention had become as sterile as had the Popean one a century before. Walt Whitman needed a new kind of form to sing the song of the vast continent of America, so he created his own: [8]

I hear America singing, the varied carols I hear,
Those of mechanics, each one singing his as it should be
   blithe and strong,
The carpenter singing as he measures his plank and beam,
The mason singing as he makes ready for work, or leaves
   off work,
The boatman singing what belongs to him in his boat, the
   deckhand singing on the steamboat deck,
The shoemaker singing as he sits on his bench, the hatter
   singing as he stands,

[8] "I Hear America Singing" from *Leaves of Grass,* by Walt Whitman. Copyright, 1926, by Doubleday, Doran and Company, Inc.

The woodcutter's song, the plowboy's on his way in the
    morning, or at noon intermission or at sundown,
The delicious singing of the mother, or of the young wife
    at work, or the girl sewing or washing,
Each singing what belongs to him or to her and to none
    else,
The day what belongs to the day—at night the party of
    young fellows, robust, friendly,
Singing with their mouths their strong melodious songs.

No one had ever written poetry just like that before.
It was a new kind of verse for a new kind of nation,
a nation where the thoughts and songs and work of
the common man mattered as never before. Since then
others have tried this kind of verse. Carl Sandburg
found that such verse was ideally suited for poems
about steel mills and stock yards. Whether you prefer
Whitman or Sandburg does not change the fact that
Whitman was the originator of a new literary form.

Emily Dickinson. Emily Dickinson, on the other
hand, frequently used the old "fourteener" stanza of
the ballads, a stanza which had been a favorite of
Wordsworth's. Here is the kind of thing she did with
it: [9]

It dropped so low in my regard
    I heard it hit the ground,
And go to pieces on the stones
    At bottom of my mind.

Yet blamed the fate that fractured less
    Than I reviled myself

[9] "Disenchantment" from *The Poems of Emily Dickinson,* 3rd
Series (Boston, 1914), p. 50. Edited by Martha Dickinson Bianchi
and Alfred Leete Hampson. Reprinted by permission of Little,
Brown & Company.

For entertaining plated wares
Upon my silver shelf.

If, in Coleridge's phrase, you "met those stanzas
running loose in the deserts of Arabia," you could have
recognized them as Emily Dickinson's—granting of
course that you knew anything about Emily Dickinson. No one else had ever taken such humble materials: the ballad stanza, the words and images from
everyday household affairs, and had used them in the
service of philosophy. Even Wordsworth had not been
so daring in his use of humble words. No poet had ever
started out so unpretentiously as was her custom, and
then suddenly had revealed some new facet of man
or the universe.

For as Professor Lowes points out in *Convention
and Revolt in Poetry*, originality may take the form of
a break with an outmoded convention, or it may be
the infusion of new life into an ancient mold. Always
it demands that the writer must examine man and
the universe for himself. He cannot be content with
the findings of others. Many writers have been imitative while learning their art. Whether or not that is
the best way is debatable; it is not debatable that all
great writing possesses the quality of originality.

Eccentricity. But simply because a work is new and
different, it is not necessarily a manifestation of genius.
Our ancestors knew, what we have sometimes forgotten, that eccentricity is a more common article than
genius. It is perhaps this modern attitude which has
often led writers of talent to strive for the different
rather than the excellent. Witness such obvious at-

tempts to be different as E. E. Cummings' avoidance
of capitals and punctuation. Such devices seem a bit
tame compared to those Herbert used in the seventeenth century. When he wrote about an altar, he
made the poem look like one; he even did two pairs
of angel wings in verse. Not only that: in spite of the
strange stanza form, the poem is rather good—something that cannot always be said for the work of modern eccentrics. Here are his "Easter Wings":

My tender age in sorrow did beginne;
And still with sickness and shame
Thou didst so punish sinne,
That I became
Most thinne.
With Thee
Let me combine
And feel this day thy Victorie:
For if I imp my wing on thine,
Affliction shall advance thy flight in me.

Lord, who createdst man in wealth and store,
Though foolishly he lost the same,
Decaying more and more,
Till he became
Most poore:
With thee
O let me rise
As larks, harmoniously
And sing this day thy victories:
Then shall the fall further the flight in me.

There is no formula to distinguish originality from
eccentricity. Critics have often mistaken one for the
other. Francis Jeffrey, a leading critic of his time, said
Wordsworth's early poems were "childish and absurd." Southey called The Ancient Mariner, "a Dutch

attempt at German sublimity." Instances of this kind have been frequent in all ages. There are however certain warning signs to indicate the bogus article. One of them is a striving for effect, an obvious attempt to shock or astonish. The famous opening to a student's short story, "Hell," said the duchess, "let go my leg!" was of this type.

One name for this false sort of originality is *tour de force*. Usually it is the work of a writer who has considerable skill, but no new idea. It can take the form of trick endings like that of Frank Stockton's "The Lady or the Tiger?" The story itself is essentially sterile; give it another ending and there is nothing left. So too are many of Poe's stories: In "The Fall of the House of Usher" or "The Masque of the Red Death" you can see the author skilfully piling strange scene upon scene, horror upon horror. Yet in the end there is nothing real; it is all a literary trick. The staging of the very excellent play, *Our Town*, was a kind of *tour de force:* the women stringing imaginary beans, the milkman carrying imaginary bottles which gave out real klinks and jingles; people climbing a stepladder to pretend they were going upstairs. There was no real need for all this as the motion picture version showed; it was only an attempt to be different. It is difficult to persuade most readers that Gertrude Stein's kind of writing is not designed more to astonish than enlighten.

Transitional writers. Perhaps, however, Miss Stein belongs to that class of writers often called transitional: writers who have tried to develop a new form, but have failed to perfect it. It is rare for a new art form to be born fully developed; the perfecting of the form is usually the work of writers who have the second kind of originality, that of infusing new life into an existing convention. Chaucer, Shakespeare, and Milton all used existing literary forms. Wyatt and Surrey used the sonnet somewhat awkwardly; Marlowe's blank verse was stiff compared tó that of Shakespeare. In more recent times you will find that an early realist like Frank Norris added a happy ending to his novel, *The Pit*, although his story does not lead in that direction. In other words he was unable to break entirely with an existing convention. Yet transitional writers have a kind of originality that is indispensable in the development of literature. They are the pioneers, and like most pioneers in the intellectual world, they are usually misunderstood in their own time. It is customary to starve them to death.

Formula literature. One thing that often distinguishes the true pioneer from the eccentric and the cultist is that the pioneer is forced into the creation of a new form because of something new he has to say. The cultist on the other hand usually makes form an end in itself. Alone or in company with others of his kind he issues a manifesto declaring that heretofore writers have been upon the wrong track, and that he has discovered the only true principles of the art. There is a good bit of this sort of thing in Wordsworth's Preface to *Lyrical Ballads*. Along with some very sound artistic principles, he stated also some literary formulas which he was trying to put into practice. Poetry, he stated, should be about rustics, and should be written in their language. To appeal to this class of people he frequently chose also their own metrical form, the ballad meter.

In accord with this theory he wrote "The Idiot Boy," "Peter Bell," "Goody Blake and Harry Gill," and "Simon Lee." Here is what happened when he wrote according to his formula: [10]

> "What can I do?" says Betty going,
> "What can I do to ease your pain?
> Good Susan tell me, and I'll stay;
> I fear you're in a dreadful way,
> But I shall soon be back again."

> "Good Betty go, good Betty go,
> There's nothing that can ease my pain."
> Then off she hies, but with a prayer
> That God poor Susan's life would spare,
> Till she comes back again.

True originality. Yet in the same year he did that he also wrote the great "Tintern Abbey," a poem written to no formula. In form it is blank verse, patterned somewhat after that of Milton; its language is not that of rustics but of other great English poems, the language of Shakespeare, of the Prayer Book, and of the King James Bible. The poem is Wordsworth's confession of faith. What he had to say was so important to him that he took the nearest way to say it—theory or no theory. He fitted the language and the form to the idea, not the idea to a theoretical form. Poetry cannot be reduced to a few doctrinal principles.

If a man has something new and vital to say, he may create a new form in which to say it as Carlyle did in

[10] Wordsworth, "The Idiot Boy."

Sartor Resartus. But if what he has to say is vital to him, you may be sure he will strive mightily to say it so that he can be understood. The newness or strangeness of his way of writing will not be an end in itself; it will grow inevitably out of what he has to say. As Carlyle puts it, "The merit of originality is not novelty; it is sincerity."

X

Restraint

"Rhetoric is the will trying to do the work of the imagination." [1]
—WILLIAM BUTLER YEATS

From one point of view, restraint is a quality of manners; from another, it is an element of morals. In some aspects it is almost synonymous with good taste. In conversation "gushing" is the absence of restraint. It may represent simply bad taste or downright hypocrisy. And so strong is the feeling against this gaucherie that it has come to be identified with false seeming. Many people accept restraint in conversation as an indication of honesty. "Still waters run deep" is the common way of saying it.

Lack of Restraint

1. Bombast. Lack of restraint is especially common in certain periods. Chief among them are the Elizabethan age and the Romantic revival. In the Elizabethan manifestation, it takes the form of bombast and turgidness. Shakespeare himself is not free from the fault. Marlowe is particularly given to it. For instance, here is Tamburlaine addressing a soldier sent out to capture him: [2]

[1] William Butler Yeats, "Ideas of Good and Evil," *Essays* (New York, The Macmillan Company, 1924).

[2] Christopher Marlowe, *Tamburlaine*, Act I, Sc. 2.

248

Forsake thy king, and do but join with me,
And we will triumph over all the world.
I hold the fates bound fast in iron chains,
And with my hand turn Fortune's wheel about:
And sooner shall the sun fall from his sphere
Than Tamburlaine be slain or overcome.
Draw forth thy sword thou mighty man-at-arms,
Intending but to raze my charmed skin,
And Jove himself will stretch his hand from heaven
To ward the blow and shield me safe from harm.
See how he rains down heaps of gold in showers,
As if he meant to give my soldiers pay!

The thing that carries one along is the poetic power, the immense enthusiasm of the author. The fault here is more easily pardoned than when it is done in cold blood. Then it becomes sheer hypocrisy. In Dryden's *Conquest of Granada,* the hero, Almanzor, comes upon Almahide in tears. His remarks are as follows:

What precious drops are those
Which silently each other's track pursue
Bright as young diamonds in their infant dew?
Your lustre you should free from tears maintain,
Like Egypt, rich without the help of rain.
Now cursed be he who gave this cause of grief;
And double cursed, who does not give relief!

Trite figures, like "diamonds" for "tears," and far-fetched comparisons are common substitutes for the true language of emotion, which more often than not is simple and homely.

Dryden's type of artificial emotion is far less dangerous, however, than is the sort in which the writer whips himself into a real frenzy without applying the curb of reason. Southey, who did not approve of Napoleon, has an "Ode Written During the Negotiations with Buonaparte, in January, 1814," which opens:

> Who counsels peace at this momentous hour,
>   When God hath given deliverance to the oppress'd,
>   And to the injured power?
> Who counsels peace when vengeance like a flood
> Rolls on, no longer now to be repress'd;
>   When innocent blood
>   From the four corners of the world cries out
>   For justice upon one accursed head;
> When Freedom hath her holy banners spread
>   Over all nations, now in one just cause
>   United; when with one sublime accord
>   Europe throws off the yoke abhorr'd,
> And Loyalty and Faith, and Ancient Laws
>   Follow the avenging sword!

Of course Southey had no intention of doing any of the fighting himself; the preachers of holy wars are not often soldiers.

Lack of restraint has its uses; its purpose is often to sell spurious emotion. It is one of the handmaidens of propaganda. There, as we shall see, it often takes the form of name-calling, appeals to prejudice, or to uncritical loyalty. For instance, it is difficult to find ethical justification for a policy of imperialism, especially by the United States with our creed of the right of self-government. Therefore when Senator Albert J. Beveridge preached imperialism, he did it this way: [3]

Fellow-Citizens—It is a noble land that God has given us; a land that can feed and clothe the world; a land whose coast lines would enclose half the countries of Europe; a

[3] Alfred Beveridge, *The Meaning of the Times* (Indianapolis, The Bobbs Merrill Company, 1936).

land set like a sentinel between the two imperial oceans of the globe; a greater England with a nobler destiny. It is a mighty people that He has planted on this soil; a people sprung from the most masterful blood of history; a people perpetually revitalized by the virile workingfolk of all the earth; a people imperial by virtue of their power, by right of their institutions, by authority of their heaven-directed purposes, the propagandists and not the misers of liberty. It is a glorious history our God has bestowed upon His chosen people; a history whose keynote was struck by Liberty Bell; a history heroic with faith in our mission and our future; a history of statesmen who flung the boundaries of the Republic out into unexplored lands and savage wildernesses; a history of soldiers, who carried the flag across blazing deserts and through the ranks of hostile mountains, even to the gates of sunset: a history of a multiplying people, who overran a continent in half a century; a history divinely logical in the process of whose tremendous reasoning we find ourselves today.

Therefore, in this campaign the question is larger than a party question. It is an American question. It is a world question. Shall the American people continue their resistless march toward the commercial supremacy of the world? Shall free institutions broaden their blessed reign as the children of liberty wax in strength until the empire of our principles is established over the hearts of all mankind? Have we no mission to perform—no duty to discharge to our fellow-man? Has the Almighty Father endowed us with gifts beyond our deserts, and marked us as the people of His peculiar favor, merely to rot in our own selfishness, as men and nations must who take cowardice for their companion and self for their deity . . . ?

Writing of that sort has about as much appeal to the intellect as a military band playing "The Stars and Stripes Forever." Shorn of his grandiloquent phrases about God and the sunset, Beveridge says that might makes right, that God has chosen America to rule the world, and that He demands the election of William McKinley. It is exactly the sort of doctrine that Hitler preached thirty years later the same use of intoxicating language—in fact even the same phrases.

2. *The pathetic fallacy.* Another favorite device among those authors who lack restraint is the *pathetic fallacy.* This name was given by Ruskin to the trick of attributing human emotion to objects incapable of feeling it. As an example he used: [4]

> They rowed her in across the rolling foam—
> The cruel, crawling foam.

Here he said that we pardon, or are even pleased by, the untrue description of foam because the feeling is true. A man who has just seen his loved ones drowned might easily think of the sea as cruel. But, says Ruskin, "There is no greater baseness in literature" than the use of the pathetic fallacy in cold blood. A man swearing at his car when it refuses to start is using the pathetic fallacy honestly; for the moment he thinks of the car as humanly perverse. Not so the writer who talks of weeping skies and smiling dawn.

Tennyson has a very famous lyric in *Maud.* It begins:

> Come into the garden, Maud,
>   For the black bat, night, has flown,
> Come into the garden, Maud,
>   I am here at the gate alone;
> And the woodbine spices are wafted abroad,
>   And the musk of the rose is blown.

[4] Charles Kingsley, *Alton Locke,* quoted in John Ruskin, *Modern Painters.*

All night have the roses heard
  The flute, violin, bassoon;
All night has the casement jessamine stirred
  To the dancers dancing in tune;
Till a silence fell with the waking bird,
  And a hush with the setting moon.

So far so good. The young lover might easily have such feelings about the flowers. But Tennyson falls in love with his figure and continues:

The slender acacia would not shake
  One long milk-bloom on the tree;
The white lake-blossom fell into the lake
  As the pimpernell dozed on the lea;
But the rose was awake all night for your sake,
  Knowing your promise to me;
The lilies and roses were all awake,
  They sighed for the dawn and thee.

There has fallen a splendid tear
  From the passion-flower at the gate,
She is coming my dove, my dear;
  She is coming, my life, my fate.
The red rose cries, "She is near, she is near";
  And the white rose weeps, "She is late";
The larkspur listens, "I hear, I hear";
  And the lily whispers, "I wait."

The lyric, musical power has almost carried you along. But the thing is essentially absurd, false. He didn't know when to stop. Tennyson's flowers act like a crowd of women waiting for a glimpse of Clark Gable.

3. *Striving for effect*. It is a striving for effect which leads writers to overdo an idea or emotion. Fitz-

Greene Halleck in "Marco Bozzaris," a poem much
admired by our ancestors, tells of a Greek attack upon
the Turks. Here is stanza three:

> They fought—like brave men, long and well;
>   They piled that ground with Moslem slain;
> They conquered—but Bozzaris fell,
>   Bleeding at every vein.
> His few surviving comrades saw
> His smile when rang their proud hurrah,
>   And the red field was won:
> They saw in death his eyelids close
> Calmly, as to a night's repose,
>   Like flowers at set of sun.

That would seem to conclude the matter. But two
more stanzas follow, the first of which goes:

> Come to the bridal chamber, Death!
>   Come to the mother, when she feels,
> For the first time, her firstborn's breath;
>   Come when the blessed seals
> That close the pestilence are broke,
> And crowded cities wail its stroke;
> Come in consumption's ghastly form,
> The earthquake shock, the ocean storm,
> Come when the heart beats high and warm,
>   With banquet-song, and dance, and wine
> And thou art terrible—the tear,
> The groan, the knell, the pall, the bier;
> And all we know, or dream, or fear
>   Of agony, are thine.

It is fortunate that air raids had not been invented,
or the poet would have got them in too. Obviously he
has searched diligently for every startling or emotional scene he could think of. None of them have any-

thing to do with his story; there had been no earthquake, childbirth, nor storm at sea.

Economy

Contrast with that a poem of Emily Dickinson's which deals with a tragedy greater than that of Marco Bozzaris.[5]

> It's such a little thing to weep,
>   So short a thing to sigh;
> And yet by trades the size of these
>   We men and women die.

That is all there is to the poem; yet many longer ones have said much less. It takes genuine restraint to have an idea as good as that, and not to become voluble on the subject.

Keats learned this quality in a hard school, the literary criticism of the *Edinburgh Review*. His early work was condemned with a violence and bitterness difficult for this age to understand. But it is very possible that this criticism showed him his weakness. His "La Belle Dame Sans Merci" is a miracle of concise story-telling. Yet far from being cold and barren, it is loaded with the richness and color of the Middle Ages. Note also the rapidity of the narrative:

> I met a lady in the meads,
>   Full beautiful—a faery's child,
> Her hair was long, her foot was light,
>   And her eyes were wild.

[5] "Life's Trades" from *The Poems of Emily Dickinson*, 3rd Series (Boston, 1914), p. 20. Edited by Martha Dickinson Bianchi and Alfred Leete Hampson. Reprinted by permission of Little, Brown & Company.

I made a garland for her head,
   And bracelets too, and fragrant zone;
She looked at me as she did love,
   And made sweet moan.

I set her on my pacing steed,
   And nothing else saw all day long
For sidelong would she bend, and sing
   A faery's song.

She found me roots of relish sweet,
   And honey wild, and manna dew,
And sure in language strange she said—
   "I love thee true."

She took me to her elfin grot,
   And there she wept, and sighed full sore,
And there I shut her wild wild eyes
   With kisses four.

And there she lulled me asleep,
   And there I dreamed—Ah! woe betide!
The latest dream I ever dreamed
   On the cold hill's side.

I saw pale kings and princes too,
   Pale warriors, death-pale were they all;
They cried—"La Belle Dame sans Merci
   Hath thee in thrall!"

On the other hand we have Scott's "William and Helen," the skeleton-in-armor story he got from the Germans. Beginning at line 33 we have:

"Oh rise, my child," her mother said,
   "Nor sorrow thus in vain;
A perjured lover's fleeting heart
   No tears recall again."

"Oh mother, what is gone, is gone,
 What's lost forever lorn:
Death, death alone can comfort me;
 O had I ne'er been born!

"Oh break, my heart—O break at once!
 Drink my life-blood, Despair!
No joy remains on earth for me,
 For me in heaven no share."

"Oh enter not in judgment, Lord!"
 The pious mother prays;
"Impute not guilt to thy frail child!
 She knows not what she says.

"O say thy pater noster, child!
 O turn to God and grace!
His will, that turn'd thy bliss to bale,
 Can change thy bale to bliss."

"O mother, mother what is bliss?
 O mother, what is bale?
My William's love was heaven on earth,
 Without it earth is hell.

"Why should I pray to ruthless Heaven,
 Since my loved William's slain?
I only pray'd for William's sake,
 And all my prayers were vain."

Note how much less has happened in these stanzas
than occurred in the same number quoted from "La
Belle Dame Sans Merci." Scott's conversation goes on
for six more stanzas, concluding:

"O mother, mother, what is bliss?
 O mother what is bale?
Without my William what were heaven,
 Or with him what were hell?"

She said much the same thing before. Not that this ends the poem; it is 264 lines long as contrasted with Keats's forty-eight lines. Length alone is not necessarily a fault; but when a minor point or a slight story is amplified to great lengths, we have a real artistic fault. As can be seen in Scott's ballad, the greater length, far from giving greater emphasis, destroys the force of the poem.

Turn from a "William and Helen" to one of the true folk ballads. In "Edward," the mother asks:

> "Why dois your brand sae drap wi bluid,
>   Edward, Edward,
>   Why dois your brand sae drap wi bluid,
>   And why sae sad gang yee O?"
> "O I hae killed my hawk sae guid,
>   Mither, mither,
>   O I hae killed my hawk sae guid,
>   And I had nae mair bot hee O."
>
> "Your hawkis bluid was nevir sae reid,
>   Edward, Edward,
>   Your hawkis bluid was never sae reid,
>   My deir son I tell thee O."
> O I hae killed my reid-roan steid,
>   Mither, mither,
>   O I hae killed my reid-roan steid,
>   That erst was sae fair and fine O."
>
> "Your steid was auld, and ye hae gat mair,
>   Edward, Edward,
>   Your steid was auld, and ye hae gat mair,
>   Sum other dule ye drie O."
> O I hae killed my fadir deir,
>   Mither, mither,
>   O I hae killed my fadir deir,
>   Alas, and wae is mee O!"

Notice that before the interest and suspense have a chance to weaken, the tragedy is revealed. In the next two stanzas Edward says he will let his towers and his hall go to ruin, and his wife and children beg through life.

"And what wul ye leive to your ain mither deir?
        Edward, Edward,
And what wul ye leive to your ain mither deir?
    My deir son, now tell me O."
"The curse of hell frae me sall ye beir,
        Mither, mither,
The curse of hell frae me sall ye beir,
    Sic counsels ye gave to me O."

There is so much here that is not said, and the poem is all the more powerful because of that. Few modern poets could have resisted the chance to put in all the details of the mother's counsel, as did Scott in "William and Helen." And few modern poets could equal the force of the surprise ending in the last three lines, lines that reveal the guilt of the mother. The name for this sort of restraint is *economy*. When it is used wisely, it helps to produce that quality which we call intensity. Good poetry to a much greater extent than prose, produces this intensity of emotion. But no kind of writing which is flabby with excess fat will achieve it.

It is the simplicity and directness of these old ballads that have attracted many generations of readers and imitators. And Scott is by no means the only fine poet who has failed to achieve these virtues. Read Wordsworth's "Idiot Boy" and then go back and read "Sir Patrick Spens" or "The Hunting of the Cheviot."

Classic Restraint

Restraint is one of the elements included in the critical term "classical." It is found in the Parthenon and in the plays of Sophocles. And as today we so often take classical models for our buildings but fail to achieve the same simplicity, we do the same with our literature. Hilda Dolittle has built a poem on Sappho's lines:

> I know not what to do:
> My mind is divided.

and the most cursory reading reveals the "too much-ness" of the modern work.[6]

> I know not what to do—
> My mind is reft.
> Is song's gift best?
> Is love's gift loveliest?
> I know not what to do,
> Now sleep has pressed
> Weight on your eyelids.
>
> Shall I break your rest,
> Devouring, eager?
> Is love's gift best?
> Nay, song's the loveliest.
> Yet, were you lost,
> What rapture could I take from song?—
> What song were left?
>
> I know not what to do:
> To turn and slake
> The rage that burns,

[6] "Hesperidies"—Fragment XXXIV from *Collected Poems by H. D.* by Hilda Dolittle (New York, 1940). Published by Liveright Publishing Corporation.

With my breath burn
And trouble your cool breath—
So shall I turn and take
Snow in my arms,
(Is love's gift best?)

Yet flake on flake
Of snow were comfortless,
Did you lie wondering
Wakened yet unawake.

Shall I turn and take
Comfortless snow within my arms,
Press lips to lips that answer not,
Press lips to flesh
That shudders not nor breaks?

Is love's gift best?—
Shall I turn and slake
All the wild longing?
Oh, I am eager for you!
As the Pleiads shake
White light in whiter water,
So shall I take you?

This goes on for forty more lines. Some poets could profit by the mythical advice given by Dr. Freud to the girl in *Gentlemen Prefer Blondes:* that is, "to cultivate some inhibitions and get more sleep."

Sentiment and Sentimentality

One of the commonest places to find this "too-muchness" is in writing designed to be tragic or pathetic. Two terms, *sentiment* and *sentimentality,* give us the difference between the genuine and the false. There is no hard and fast rule that enables us to distinguish between them. To one person a passage may speak genuine emotion; to another the same thing may be goo. Different ages judge by differing standards. Our own period is often called hard-boiled. In any case we are today suspicious of Fourth-of-July oratory and of Little-Eva-Going-to-Heaven passages.

Tearing a passion to tatters. One reason that we now laugh at nineteenth-century melodramas is that their authors "tore a passion to tatters." Shakespeare as he matured discovered that true passion speaks a simple language. Read this from *Romeo and Juliet:* [7]

> Ah! dear Juliet,
> Why art thou yet so fair? Shall I believe
> That unsubstantial Death is amorous,
> And that the lean abhorred monster keeps
> Thee here in dark to be his paramour?
> For fear of that, I still will stay with thee,
> And never from this palace of dim night
> Depart again: here, here will I remain
> With worms that are thy chamber-maids; O! here
> Will I set up my everlasting rest,
> And shake the yoke of unauspicious stars
> From this world-wearied flesh. Eyes, look your last!
> Arms, take your last embrace! and, lips, O you
> The doors of breath, seal with a righteous kiss
> A dateless bargain to engrossing death!
> Come, bitter conduct, come unsavory guide!
> Thou desperate pilot, now at once run on
> The dashing rocks thy sea-sick weary bark!
> Here's to my love! . . .

This is good of its kind, but it seems about as real as the final scene of an opera where the dying tenor shakes the chandeliers. *Romeo and Juliet* was one of

[7] *Romeo and Juliet,* Act V, Sc. 3.

Shakespeare's earliest tragedies; after he perfected his art, he gave us another kind of death scene. Horatio, seeing Hamlet dying of poison, says that he will follow his friend in death. Hamlet answers: [8]

> O good Horatio, what a wounded name,
> Things standing thus unknown, shall live behind me!
> If thou dids't ever hold me in thy heart,
> Absent thee from felicity awhile,
> And in this harsh world draw thy breath in pain,
> To tell my story.

In place of the polysyllabic, high-flown diction of Romeo, the poet has here used simple, everyday words; there are no far-fetched figures of speech. As Dr. Johnson said, "passion [emotion] runs not after remote allusions and obscure opinions . . . Where there is leisure for fiction there is little grief." Some of the most powerful emotional effects in all literature have been attained by very simple language. King Lear is nursed back to sanity by Cordelia, the daughter he had grievously wronged. When he first regains his senses, he falls on his knees before her.[9]

CORDELIA. . . . No sir, you must not kneel.
LEAR.   Pray do not mock me,
  I am a very foolish fond old man,
  Fourscore and upward, not an hour more nor less;
  And, to deal plainly
  I fear I am not in my perfect mind.
  Methinks I should know you, and know this man;
  Yet I am doubtful, for I am mainly ignorant
  What place this is; and all the skill I have

[8] *Hamlet,* Act V, Sc. 2.
[9] *King Lear,* Act V, Sc. 7.

Remembers not these garments; nor I know not
Where I did lodge last night. Do not laugh at me;
For, as I am a man, I think this lady
To be my child Cordelia.
CORDELIA.   And so I am, I am.
LEAR. Be your tears wet? Yes, faith, pray weep not:
If you have poison for me, I will drink it.
I know you do not love me; for your sisters
Have, as I do remember, done me wrong:
You have some cause, they have not.

Many critics select this as the most moving scene
in all Shakespeare. To get its full effect you must read,
or, better still, see the whole play; then you will understand the way in which it shows the regeneration
of a man who through his own folly and pride brought
down upon himself a terrible punishment. At a junc-
ture like this in a story, most writers would have been
tempted to pull out all the stops on the mighty Wur-
litzer.

Criteria. Although there is no unfailing rule to indicate just when a writer is exceeding the mark, there
are certain guideposts. The chief indication of sentimentality is the writer's love of weeping for its own
sake. Often it is the substituting of emotion for action.
It is from the man who is half-seas over that we are
most likely to hear an impassioned discourse on "all
that I am, I owe to my mother."

The verbal weeping over the lot of the poor and
the downtrodden seldom comes from the welfare
worker, but is more likely to be heard from the lady
whose diminished dividends "force her to cut" her con-
tribution to the community chest.

In "The Cotter's Saturday Night," Robert Burns draws a picture of a peasant's home that is genuinely moving.

But hark! a rap comes gently to the door
   Jenny, wha kens the meaning o' the same,
Tells how a neibor lad cam o'er the moor,
   To do some errands, and convoy her hame.
The wily mother sees the conscious flame
   Sparkle in Jenny's ee, and flush her cheek;
   Wi' heart-struck anxious care, inquires his name,
While Jenny hafflins is afraid to speak;
Weel pleased the mother hears, it's nae wild worthless
   rake.

Wi' kindly welcome Jenny brings him ben;
   A strappin youth; he takes the mother's eye;
Blithe Jenny sees the visit's no ill taen;
   The father cracks of horses, pleughs, and kye.
   The youngster's artless heart o'erflows wi' joy,
But, blate and laithfu', scarce can weel behave;
   The mother, wi' a woman's wiles, can spy
What makes the youth sae bashfu' an' sae grave;
Weel-pleased to think her bairn's respected like the lave.

But in the same poem he also gives us:

O happy love! where love like this is found!
   O heart-felt raptures! bliss beyond compare!
I've pacèd much this weary, mortal round,
   And sage experience bids me this declare—
"If Heaven a draught of heavenly pleasure spare,
One cordial in this melancholy vale,
   'Tis when a youthful, loving, modest pair,
In other's arms breathe out the tender tale,
Beneath the milk-white thorn that scents the evening
   gale."

Is there, in human form, that bears a heart,
  A wretch! a villain! lost to love and truth!
That can with studied, sly, ensnaring art
  Betray sweet Jenny's unsuspecting youth?
  Curse on his perjured arts! dissembling smooth!
Are honor, virtue, conscience, all exiled?
  Is there no pity, no relenting ruth,
Points to the parents fondling o'er their child,
Then paints the ruined maid, and their distraction wild?

Note the striving for effect, the "fine language" as contrasted with the simplicity of the former stanzas. True feeling does not need so many exclamation points. That Burns was revelling in emotion for its own sake is only too evident when we consider his life. Instead of the parents "weeping over the ruined maid," and "their distraction wild," Jean Armour's father chased Robert from the house and tried to prevent Jean from marrying him. And only too often he was "the wretch in human form." A psychologist would call this outpouring "compensation." Burns tried to compensate for his own lack of virtue by declaiming against seducers. It is probably the same sort of motive which leads robber barons to make lavish gifts to churches and charities. In literature many a sentimental or ranting passage grows out of the writer's feelings of inferiority or guilt. Like the Puritans in *Hudibras* they [10]

> Compound for sins they are inclined to
> By damning those they have no mind to.

So in the end we have come round to sincerity. Sentimentality and lack of restraint are dangerously close to dishonesty.

[10] Samuel Butler, *Hudibras.*

XI

Sincerity and Propaganda

Sincerity, always difficult, is perhaps even harder to achieve today than ever. Stuart Chase, in his essay, *The Luxury of Integrity*, has suggested that our present economic order, in which the vast majority of men are employees, is the cause. The "yes man," the publicity man, the advertising writer, are always in danger of writing what is asked of them rather than what they really believe.

Types of Insincerity

The danger threatens literature at many points. There is the editorial writer who works for a newspaper whose doctrines are quite opposed to his own. There is the essayist who imitates the views and even the style of the periodical which gives him the best market for his wares. There is the novelist who turns out books according to the pattern which his publishers tell him is most salable. And the ghost-writer is ever with us.

Not all these are new phenomena, but there is reason to believe them more prevalent today than formerly. A society in which wealth is the most frequent basis for judging a man is not the safest for literary men. And because the financial rewards of literary success are larger today than ever before, the temptations are greater. The wonder is not that men fall, but that so many modern writers stand firm. For, in spite of all temptations, there is much honest and thoughtful contemporary writing. Our job is to recognize it.

1. Forcing emotions into a mold. As it is easier to make decisions after all the returns are in, let us first examine past productions that are generally recognized as excellent or the reverse.

When Wordsworth was a young man, he found himself at once separated from the woman he loved and disillusioned in his ideals of humanity because of the excesses of the French Revolution. After much mental turmoil he found peace: [1]

> In nature and the language of the sense,
> The anchor of my purest thoughts, the nurse,
> The guide, the guardian of my heart, and soul
> Of all my moral being.

Believing this, he wrote some of the finest poetry in the English language. But this was a radical doctrine in a time when most people believed that a man's senses were at war with his spiritual nature. Radical doctrines are likely to make their holders unpopular or even persecuted. Wordsworth had no martyr complex, and he dearly loved comfort. Therefore he began to mold his opinions closer to those of his neighbors and of his patron, a conservative landholder. The result was spiritual tragedy. Intellectually he came to identify himself with Tory opinion, but it killed his

[1] "Lines Composed a Few Miles Above Tintern Abbey."

emotional life, and emotional sincerity is at the basis of all sincerity. A man may convince his mind that the safe course is the wise one; but if his sympathies be elsewhere, he is unlikely to write convincingly of what he does not really feel. He may decide that it is wise to marry "the nut brown maid" with the rich estate, but he does not write immortal verse to her; yet a Robert Burns, though loving unwisely, can create great love songs because of his, at least momentary, emotional sincerity.

To come down to specific cases. Here is a passage from "that drowsy, frowsy poem" called *The Excursion,* a passage that denies the whole creed of "Tintern Abbey":

> One adequate support
> For the calamities of mortal life
> Exists—one only, an assured belief
> That the procession of our fate, howe'er
> Sad or disturbed, is ordered by a Being
> Of infinite benevolence and power;
> Whose everlasting purposes embrace
> All accidents, converting them to good.

That is the language not of emotion, but of rationalization—it is prose masquerading as poetry. When Wordsworth let his emotions speak, as he did in "Tintern Abbey," he could write:

> And I have felt
> A presence that disturbs me with the joy
> Of elevated thoughts; a sense sublime
> Of something far more deeply interfused,
> Whose dwelling is the light of setting suns,

And the round ocean and the living air,
And the blue sky, and in the mind of man:
A motion and a spirit, that impels
All thinking things, all objects of all thought,
And rolls through all things.

True, Wordsworth's contemporaries found this unorthodox, pantheistic, whereas *The Excursion* was sound doctrine. But sound doctrine is not necessarily sincerity—nor is radicalism therefore truth. For the writer, the platitude of Polonius "to thine own self be true," is the only sincerity.

Perhaps the reason that there is so little good religious poetry is that it more often springs from doctrine than from the heart. The author of a truly great poem like the Twenty-Third Psalm was not arguing theology; he was expressing the immemorial longing of the soul of man for peace: "He leadeth me beside the still waters."

2. *Fashionable opinions.* Our age, however, is less in danger of insincere orthodoxy than of fashionable unorthodoxy. Because many of our ablest writers are disillusioned and cynical, disillusion and cynicism have become the tone of smart writing. Now both have their place in literature if literature is to be a complete mirror of man. Throughout the ages there have been times when to every man: "Vanity of vanities, saith the Preacher, vanity of vanities; all is vanity."

There is no questioning the honesty of these verses from the second chapter of Ecclesiastes: [2]

I said in mine heart, Go to now, I will prove thee with mirth, therefore enjoy pleasure: and, behold, this also is

[2] Ecclesiastes II:1–17.

vanity. I said of laughter, It is mad: and of mirth: What doeth it? I sought in mine heart to give myself unto wine, yet acquainting mine heart with wisdom; and to lay hold on folly, till I might see what was that good for the sons of men, which they should do under the heaven all the days of their life. I made me great works; I builded me houses; I planted me vineyards: I made me gardens and orchards, and I planted trees in them of all kind of fruits: I made me pools of water, to water therewith the wood that bringeth forth trees: I got me servants and maidens, and had servants born in my house; also I had great possessions of great and small cattle above all that were in Jerusalem before me: I gathered me also silver and gold, and the peculiar treasure of kings and of the provinces: I gat me men singers and women singers, and the delights of the sons of men, as musical instruments, and that of all sorts. So I was great, and increased more than all that were before me in Jerusalem: also my wisdom remained with me. And whatsoever mine eyes desired I kept not from them, I withheld not my heart from any joy; for my heart rejoiced in all my labour: and this was my portion of all my labour. Then I looked on all the works that my hands had wrought, and on the labour that I had laboured to do: and, behold, all was vanity and vexation of spirit, and there was no profit under the sun. And I turned myself to behold wisdom, and madness, and folly: for what can the man do that cometh after the king? even that which hath been already done. Then I saw that wisdom excelleth folly, as far as light excelleth darkness. The wise man's eyes are in his head; but the fool walketh in darkness: and I myself perceived also that one event happeneth to them all. Then said I in my heart, As it happeneth to the fool so it happeneth even to me; and why was I then more wise? Then I said in my heart, that this also is vanity. For there is no remembrance of the wise more than of the fool for ever; seeing that which now is in the days to come shall all be forgotten. And how dieth the wise man? as the fool.

But we must gravely question the authenticity of Ernest Dowson's emotion when, in his "Villanelle of the Poet's Road," he says: [3]

Wine and women and song,
    Three things garnish our way;
Yet is the day over long.

Lest we do our youth wrong,
    Gather them while we may:
Wine and woman and song.

Three things render us strong,
    Vine leaves, kisses and bay;
Yet is the day over long.

Unto us they belong,
    Us the bitter and gay,
Wine and woman and song.

We, as we pass along,
    Are sad as they will not stay;
Yet is the day over long.

Fruits and flowers among,
    What is better than they:
Wine and woman and song?
    Yet is day over long.

There is no doubt the poet thought he was being very shocking when he wrote those lines. There is about them a sophomoric delight in fancied iniquity. It was this attitude that gave Dowson's age the name of "the naughty nineties."

But if the nineties had its *Yellow Book* school, the

[3] Ernest Dowson, "Villanelle of the Poet's Road" (New York, 1905). Reprinted by permission of Dodd, Mead & Company, Inc.

1920's had the *American Mercury* school. Taking Mr. H. L. Mencken much more seriously than he took himself, a whole group of essayists imitated him and his imitators. These writers invariably referred to the common people as the "booboise"; the South was "the Bible belt"; and any preacher was ironically "an eminent doctor," or a "witch doctor." In other words, the writers borrowed a whole set of ideas and terms because these were at the time regarded as clever. In their way they were just as false as the carry-me-back-to-the-dear-old-southland of song writers who had never been south of Jersey City.

3. *Profitable opinions "slanting."* If an assumed cynicism has, however, been too often the fault of one group of writers, the reverse has been equally true of another school. The professional optimist has made such a nuisance of himself that he is perhaps a major cause of the reaction toward pessimism. From a financial standpoint, optimism in writing has been profitable. Syndication has been the reward of the booster. True, he has appealed to a less educated public; and he has not usually deceived the critics, whereas his equally insincere cynical contemporary has too frequently succeeded in doing just that.

As a nation though, we can most often be accused of the more dangerous of these two dishonesties. For it is more disastrous to be told that all is well, when it is not, than to be warned of the evils around us. The false prophets that led the nation into the panic of 1929 were the professional optimists. It is well to be able to recognize them. There is no magic formula, but there are certain earmarks of the species.

When we read: "What has been going on quite openly for the last twenty-five years is the spiritualization of business . . . the gradual emergence of a mystical attitude toward the mastery of economic environment," [4] we see one of the infallible signs—a sweeping eulogy of one person, group, or institution. The writer who finds everything terrible or perfect is being dishonest either with himself or with his reader. Newspapers and periodicals reflecting only one opinion are the hotbeds of such false prophets. It is only the stupid and the dishonest who fashion their opinions exactly after those of some one creed. And if one set of opinions is likely to be profitable, its holders are open to suspicion.

It is only human to believe that anyone disagreeing with your ideas is a hypocrite. However it is safer to look for the deceivers among those of your own beliefs. They alone are dangerous. When you can recognize insincerity even in your camp, and sincerity among your foes, you may read where you will without danger. The thing to look for is not whether the writer agrees or disagrees with you, but for sweeping generalities, the bland assumption that everything is either black or white. We must be on the alert for the omission of important facts, or for the implication that these facts are unimportant. It may be quite true that every cloud has a silver lining; but if the cloud happens to be part of a hurricane, the silver lining is not the important fact. The writer who dismisses panics and wars with the statement that they will be followed by better times is refusing to face the problems before him. It

[4] Mary Austin, quoted in *Forum*, May, 1931.

is this failure to face facts, however unpleasant, which is at the core of dishonest optimism.

4. *Writing down to the reader*. Writing down to the reader is another and less virulent type of insincerity —less virulent but not less contagious; the thing leads more frequently to poor workmanship than to dishonesty in opinions. The temptation is great, for the author usually desires to reach as many people as possible. Even Shakespeare has scenes addressed to the groundlings, those ignorant fellows in the pit who, he said, were "incapable of anything but inexplicable dumb shows and noise." Despising such want of taste, Shakespeare nevertheless gave them on occasion their beloved dumb shows and noise.

There is a name for this kind of writing—a "pot boiler." Some novelists turn out a pot boiler or two to support themselves while they are working on something really good. This is perhaps excusable; even a Shakespeare must eat. What is more difficult to pardon—perhaps it is *the* unpardonable sin in a writer— is complete surrender. Arnold Bennett is accused of this, for after making his reputation with *The Old Wives' Tale* he seemed to be content with rather tawdry writing.

In the "slick paper" magazine field, the temptation is especially great. There is an extremely limited market for excellent work, and a very large and profitable one for clever trivialities, especially if the writer has a name to sell. We must learn, then, not to be misled by labels—a famous name does not insure a fine piece of writing.

It is probable that writers frequently insult the reader's intelligence—that even the common man has a respect for genuine worth. Countless men and women have been moved by St. Paul's familiar words: [5]

Thrice was I beaten with rods, once was I stoned, thrice I suffered shipwreck, a night and a day I have been in the deep; In journeyings often, in perils of waters, in perils of robbers, in perils by mine own countrymen, in perils by the heathen, in perils in the city, in perils in the wilderness, in perils in the sea, in perils among false brethren; In weariness and painfulness, in watchings often, in hunger and thirst, in fastings often, in cold and nakedness.

This was described by Bruce Barton in a popular magazine as the vocabulary of the athletic field and the arena. He believed that Paul would have liked the slang phrase, "taking it on the chin." But even Bruce Barton cannot make Paul talk like a football coach. An immense gulf is fixed between the two men. Paul was not trying to write like a gladiator to curry favor with the mob. He was not writing down to his public. It is Barton who insults the reader's intelligence by assuming that he cannot accept dignity of thought and language.

This is the reason the play *Tobacco Road* is essentially third-rate. A serious study of a social problem has been turned into a humorous, risqué farce to bring in the cash customers. It succeeded, in bringing them in, but as a play it is more dishonest than a burlesque show, which makes no pretense at being a social document. A trick as old as the miracle plays, and as modern as Hollywood, is to end a risqué story with a moral preachment.

[5] II Corinthians XI:25–27.

Propaganda

More dangerous than any of these types of insincerity is the deliberate attempt to mislead or deceive —commonly called *propaganda*. It is necessary here to define our terms. *Propaganda* in its original sense is related to *propagate;* originally it meant propagating an idea or doctrine. In that sense nearly all writing is propaganda. However, probably because in the First World War propaganda was often intended to deceive, the word has taken on an unpleasant connotation. In this chapter we shall not concern ourselves with open and honest efforts to present ideas, but with insincere and deceptive writing. It is in this sense that the word *propaganda* will be used.

Unsupported generalizations. The first mark of such writing is a lack of specific statements and a reliance upon unsupported generalization. Thus Dr. Johnson, who preferred monarchies to republics, wrote of Milton: [6]

His political notions were those of an acrimonious and surly republican, for which it is not known that he gave any better reason than "a popular government was the most frugal; for the trappings of monarchy would set up an ordinary commonwealth." It is surely very shallow policy that supposes money to be the chief good; and even this, without considering that support and expense of a court is, for the most part, only a particular kind of traffic by which money is circulated without any national impoverishment.

Milton's republicanism was, I am afraid, founded in an envious hatred of greatness, and a sullen desire of inde-

[6] Johnson, "The Life of Milton," *Lives of the English Poets.*

pendence; in petulance impatient of control, and pride disdainful of superiority. He hated monarchs in the state, and prelates in the church; for he hated all whom he was required to obey. It is to be suspected that his predominant desire was to destroy rather than establish, and that he felt not so much the love of liberty as repugnance to authority.

Note that Johnson selects only one of Milton's statements about government, and dogmatically states that this was the only reason Milton preferred a republic. Yet anyone has only to turn to the *Areopagitica* to find a large part of his argument based on the theory that the individual has the right and duty to choose for himself. He believed that "God, therefore, left him free," and that "God sure esteems the growth and completing of one virtuous person, more than the restraint of ten vicious." Johnson had a perfect right to disagree with this theory, but he had no right to disregard it and state that Milton's chief reason for opposing monarchy was that it cost too much money. And to charge that Milton believed money "the chief good" is absurd in view of Milton's remark in *Paradise Lost:* [7]

> Let none admire
> That riches grow in Hell; that soil may best
> Deserve the precious bane.

Likewise Johnson's statement that Milton's predominant desire was "to destroy rather than establish" fails to account for the fact that Milton for twenty years laid aside his dream of creating a great poem to devote himself to establishing a commonwealth.

[7] *Paradise Lost,* Book I.

Question-begging words. Johnson's attack shows another common element of misleading and biased writing—the use of question-begging words. Question-begging is a form of argument that assumes as true that which is to be proved. It often takes the form of name-calling. Johnson's phrases—"an acrimonious and surly republican"; "sullen desire of independence"; "petulance impatient of control"—are designed to prejudice the reader even before reasons are presented. The fact that Johnson regarded all republicanism as sullen, surly, and petulant does not justify this sort of writing. A person may have excellent reasons for distrusting communists or fascists, but such terms as "dirty red" or "fascist boll weevil" are aimed at the emotions of hate and fear. They appeal to passion and prejudice in the same way that "gringo" does in Mexico or "foreign devil" in Japan. They are excellent material for starting wars, but they are unfitted for a rational, peaceful society. Emotion has its place in life, but social problems must be solved by the rational faculty.

Thus a widely syndicated columnist writes about a mining operation in Minnesota: [8]

A parlor pink college professor once came here, watched a man work, asked how much he mined, his day's pay, and then blandly announced that the mining companies were robbers because it cost, according to his calculation, 2 cents a ton to mine the ore. He forgot the millions of dollars in equipment, railroads, trains, cars, scoops, trucks, shops and machinery. He forgot the schools, new homes, good roads. He disregarded the taxes of the grasp-

[8] Boake Carter, in The Philadelphia *Evening Public Ledger.*

ing politicians. He forgot them all—just like the Washington politicians, who never operated a business in their lives but have spent six years informing industry how to operate!

We recognize at once that this is an appeal to prejudice. "Parlor pink," "blandly announced," "grasping politicians"—these are not terms which could help in clearing up the difficult problems of fair wages and wise taxation.

The same method can be used in reverse: question-begging words may eulogize as well as attack. Thus the same columnist writes: [9]

Stupendous wealth has come out of this range and these iron mines. But stupendous has been the investment to bring out this wealth—wealth which is shared by every American. It isn't a matter of dollars and cents. To be sure, the mining companies have made money. But they were run by men who risked much, showed courage, worked hard with their hands, and the profits they have made are their due and just desert. But they made it possible for Americans to obtain the greatest profit—they mined something which resulted in creating engineering marvels that lifted our standard of material living one-third higher than the next richest nation in the world.

"Courage," "worked hard with their hands," "engineering marvels," "richest nation in the world"—all these assume as true exactly what the writer is trying to prove: that the mining companies deserve the profits they have obtained. As is usual in such writing, the question-begging is combined with assertions unsupported by evidence. No examples or statistics are given to back up the statements that the owners

[9] *Ibid.*

worked hard with their hands and that "the profits they have made are their due and just desert." Whether the columnist is right or wrong is not the question; the point is that he has given us nothing which would hold in a court of law or weigh before an arbitration board.

Appeals to loyalties. Especially dangerous are appeals to loyalties, to patriotism, to love of child and kin. These are often used to obscure the fact that the writer has some design upon us. Thus the maker of nostrums is likely to say, "Don't risk your child's health" or "You want the best for your family" instead of demonstrating that his product is beneficial or the best.

And when the advertiser assures us that his only desire is for our own welfare, or simply to serve the public, we have every right to doubt his sincerity. As has been said, a writer may legitimately try to win us to his point of view, but he is dishonest if he pretends to one aim and serves another. Thus he has no right to pretend that his object is patriotic service when he is really trying to sell goods or get a political job. When Southey in "Vision of Judgment" has the ghost of Washington address George III:

Thou, too, didst act with upright heart, as befitted a Sovereign
  eign
True to his sacred trust, to his crown, his kingdom, and
  people.

we are reminded that Southey held a government pension. We should be equally suspicious of the editorial writer who, employed by a wealthy man, assures us that higher taxes on large incomes are against the national interest.

Prettification. Appeals to admirations and loyalties are often used to cause us to accept things which our intellects tell us are wrong. Machine-gunning of refugees cannot be justified, but it can be obscured by praise of the courage of the defenders of the fatherland. The blood and savagery of war can be wrapped in sentimental phrases and pleasant imagery: [10]

> How sleep the brave, who sink to rest,
> By all their country's wishes blest!
> When Spring, with dewy fingers cold,
> Returns to deck their hallowed mold,
> She there shall dress a sweeter sod
> Then Fancy's feet have ever trod.
>
> By fairy hands their knell is rung;
> By forms unseen their dirge is sung;
> There Honor comes, a pilgrim gray,
> To bless the turf that wraps their clay;
> And Freedom shall a while repair,
> To dwell a weeping hermit there!

That is a lovely poem—too lovely in fact for the ugly reality of death in battle. This sentimentalizing of war is one of the things that make it possible. Equally dangerous is the sentimentalizing of peace, the fiction that except for the war lords all men desire to live as brothers. The difficult text of truth is not made clearer by trying to see it through rose-colored spectacles.

More recently Ernest Hemingway has written about bull-fighting in a pseudo-scientific manner which covers up its barbarity. Gored horses getting tangled in

[10] William Collins, "Ode Written in the Beginning of the Year 1746."

their own entrails are calmly likened to the clowns in a circus. The writer's objectivity is designed to trick the reader into a mood that will accept cruelty as a kind of scientific experiment.

Propaganda in fiction and drama. Propaganda appears also in fiction and the drama. Here it is more difficult to analyze unless the writer introduces commentary presenting his ideas. When a character states a point of view, it may, as we have seen in other chapters, be simply dramatic, designed only to reveal the mind of the character. Hamlet's remarks upon suicide are not intended to convince the audience, but to show Hamlet's state of mind. Often, however, we can find a character talking at the reader, arguing the author's own point of view. Jim Laird, the drunken lawyer in Willa Cather's "The Sculptor's Funeral," does this when he tells fellow-townsmen why their boys seldom amount to much, and condemns the whole money-grubbing code of the small Kansas town. The value and sincerity of such things can be judged by the same standards we apply to any presentation of a point of view. If the writer is honest, he will not appeal to prejudice, will not try to hide the facts in a cloud of emotion.

We cannot ask the writer of fiction to give us facts and figures, although he may do so, but we do require him to give an honest picture of life. If his manufacturers and business men are all scoundrels and libertines, and his workmen all fine, honest fellows, we should be on our guard. We well know that men are neither all good nor all bad; if, therefore, a writer tries to show us such people, he is falsifying life, either because he is an inferior artist or more often because he wants to win us to his own point of view. His point of view may or may not be correct, but if he falsifies his picture of life he is using dishonest means. Thus Wordsworth, who disagreed with the theology of the Reverend Joseph Fawcett, introduced him into *The Excursion* as a person of low morals as well. Sinclair Lewis has done the same sort of thing with Elmer Gantry; he has made him so great a shyster that he is hardly credible. And so Lewis' criticism of organized religion has much less force than his criticism of business in *Babbitt*. George Babbitt, for all his crassness and dishonesty, is essentially a decent fellow. The picture is closer to reality.

One reason for the paucity of good proletarian novels is that the writers have so often twisted their characters and situations to prove a point. On the other hand, Galsworthy's study of labor trouble in *Strife* is still vital because he has shown the good and bad on both sides. The play is not a struggle between vice and virtue, but between an honest but overbearing employer and a sincere but pig-headed labor leader. They are human beings, not abstractions out of Karl Marx. Galsworthy's sympathies in the play seem to lie with the workmen, but he is honest enough to recognize their faults also.

The problem is not solely one of the sincerity of the writer's convictions. Obviously those writers who can adjust their point of view overnight to suit a different publication or to follow the party line are propagandists of the baser sort. However, many a man, sincerely believing a certain thing, has used essentially dishonest means to attain it: appeals to prejudice, fallacious reasoning, or, in fiction, false portrayal of characters or social institutions. A literary artist has no greater right to use shoddy material, however effective on the surface, than has a carpenter to support his structure with rotten lumber.

Safeguards against propaganda. Earlier we spoke of the common man's respect for worth. The trouble is that he is at times misled—he cannot always distinguish the plated ware from true metal. This chapter has suggested some of the tests that may help, but there are no infallible rules. Literature is not like a compound that can be analyzed chemically. The diamond expert learns to distinguish the grades of stones by long practice, by familiarizing himself with the best. The reader who would protect himself against intellectual cheats must do the same. He must be acquainted with the best, must value the genuine.

Of the dangers in accepting shoddy ideas we have spoken; of the reward for knowing and loving the finest many have testified; the experts in every line, from good food and wines to masterpieces in art and music and literature, know a joy untasted by the ignorant. In a time when the specious is often skilfully processed to look like the real thing, and when propaganda is frequently backed by millions of dollars, sound, honest writing is best described in Edna St. Vincent Millay's words: [11]

> Oh, the good smack of truth on the tongue again,
> After a winter of lies!

[11] From *The King's Henchman*, published by Harper & Brothers. Copyright, 1927, by Edna St. Vincent Millay.

Exercises

The following exercises are offered merely as aids to an understanding of some of the principles discussed in the foregoing chapters; they are not intended to be the staple of a course in literature. It seems to me that the first job of the student is to understand the meaning of the works studied. Some of the exercises are designed to help him do that; more of them are intended to develop a discriminating sense of values. Therefore, whatever the assignment, the student should first master the content of what he has read. Then he may turn to these exercises for drills and techniques in the interpretation of his reading.

For this study he should own or have readily available either a comprehensive anthology of English (or English and American) literature or several volumes, including an anthology of poetry, one of the short story, one of modern drama, and a collection of Shakespeare's plays. In addition, it is suggested that he read several novels representing some of the more important writers in English. Although the questions are usually keyed to certain anthologies, the poems, plays, or stories mentioned are those found in many collections. A few questions are designed to send the student to the library for collateral reading. Therefore the exercises should be useful whatever texts are adopted for a course devoted to literature in English.

ANTHOLOGIES REFERRED TO IN THE EXERCISES

THOMAS, Wright and BROWN, Stuart Gerry, *Reading Poems* (New York, Oxford University Press, 1941). (Referred to as R.P.)

UNTERMEYER, Louis, *The Book of Living Verse* (New York, Harcourt, Brace and Company, Inc., 1939). (L.V.)

BULLETT, Gerald, *The English Galaxy of Shorter Poems* (London, Everyman, 1939). (E.G.)

BURRELL, Angus and CERF, Bennett, *The Bedside Book of Famous American Stories* (New York, Random House, Inc., 1936). (B.B.F.A.S.)

WATSON, E. B. and PRESSEY, W. B., *Contemporary Drama* (New York, Charles Scribner's Sons, 1941). (C.D.)

BUCK, Philo M., GASSNER, J. and ALBERTSON, H. S., *A Treasury of the American Theatre* (New York, Simon and Schuster, Inc., 1940). (T.T.)

HATCHER, Harlan, *Modern American Drama* (New York, Harcourt, Brace and Company, Inc., 1941). (M.A.D.)

BROOKE, Tucker, CUNLIFFE, John William, and MAC-CRACKEN, Henry Noble, *Shakespeare's Principal Plays* (New York, D. Appleton-Century Company, Inc., 1935).

CHAPTER I

THE NATURE OF LITERATURE

1. Write an essay on some book or poem you especially like, pointing out specifically some of the elements which in your opinion make it a work of true literature.

2. After the essay is returned to you, file it away until the end of the semester. Then re-read it to determine if in the light of further studies of literary values, you have modified any of your opinions. Write a paragraph or two of comment on this point.

3. Read Psalms I, XXVII, and CIV. Which ones of the elements discussed in this chapter do you find in these

poems? What was the writer's primary purpose? Had he any objectives other than the primary one?

4. In *The English Galaxy of Shorter Poems*, the first two lyrics are "Western Wind, When Wilt Thou Blow," and "The Maidens Came" (p. 3). After reading them, tell why you think the editor chose them.

Other suggested poems:

"Full Fathom Five, Thy Father Lies" (140)

"Break, Break, Break" (409)

"So, We'll Go No More a Roving" (370)

In *Reading Poems* the following may be used:

"Western Wind, When Wilt Thou Blow" (42)

"Full Fathom Five, Thy Father Lies (9)

"Break, Break, Break" (16)

"So, We'll Go No More a Roving" (64)

O, My Luv Is Like a Red, Red Rose" (63)

In *The Book of Living Verse:*

"Full Fathom Five, Thy Father Lies" (61)

"Hark! Hark! the Lark" (61)

"Break, Break, Break" (331)

"Sweet Afton" (194)

"To Night" (267)

5. Select a poem from a newspaper or popular magazine; then in the anthology you are using, try to find one expressing a similar idea or emotion. Which one has more thought, emotion, or imagination? Be prepared to explain why you think so.

CHAPTER II

POETRY: ITS NATURE

The following exercises are keyed to the anthologies listed below, but they can be readily adapted for use with other standard collections of verse in English.

UNTERMEYER, Louis, *The Book of Living Verse* (New York, Harcourt, Brace and Company, Inc., 1939). (Referred to as L.V.)

THOMAS, Wright and BROWN, Stuart Gerry, *Reading Poems* (New York, Oxford University Press, 1941). (R.P.)

BULLETT, Gerald, *The English Galaxy of Shorter Poems* (London, Everyman, 1939). (E.G.)

1. Rewrite the following poems in prose form:
"Sigh No More, Ladies, Sigh No More" (E.G. 149; L.V. 59)
"To the Virgins, to Make Much of Time" (R.P. 53; E.G. 227)
"Back and Side Go Bare, Go Bare" (E.G. 21)
"Sumer Is Icumen In" (R.P. 152)
"The Passionate Shepherd to His Love" (R.P. 445; L.V. 73; E.G. 118)
"To an Athlete Dying Young" (R.P. 12; L.V. 484)
What effect has the loss of rhythm on the mood or emotion?

2. Comment on the use of onomatopoeia in the following poems. In any of them does it seem forced or too obvious?
Poe: "The Bells"
Tennyson: "Break, Break, Break" (R.P. 16; L.V. 331; E.G. 409)
"Morte d'Arthur," 11, 181-92 (L.V. 348)
"The Lotus Eaters" (R.P. 249)
Swinburne: "When the Hounds of Spring" (L.V. 423)
Shelley: "The Cloud" (R.P. 26; L.V. 276)
Herrick: "Upon Julia's Clothes" (R.P. 52; L.V. 97; E.G. 240)

3. In *The Rime of The Ancient Mariner*, point out the stanzas in which Coleridge has used onomatopoeia. List the various sound effects he has imitated (R.P. 224; L.V. 230).

4. What effect on the thought or emotion has the rhythm of the following stanzas from Wigglesworth's "The Day of Doom"?

"But Nature's light shin'd not so bright, to teach us the
    right way:
We might have lov'd it and well improv'd it, and yet have
    gone astray."
The Judge most High makes this Reply: "You ignorance
    pretend,
Dimness of sight, and want of light, your course Heav'n-
    ward to bend.

"How came your mind to be so blind? I once you knowl-
    edge gave,
Clearness of sight and judgment right: who did the same
    deprave?
If to your cost you have it lost, and quite defac'd the same,
Your own desert hath caus'd the smart; you ought not me
    to blame.

"Yourselves into a pit of woe, your own transgression led,
If I to none my Grace had shown, who had been injured?
If to a few, and not to you, I shew'd a way of life,
My Grace so free, you clearly see gives you no ground of
    strife."

5. Compare these two versions of the same stanzas.
Which has the more regular beat? Which is the better?

> But still he holds the wedding guest—
>   There was a Ship, quoth he—
> "Nay if thou'st a gladsome tale,
>   "Marinere! come with me."
>
> He holds him with his skinny hand,
>   Quoth he, there was a Ship—
> "Now get thee hence, thou grey-beard Loon!
>   Or my staff shall make thee skip."
>
>
> He holds him with his skinny hand,
> "There was a ship," quoth he.
> "Hold off! unhand me, grey-beard loon!"
> Eftsoons his hand dropt he.

He holds him with his glittering eye—
The Wedding-Guest stood still,
And listens like a three years' child:
The Mariner hath his will.[1]

Coleridge wrote three versions of the following stanza.
Which is the best? (They are not given in the order of
composition.)

Are those her ribs through which the Sun
Did peer, as through a grate?
And is that Woman all her crew?
Is that a Death? and are there two?
Is Death that Woman's mate?[2]

Are those *her* naked ribs, which fleck'd
The sun that did behind them peer?
And are those two all, all her crew,
That woman and her fleshless Pheere?

Are those *her* Ribs, thro' which the Sun
Did peer, as thro' a grate?
And are those two all, all her crew,
That Woman, and her Mate?

What improvements has Coleridge made in the expanded
version of the following stanza? Observe such things as
rhythm, imagery, vivid diction, and relation of sound to
sense. (As Lowes has shown, Coleridge is representing
the passage of time from sunset to the rising of a waning
moon long after midnight.)

With never a whisper in the Sea
Off darts the Spectre-ship;
While clomb above the Eastern bar
The horned Moon, with one bright Star
Almost atween the tips.

[1] *The Rime of the Ancient Mariner*, Part I.
[2] *Ibid.*, Part III.

The Sun's rim dips; the stars rush out:
At one stride comes the dark;
With far-heard whisper, o'er the sea,
Off shot the spectre-bark.

We listened and looked sidewise up!
Fear at my heart, as at a cup,
My life-blood seemed to sip!
The stars were dim, and thick the night,
The steersman's face by his lamp gleamed white;
From the sails the dew did drip—
Till clomb above the eastern bar
The horned Moon, with one bright star
Within the nether tip.[3]

6. On the basis of word-sound why do you think Tennyson changed the following stanza?

On either side the river lie
Long fields of barley and of rye,
That clothe the wold, and meet the sky.
And thro' the field the road runs by
    To many towered Camelot.
The yellowleaved waterlily,
The greensheathed daffodilly,
Tremble in the water chilly,
    Round about Shalott. (1833)

On either side the river lie
Long fields of barley and of rye,
That clothe the wold and meet the sky;
And through the field the road runs by
    To many-towered Camelot;
And up and down the people go,
Gazing where the lilies blow

[3] *Ibid.*

Round an island there below,
The island of Shalott.[4] (1842)

7. Choose a short poem and substitute three or four synonyms for the original words. If possible keep the same number of syllables in the lines you change. Does the change of word-sound affect the mood or emotion?

8. In Gray's "Elegy" compare stanzas 1–3 with 8–11. Which ones give the more vivid pictures? List the images in each group (R.P. 123; L.V. 173).

9. Do the same for the three stanzas of Wordsworth's "She Dwelt Among the Untrodden Ways" (R.P. 10; L.V. 217; E.G. 356).

10. Look up Longfellow's "A Psalm of Life." Comment on:

The effectiveness of the rhythm
The use of images

11. In Shelley's "To a Skylark" point out the images that suggest beauty and joy (R.P. 37; L.V. 268).

12. In a sentence for each, state the mood of each of the five sections of Shelley's "Ode to the West Wind." Now list his images which suit with each mood (R.P. 98; L.V. 274).

13. In Eliot's "The Love Song of J. Alfred Prufrock," point out four images which suggest boredom; four which suggest hesitation or timidity. What image suggests the element Prufrock has missed in life?

Now read the poem as a whole, and note the cumulative effect of these images.

14. In "Memorial Rain" by MacLeish, point out trite phrases in the ambassador's speech, and vivid images and fresh diction in other parts of the poem. What purpose is served by this contrast? How does the contrast help us to understand the meaning of the poem (L.V. 550)?

[4] Tennyson, "The Lady of Shalott," Part I.

A similar study may be made of Eliot's *The Waste Land* (R.P. 591).

15. Coleridge said that the images in Wordsworth's "Ode on Intimations of Immortality," 11. 108–121, were obscure and unsuited to a description of a child. Do you agree? Compare them with the image in 11. 1–76 (R.P. 88; L.V. 221).

16. In Shakespeare's sonnet No. LXXXVII point out the legal terms used. Do these give any freshness or vividness to the poem? Does this sonnet support or refute Wordsworth's theory that a poet should employ "language really used by men" (L.V. 70 or in any edition of Shakespeare's works)?

Other poems which may be studied for the use of language from daily life:

Drayton: "Since There's No Help" (E.G. 117)

MacLeish: "Speech to Those Who Say Comrade" (R.P. 109)

Milton: "Lycidas," 11. 113–131 (R. P. 445; L.V. 117)

Frost: "Mending Wall" (R.P. 286)

"Two Tramps in Mud Time" (L.V. 519)

17. In sonnet No. CXXX Shakespeare made fun of the trite figures of speech used in love poetry. How many of them are still used in popular songs? (Found on p. 50 above).

CHAPTER III

POETRY: FORM AND FUNCTION

1. After reading some of the old ballads (R.P. 191–202; L. V. 3–25), turn to Housman's "The True Lover" (L.V. 482) or "White in the Moon the Long Road Lies" (R.P. 71) or "Grenadier" (E.G. 471). Give reasons why the poet may have chosen the meter of the old ballads. What similarities besides that of form do you note?

2. Find a poem by Burns and one by Wordsworth

which use ballad meter. What in the subject or the treatment suits with the ballad form?

3. Look up Spenser's *Faerie Queen,* and read Canto I, stanzas 38–46. Then read Keats's "The Eve of St. Agnes" (R.P. 320; L.V. 311). What effects that Keats wanted to achieve are found in Spenser's work?

Do the same for Tennyson's "The Lotus Eaters" (R.P. 249; L.V. 337).

4. Study the division of thought in a Shakespearean sonnet (R.P. 160–167; L.V. 65–72; E.G. 122–139), and that of an Italian type of sonnet "On His Being Arrived to the Age of Twenty-Three" (R.P. 169; E.G. 278) or "It Is a Beauteous Evening" (R.P. 137; L.V. 215). Then turn to some modern sonnets (R.P. 185–187; L.V. 536, 547–548, 498–500) to determine if the poets have chosen one or the other form to suit the thought-pattern.

5. In Exercise IX, Chapter II, you were asked to compare the imagery in the three stanzas of Wordsworth's "She Dwelt Among the Untrodden Ways" (R.P. 10; L.V. 217; E.G. 35). Now compare the metrical patterns of the same three stanzas. Which has the greatest regularity; which the greatest variety? Does the variety make the stanza more or less musical? Is the stanza you think the most musical the same one you found to have the best imagery?

6. From *The Rime of the Ancient Mariner* (R.P. 224; L.V. 230), select five stanzas which show variations from the basic ballad stanza pattern. Have these variations any relation to the thought or mood of the stanzas in which they appear?

7. In any poem, find a stanza in which one or more anapests appear. Had the poet any reason for seeking a lilting or rollicking effect?

Find a stanza containing a trochee. Why do you think the poet used it?

8. Study the metrical variations in "Lycidas" (R.P. 445; L.V. 117). Does the variation in rhyme pattern make the

poem more or less musical? Do the short lines add emphasis?

9. Is the heroic couplet as well suited to Pope's "Eloisa to Abelard" (R.P. 568) as to his *The Rape of the Lock* (R.P. 374; L.V. 161)? Is the form suited to Dryden's "Mac-Flecknoe (R.P. 357); to Pope's "Epistle to Dr. Arbuthnot" (R.P. 363)?

10. Criticize the following stanza, discussing such things as regularity, feminine rhyme, and types of feet used.[5]

> The skies they were ashen and sober;
>> The leaves they were crispèd and sere—
>> The leaves they were withering and sere;
> It was night in the lonesome October
>> Of my most immemorial year;
> It was hard by the dim lake of Auber,
>> In the misty mid region of Weir—
> It was down by the dank tarn of Auber,
>> In the ghoul-haunted region of Weir.

11. What is the prevailing meter of the following stanzas? Is it suited to the subject: a memorial to Robert Emmet, an Irish rebel against England? [6]

Oh, breathe not his name! let it sleep in the shade,
Where cold and unhonored his relics are laid;
Sad, silent, and dark be the tears that we shed,
As the night-dew that falls on the grass o'er his head.

But the night-dew that falls, though in silence it weeps,
Shall brighten with verdure the grave where he sleeps;
And the tear that we shed, though in silence it rolls,
Shall long keep his memory green in our souls.

12. Judge the following stanzas from "A Friend's Greet-

---

[5] Edgar Allan Poe, "Ulalume—A Ballad."
[6] Thomas Moore, "Oh Breathe Not His Name."

ing" by Edgar A. Guest on the basis of the following
things: [7]

> variety of music
> harmony of sentence and verse rhythm
> naturalness of word order
> imagery
> freshness of diction

I'd like to be the sort of friend that you have been to me;
I'd like to be the help that you've been always glad to be;
I'd like to mean as much to you each minute of the day
As you have meant, old friend of mine, to me along the
way.

I'd like to do the big things and the splendid things for
you,
To brush the gray from out your skies and leave them only
blue;
I'd like to say the kindly things that I've so often heard,
And feel that I could rouse your soul the way that mine
you've stirred.

CHAPTER IV

POETRY: ITS INTERPRETATION

1. What emotions or ideas are symbolized for you by
the lark, the nightingale, a ship, the moon, a fireplace or
hearth? In your anthology, find poems using one or more
of these. Has the poet used them for their symbolic or
their literal meaning?

2. Read the Twenty-Third Psalm. What phrases have
symbolic meaning?

3. In "Lycidas" (R.P. 445; L.V. 117) Milton has used
the following symbols: laurels, sisters of the sacred well,
string (of a musical instrument), urn, satyrs, fauns, the
shepherd, the tangles of Nearea's hair, shears, the two

[7] From Mr. Guest's book *A Heap O'Livin'*. Copyright, 1916.
Used by permission of The Reilly & Lee Co., Chicago, Ill.

massy keys, the mitre (in "mitred locks"), shearers' feast, sheep hook (a shepherd's crook). With the help of a dictionary and a guide to mythology, explain briefly the meaning of each as it is used in the poem. Which ones are from classical mythology; from the Bible; of Milton's own creation? Are any of them the same as you found in the Twenty-Third Psalm?

Many of these symbols are used throughout literature. When you meet them, note whether or not they have the same meaning as in "Lycidas."

4. In Sandburg's "Four Preludes on Playthings of the Wind" (L.V. 527) point out four things you believe to have symbolic meaning. Give your interpretation of what they symbolize.

Other poems which may be studied in a similar way:

MacNeice: "Song: The Sunlight on the Garden" (R.P. 523)

Eliot: "Sweeney among the Nightingales" (R.P. 534; L.V. 544)

Fitzgerald: The Rubáiyát of Omar Khayyám (R.P. 139; E.G. 402)

5. Professor Lowes has said that in The Rime of the Ancient Mariner (R.P. 224; L.V. 230), the Albatross "has a profoundly symbolic meaning." Study the poem to determine what that meaning is.

6. To a greater or less degree each of the following poems suggest moods, feelings, or ideas not specifically stated. Choose two of the poems and try to state the moods, feelings, or ideas suggested.

MacLeish: "Memorial Rain" (L.V. 550)

Hopkins: "I Wake and Feel the Fell of the Dark" (R.P. 587)

"The Windhover" (R.P. 505)

"Binsey Poplars" (E.G. 458)

Eliot: "La Figlia Che Piange" (L.V. 543)

"Marina" (R.P. 535. Cf. also note, *ibid.*, 708)
Yeats: "The Arrow" (E.G. 470)

7. In any of the above poems, point out an example of "free association": one image or idea suggested by another rather than by logical thought processes.

8. Judged by modern standards do any of the following poems have too obvious a design upon us? Would it have been better had the poet suggested the idea instead of stating it? Is the point or moral dragged in or is it an integral part of the poem?

Bryant: "To a Waterfowl" (L.V. 433)
"Thanatopsis (L.V. 434)
"The Yellow Violet" (R.P. 35)
Lamb: "The Old Familiar Faces" (E.G. 364)
Bunyan: "The Shepherd Boy Sings in the Valley of Humiliation" (E.G. 326)

Or look up the following poems for similar consideration:
Wordsworth: "Resolution and Independence"
"To a Skylark"
Browning: "The Statue and the Bust"
Longfellow: "A Psalm of Life"
Whittier: "The Barefoot Boy"

9. Find poems on themes similar to two of those in Exercise VIII, but poems which present the theme in a more subtle manner. Compare the two groups in such qualities as varied music, vivid imagery, vivid diction.

10. Coleridge once said that he thought *The Rime of the Ancient Mariner* had "entirely too much moral." What stanzas may he have had in mind? Do you agree?

11. The following poems are simple in verse form and phraseology. Do they deal with simple or complex ideas or emotional states?

"Western Wind, When Wilt Thou Blow"
(R.P. 42; E.G. 3)

Wordsworth: "A Slumber Did My Spirit Seal" (R.P. 10; L.V. 218; E.G. 356)

Housman: "The Night Is Freezing Fast" (R.P. 10; E.G. 473)

"Oh, When I Was in Love with You" (L.V. 485)

"Could Man Be Drunk Forever" (E.G. 476)

Stevenson: "Requiem" (R.P. 16)

Burns: "John Anderson, My Jo" (R.P. 60; L.V. 198)

"Sweet Afton" (L.V. 194)

"O, Wert Thou in the Cauld Blast" (R.P. 61; L.V. 200)

"Ye Flowery Banks o' Bonnie Doon" (E.G. 349)

Now take a group of poems of complex form and phraseology, and determine if they reflect more complex ideas or emotions:

Donne: "A Valediction: Of Weeping" (E.G. 190)

"The Sun Rising" (L.V. 83)

"The Funeral" (R.P. 215)

Wylie: "Hymn to Earth" (R.P. 583; L.V. 534)

Eliot: "La Figlia Che Piange" (L.V. 543)

"The Love Song of J. Alfred Prufrock" (R.P. 530)

12. The old ballads were simple in form, and dealt with simple emotions or situations: love, treachery, jealousy, murder, sudden death, ghost stories. After reading some of the ballads (R.P. 191–204; L.V. 3–25), select from the daily paper two or three stories which might be handled successfully in ballad form.

Can you find any folk ballad, ancient or modern, dealing with a similar situation?

13. Now from the fields of sociology, economics, or psychology, suggest certain themes (for example, poverty, paranoia) which might require complex forms or phraseology. Can you find any poems dealing with any of these themes? Are these poems simple or complex?

14. Wordsworth's sonnet, "The World Is Too Much with Us" (R.P. 172) and T. S. Eliot's *The Waste Land*

(R.P. 591) both picture their own periods as emotionally sterile, and show man out of tune with the world about him; both use literary allusion to evoke a past allegedly more filled with beauty and imagination. Using Mr. Eliot's own notes to *The Waste Land* (R.P. 720–731), make a study of Section II, "A Game of Chess," to show how he has used such things as symbolism, suggestion, free association, and literary allusion. Then turn to Wordsworth's sonnet to note how the poet has used the more traditional methods of direct statement and logical reasoning. Can you point to any lines of Eliot's which *suggest* ideas *stated* by Wordsworth?

Wordsworth says, "For this, for everything, we are out of tune." Which poet makes us share the experience of being out of tune?

Is the greater clarity of Wordsworth's poem balanced by any advantages on Eliot's part, such as more vivid imagery or greater challenge to the imagination?

CHAPTER V

PROSE STYLE

1. Find a composition written by a child, and compare its sentence patterns with those of the Anglo-Saxon *Chronicle* (p. 97 above). Now examine a few paragraphs of a theme or term report of your own to determine the extent to which you follow the same primitive patterns.

2. Here are two excerpts on a similar topic: American subservience to European culture. One was written in 1837, the other in 1940. Point out the characteristics of style of each period. In both point out the elements of good style regardless of period.

Furthermore, those things on which the mind and imagination fed were to be found, so educated Americans came to feel, chiefly in Europe. At college, literature meant chiefly English literature; even in childhood young Americans were brought up on Dickens and Scott and Thackeray, and pictures of English country houses and cathedrals. When people built fine houses were they not ambitiously imitative? Were not churches Gothic, and banks Greek? Why should it not seem natural to go to Europe to find their originals and to drink deep from the fountain whence the original inspiration of these things came? Henry Adams may have protested later that he got no education from England and Italy or Germany, though he confessed he did get Beethoven by accident in a German beer garden. But for many others a sense that the cherishable past was European was combined with a conviction that nothing worth cherishing was being thought or felt in expanding industrial America. All the young men of the genteel tradition (and their mothers and sisters too) went to Europe—their fathers were too busy making money for its own sake and too busy paying for the trip.[8]

We have listened too long to the courtly muses of Europe. The spirit of the American freeman is already suspected to be timid, imitative, tame. Public and private avarice make the air we breathe thick and fat. The scholar is decent, indolent, complaisant. See already the tragic consequence. The mind of this country, taught to aim at low objects, eats upon itself. There is no work for any but the decorous and the complaisant. Young men of the fairest promise, who begin life upon our shores, inflated by the mountain winds, shined upon by all the stars of God, find the earth below not in unison with these, but are hindered from action by the disgust which the principles on which business is managed inspire, and turn drudges, or die of disgust, some of them suicides. What is the remedy? They did not yet see, and

[8] Irwin Edman, "Look Homeward America," *Harper's Magazine*, December, 1940.

thousands of young men as hopeful now crowding to the barriers for the career do not yet see that if the single man plant himself indomitably on his instincts, and there abide, the huge world will come round to him.[9]

3. In one of your textbooks find a paragraph which you regard as an example of good, clear prose. Justify your choice.

4. Do the same for a passage of bad prose.

5. From an editorial or political speech select some examples of weasel words.

6. Compare the opening paragraphs of Poe's "The Purloined Letter" with those of Twain's "The Celebrated Jumping Frog of Calaveras County" (*The Bedside Book of Famous American Stories,* p. 126 and p. 254). What elements make Twain's style seem more modern than Poe's?

7. From the writings of Paul in the New Testament, find a passage to illustrate Luther's statement: "Paul's words are alive, they have hands and feet; if you cut them they bleed."

8. From an article in a current magazine select a paragraph containing images and concrete diction.

9. Compare the four opening paragraphs of Thomas Henry Huxley's *On the Physical Basis of Life* with some paragraphs in a textbook of biology; with a recent essay on science. Comment on such things as clarity, use of technical language, concrete diction, vividness.

10. Thomas Wolfe's style has been praised and condemned by critics. Read the last half-dozen paragraphs of "A Portrait of Bascom Hawke" (B.B.F.A. S. 1205–1206). What unusual qualities do you find? Does it seem musical to you? Are there any characteristics you dislike or think overdone?

[9] Ralph Waldo Emerson, *The American Scholar.*

CHAPTER VI

FICTION

Many of the following exercises should be regarded as suggestions rather than prescriptions. In contrast to the study of poetry, the study of fiction does not revolve around a standard body of material. Certain poems, for instance, appear in nearly all anthologies; there is much less agreement among the anthologists of the short story. And in the field of the novel the problem becomes greater. Only a few novels can be included in any general course in literature. What shall they be? Assuming that such a course might contain as many as six novels representing the development from the eighteenth century to the present, it is obvious that no two persons would agree upon the same novels or even novelists. Should the nineteenth century be represented by Scott, Emily Brontë, Jane Austen, Dickens, Thackeray, George Eliot, Trollope, Meredith, Henry James, Mark Twain, Melville, or Hardy? And if Dickens, what novel? The permutations and combinations become astronomical. If, on the other hand, fiction is studied only through the short story, one must omit some of the most significant writers in the English language. And there are problems in the study of the novel which do not appear in the short story: the complete analysis and development of character, for example.

Furthermore, novels are often assigned as collateral reading instead of being subjected to careful analysis in the classroom. When that practice is followed, there is little room for detailed exercises such as those offered for the chapters on poetry.

The following exercises are presented then with these suggestions:

1. That whatever materials are used for study, the student be asked to answer the questions relating to value (pp. 160–161, above).

2. That the student should be able to point out and discuss such things as the exposition, setting, plot structure, characterization, use of dialogue, style, and purpose.

3. That the student should present at least one written criticism of some work studied. This criticism should show a knowledge of some of the criteria discussed in the chapter on fiction.

The more detailed exercises below are keyed to *The Bedside Book of Famous American Stories*, edited by Angus Burrell and Bennett Cerf (New York, Random House, Inc., 1936). All page references are to this volume. However a number of the stories appear in other anthologies so that the usefulness of the exercises does not depend upon the adoption of a specific anthology. With slight changes many of the exercises can be used for any stories selected by the instructor. (That is, questions 6, 8, 9, 10, 11)

1. Compare Poe's "The Pit and the Pendulum" (p. 113) with Faulkner's "A Rose for Emily" (p. 1122). Point out in detail the greater depth and meaning of the latter story.

2. In a fantasy such as "Rip Van Winkle" (p. 28), "The Great Stone Face" (p. 44), or "The Arrow" (p. 993), show how the author has brought out some truth or some criticism of real life.

3. Find a news item which, though possibly true, might not be good material for a story because it would not seem true. Be prepared to give reasons.

4. Find a news item which might be developed into a story or novel.

5. In *The Bedside Book of Famous American Stories* only one of sixty-seven stories deals with the boy-meets-girl, boy-loses-girl, boy-wins-girl theme. How does that percentage compare with that of the stories in a popular magazine? What significance do you find in the result of your comparison?

6. What principles of economics, sociology, or psychology are involved in the following stories? Could any of the stories have had a different ending without running counter to these laws or principles?

William Dean Howells: "Edithia" (p. 316)
Willa Cather: "Paul's Case" (p. 681)
Sherwood Anderson: "I'm a Fool" (p. 712)
Edna Ferber: "The Afternoon of a Faun" (p. 881)
Dorothy Parker: "Big Blonde" (p. 974)
Ruth Suckow: "The Little Girl from Town" (p. 1070)
Erskine Caldwell: "Kneel to the Rising Sun" (p. 1218)

7. Compare the following stories to determine which is more dependent upon coincidence for its conclusion. Which one shows the better development of character?

O. Henry: "The Furnished Room" (p. 493)
            "A Municipal Report" (p. 511)

8. Discuss the relative importance of setting in the following stories. Would a change of scene make any great difference?

Washington Irving: "The Legend of Sleepy Hollow" (p. 3)
George Ade: "Effie Whittlesy" (p. 550)
Ring Lardner: "Some Like Them Cold" (p. 897)
William Faulkner: "A Rose for Emily" (p. 1122)
Ernest Hemingway: "The Killers" (p. 1130)
Erskine Caldwell: "Kneel to the Rising Sun" (p. 1218)

9. In the following stories point out:
    Typical characters
    Individualized characters

Symbolic characters (representing some idea or quality)

Nathaniel Hawthorne: "The Great Stone Face" (p. 44)

Herman Melville: "Billy Budd, Foretopman" (p. 141)

Mark Twain: "The Man that Corrupted Hadleyburg" p. 260)

Booth Tarkington: "Little Gentleman" (p. 556)

Willa Cather: "Paul's Case" (p. 681)

Ring Lardner: "The Golden Honeymoon" (p. 913)

Dorothy Parker: "Big Blonde" (p. 974)

F. Scott Fitzgerald: "The Rich Boy" (p. 1086)

William Faulkner: "A Rose for Emily" (p. 1122)

Ernest Hemingway: "The Killers" (p. 1130)

Katherine Brush: "Night Club" (p. 1207)

10. Compare the proportion of dialogue in two of the older short stories with the proportion in two recent ones.

11. In the following stories point out passages that cause the reader to share the physical sensations of the characters: to feel that he is experiencing the situation:

Stephen Crane: "The Open Boat" (p. 580)

Conrad Aiken: "Silent Snow, Secret Snow" (p. 959)

John Dos Passos: "The Body of an American" (p. 1117)

Erskine Caldwell: "Kneel to the Rising Sun" (p. 1218)

12. From your reading select a story which best represents each of the following methods of writing:

The romantic

The sentimental

The realistic

The naturalistic

The stream-of-consciousness

(See also question 9, Chapter XI)

CHAPTER VII

DRAMA

Exercises are keyed to the following anthologies, but can be used with other standard collections of plays:

Buck, Philo M., Gassner, J., and Albertson, H. S., *A Treasury of the American Theatre* (New York, Simon and Schuster, Inc., 1940). (T.T.)

Hatcher, Harlan, *Modern American Drama* (New York, Harcourt, Brace and Company, Inc., 1941). (M.A.D.)

Watson, E. B. and Pressey, W. B., *Contemporary Drama* (New York, Charles Scribner's Sons, 1941). (C.D.)

Brooke, Tucker, Cunliffe, John William, and Mac-Cracken, Henry Noble, *Shakespeare's Principal Plays* (New York, D. Appleton-Century Company, Inc., 1935). (Or any complete Shakespeare)

1. On page 169 it was stated that the essence of a dramatic situation is conflict. For each play you read, state in a sentence the central conflict on which the action is based.

2. Pick out three passages of dialogue which characterize the persons talking. Pay special attention to phrases or points of view which are individual to a character.

3. Name several characters in current radio or motion picture comedies which are "humor" characters in the Jonsonian sense. (See p. 182 above)

4. In the following comedies, which characters are individuals and which are personified "humors"?

Odets: *Awake and Sing!* (T.T.; M.A.D.)
Shaw: *Candida* (T.T.)
Barrie: *What Every Woman Knows* (C.D.)
Maugham: *The Circle* (C.D.)
Wilder: *Our Town* (M.A.D.)
Shakespeare: *Twelfth Night*
Much Ado About Nothing
The Merchant of Venice

5. Using the same plays, select two characters who are complex persons, and write character sketches of them. Does their complexity add interest to the plays in which they appear?

6. Do the following tragedies support Maxwell Ander-

son's theory (see pp. 184–185 above) that great plays show man in conflict with the great forces of the universe?

Shakespeare: *Hamlet*
              King Lear
Anderson: *Winterset* (M.A.D.)
          Elizabeth the Queen (T.T.)
O'Neill: *Beyond the Horizon* (M.A.D.)
         The Hairy Ape (C.D.)
Galsworthy: *Justice* (C.D.)
            Escape (T.T.)
Rice: *Street Scene* (C.D.)

7. In one of the following plays show how the dramatist has built his plot structure to meet the needs of the theater. For instance, how could the structure differ if the story were presented in a novel?

Odets: *Awake and Sing!* (T.T.; M.A.D.)
Sherwood: *Abe Lincoln in Illinois* (C.D.; M.A.D.)
Galsworthy: *Escape* (T.T.)
Howard: *The Silver Cord* (C.D.)

8. In two plays you have read, point out examples of foreshadowing.

9. Compare the exposition in the following pairs of plays. Which one in each pair shows the more skilful handing of the problem? Explain.

Shakespeare: *Henry IV*, Part I
Sherwood: *Abe Lincoln in Illinois* (C.D.; M.A.D.)
Shakespeare: *The Merchant of Venice*
             Macbeth
O'Neill: *Anna Christie* (T.T.)
              or
Lewis & Howard: *Dodsworth* (M.A.D.)
Odets: *Awake and Sing!* (T.T.; M.A.D.)
Maugham: *The Circle* (C.D.)
Galsworthy: *Justice* (C.D.)

10. Report on some play or movie you have seen which had one or more of the following weaknesses:

A character doing something contrary to his own nature

An unlikely coincidence

A *deus ex machina* (see p. 195 above)

Stock characters

A stock situation

11. From your reading, select three plays which have some value or meaning beyond mere entertainment. Write a paragraph on each, giving your interpretation of that value or meaning. Does' this added "weight" add to or detract from the interest of the plays?

12. Compare an older comedy of manners like Congreve's *The Way of the World*, Sheridan's *The Rivals* or *The School for Scandal* with a modern one like the following:

Shaw: *Candida* (T.T.)

Maugham: *The Circle* (C.D.)

O'Neill: *Ah, Wilderness*

Sherwood: *Reunion in Vienna*

Barry: *The Philadelphia Story*

In what respects are the purposes and methods of the older and newer writers alike? Has the modern writer any added purpose or weight not characteristic of older comedy?

13. On the basis of your reading, write an essay on the modern dramatist's interest in social and economic problems.

14. After reading several modern problem plays such as:

Rice: *Street Scene* (C.D.)

The Adding Machine (M.A.D.)

Galsworthy: *Justice* (C.D.)

Escape (T.T.)

Odets: *Awake and Sing!* (T.T.; M.A.D.)

Howard: *The Silver Cord* (C.D.)

turn to Shakespeare's *Othello, Hamlet,* or *Measure for Measure.* What similarities and what differences do you find in the choice of materials; in the writer's purposes?

15. On the basis of the plays you have read and recent movies you have seen, discuss the comparative values of

the two mediums. Which one gives a more valid picture of life?
(See also question 10, Chapter XI)

CHAPTER VIII

HUMOR

1. How many of the different types of humor listed in Chapter VIII can you find in Shakespeare's *Henry IV, Part I* (that is, wise-cracks, mock-heroic style, humorous characters)?

2. In some current magazine, newspaper column, or recent book, find examples of two of the following:

> mock-heroic style
> parody
> irony
> satire

3. In any one of the books of Swift's *Gulliver's Travels*, point out elements of universal satire—things that still apply to persons or institutions.

4. Analyze the humor in some current radio program to determine to what extent the humor depends upon such devices as making fun of physical defects, topical allusions, gags, puns, dialect, peculiar mannerisms, and so forth, and to what extent it contains the more enduring elements like epigrams, satire on human foibles or institutions, portrayal of humorous characters.

5. What type or types of humor are represented by each of the following? Point out any universal or enduring elements you find.

Pound: "Ancient Music" (R.P. 152)
Robinson: "Miniver Cheevy" (R.P. 281)
Dryden: "Mac-Flecknoe" (R.P. 357)
Pope: "Epistle to Dr. Arbuthnot" (R.P. 363)
      "The Rape of the Lock" (R.P. 374; L.V. 161)
Byron: "The Vision of Judgment" (R.P. 395)

Suckling: "Why So Pale and Wan, Fond Lover?" (R.P. 54; E.G. 284)

"Out Upon It, I Have Lov'd" (R.P. 55; E.G. 285)

6. Select two of the following stories and discuss the qualities which have made them enduring pieces of humorous writing. (All are in *The Bedside Book of Famous American Stories*.)

Irving: "The Legend of Sleepy Hollow"
"Rip Van Winkle"
Twain: "The Celebrated Jumping Frog of Calaveras County"
Harris: "Brer Rabbit, Brer Fox, and the Tar Baby"
Lardner: "Some Like Them Cold"
"The Golden Honeymoon"

7. Do the same for one of the following plays:
Shakespeare: *A Midsummer Night's Dream*
Much Ado about Nothing
Shaw: *Candida* (T.T.)
Connelly: *The Green Pastures* (T.T.)
Maugham: *The Circle* (C.D.)

8. E. B. White says: "There is hardly a paragraph of *Walden* which does not seem humorous to me . . . Thoreau makes me laugh the inaudible, enduring laugh."

After reading *Walden,* discuss this statement. Can you name any other work that produces "the inaudible, enduring laugh"?

9. Go to a library and get a volume of *The New Yorker* at least five years old. Are any of the pieces in "The Talk of the Town" section still amusing? If so, what enduring elements do they contain?

10. Try the same test on the humor in a newspaper or in *The Saturday Evening Post* of the same vintage.

11. From your reading select some example of humor that seems to you characteristically American. Explain why you think so.

12. After reading some of the poems, plays, stories, and

humorous bits suggested in Chapter VIII and in the foregoing exercises, turn to the humorous writing in your college newspaper or magazine. To what extent does this
writing show the civilized wit, the enduring qualities of
good humorous writing?

CHAPTER IX

CONVENTION AND ORIGINALITY

1. In one or two articles on the sports page of a current
newspaper, point out elements that are conventional in
writing about sport.

2. Choose two sonnets from each: Shakespeare, Elizabeth Barrett Browning, and Edna St. Vincent Millay.
What ideas conventional to each period do you find in
them? What ideas seem individual to each writer?

3. Compare the diction, sentence structure, images,
point of view, and choice of subject in the sonnets of Edna
St. Vincent Millay (R.P. 187, 498, 580; L.V. 547) with
the same elements in the work of any other poet of the
same period (such as Sandburg, Lindsay, Amy Lowell,
Masters, MacLeish, Eliot). Do any of the conventions of
the sonnet carry over into Millay's work that are absent
in the poetry of her contemporaries? Does her writing
seem in any way more old-fashioned than that of the
others?

4. In Chaucer's Prologue to *The Canterbury Tales*
(L.V. 27), point out two characters who seem to represent
types, and two who are individualized.

5. Find five characters in contemporary magazine
stories who represent conventional types.

6. Now in some of the fiction you have read for this
course, pick out five characters which seem to you to be
drawn from life rather than from other stories.

Exercises V and VI may be applied to the movies and
to plays read for this course. (See also question 9, Chapters VI and X, Chapter VII.)

7. Examine several "short-short stories" to determine if they follow a conventional pattern.

8. Read Poe's "The Purloined Letter" (B.B.F.A.S.). What elements of his creation have since become conventions of the detective story?

9. Do any of the stories in a current magazine or in college publications follow the O. Henry pattern of the surprise ending?

10. Now turn to recent stories in any good anthology or to those in "quality" magazines like *The Atlantic Monthly, Harper's Magazine,* or *Story.* Do any of these follow the O. Henry pattern? Do you find any elements in these stories which seem to be conventions peculiar to highbrow magazines? (That is, choice of theme, point of view, characters, style, plot structure.) Also compare question 5, Chapter VI.

11. In your anthology of verse, find two poems in which an old form (such as the sonnet, blank verse, ballad meter) has been used in a new way or for new ideas. Find two poems in which the poet has a new or unusual verse form. Using these poems for illustrations, discuss the advantages and disadvantages of each method. (See also questions 2, 3, 4, 6, 8, 9 in Chapter III.)

CHAPTER X

RESTRAINT

1. In *The Merchant of Venice,* compare the speeches of Portia's three suitors (Act II, Scs. 7 & 9, and Act III, Sc. 2). Which suitor uses the most bombast? Which the least? What does this reveal about the characters of the three men?

2. In Sherwood's *Abe Lincoln in Illinois,* Act III, Sc. 9, compare the speeches of Douglas and Lincoln. Which shows the greater restraint? Aside from the question of your agreement or disagreement with either of the speak-

ers, which speech is the more effective? Do you find one more sincere than the other? (M.A.D.; C.D.)

3. Look up and compare Carlyle's chapter, "Democracy" (Ch. XIII) in *Past and Present* with Mill's "On the Liberty of Thought and Discussion" (Ch. II) in *Liberty*. Is Carlyle's violence more or less convincing than Mill's restraint? Is Carlyle's appeal chiefly to the emotions or to the intellect? Does he use any of the devices of propaganda such as name-calling or appeals to prejudice?

4. Find two editorials or speeches on the same topic: one showing emotional restraint; the other the lack of it.

5. William Butler Yeats said that in Shelley's *Swellfoot the Tyrant,* "there is nothing but the cold rhetoric of obsession." Can you find any passages which support this statement?

6. Read Shelley's "The Masque of Anarchy" and "Song to the Men of England." Which has the greater restraint? Which is the more effective?

7. In one of the poems in your anthology, find an example of the pathetic fallacy. Does it seem to you one of those which represents true emotion, or is it one done in cold blood?

8. Compare the following pairs of poems. In each pair, which poem has the greater economy of statement? The criterion is not length, but the amount of space given to each idea or emotion. Do you find any relation between economy and effectiveness? Is there any relation between economy and effective diction or vivid imagery? (Compare Chapter II.)

Swinburne: "The Garden of Proserpine" (R.P. 4; L.V. 426)

H.D.: "Lethe" (R.P. 7)

> or

Christina Rossetti: "When I Am Dead, My Dearest" (L.V. 421)

Keats: "Ode to a Nightingale" (R.P. 84; L.V. 307)

Swinburne: "Itylus" (R.P. 80)

or

"A Forsaken Garden" (L. 429)

Poe: "To Helen" (R.P. 66; L.V. 441)

"The City in the Sea" (R.P. 31; L.V. 442)

Bryant: "The Yellow Violet" (R.P. 35)

Herrick: "To Daffodils" (R.P. 35)

Wordsworth: "A Slumber Did My Spirit Seal" (R.P. 10; L.V. 218; E.G. 356)

"Three Years She Grew" (R.P. 10)

or

"I've Watched You Now" (E.G. 353)

or

"To the Cuckoo" (L.V. 212)

9. Compare these poems by Byron from the point of view of sentiment and sentimentality. In either one does the poet seem to be indulging in weeping for its own sake? Do you find any relation between sentimentality and wordiness?

Think'st thou I saw thy beauteous eyes,
　Suffused in tears, implore to stay;
And heard unmoved thy plenteous sighs
　Which said far more than words can say?

Though keen the grief thy tears exprest,
　When love and hope lay both o'erthrown,
Yet still, my girl, this bleeding breast
　Throbb'd with deep sorrow as thine own.

But when our cheeks with anguish glow'd,
　When thy sweet lips were join'd to mine,
The tears that from my eyelids flow'd
　Were lost in those which fell from thine.

Thou couldst not feel my burning cheek,
　Thy gushing tears had quench'd its flame;
And as thy tongue essay'd to speak,
　In sighs alone it breathed my name.

And yet, my girl, we weep in vain,
  In vain our fate in sighs deplore;
Remembrance only can remain,—
  But that will make us weep the more.

Again, thou best beloved, adieu!
  Ah! if thou canst, o'ercome regret;
Nor let thy mind past joys review,—
  Our only hope is to forget.[10]

So, we'll go no more a roving
  So late into the night,
Though the heart be still as loving
  And the moon be still as bright.

For the sword outwears its sheath,
  And the soul wears out the breast,
And the heart must pause to breathe,
  And love itself have rest.

Though the night was made for loving,
  And the day returns too soon,
Yet we'll go no more a roving
  By the light of the moon.[11]

10. Find a passage in a novel or short story which seems to you to show sentimentality, and one which shows genuine sentiment. Give reasons for your choice.

CHAPTER XI

SINCERITY AND PROPAGANDA

1. In a Sunday supplement find a discussion of science written by a university professor or some other authority in the field. Has he written down to his audience? Look

---

[10] Byron, "To Caroline."
[11] Byron, "So, We'll Go No More a Roving."

for such devices as slang, wise-cracks, sensational statements.

2. In Shakespeare's *The Merchant of Venice* or in Marlowe's *Dr. Faustus*, pick out scenes designed primarily to please the groundlings.

3. Using the *Reader's Guide*, find two magazine articles by the same author, one in a popular periodical, the other in one like *Harper's Magazine* or *The Atlantic Monthly*. Has the writer written down to the readers of the popular magazine?

4. As a basis of comparison use a novel you have read by some recognized writer like Sinclair Lewis, Pearl Buck, Ernest Hemingway, or William Saroyan. Using the *Reader's Guide*, find a story by the same writer in a popular magazine of the past five years. (Such as *The Saturday Evening Post, The Woman's Home Companion, Esquire*.) Is the story in the slick paper magazine as honest a picture of life as the novel? Support your opinion by evidence from the two works.

5. From any source, select a passage of genuine worth that could be appreciated by the common man or by the connoisseur.

6. In *The Fountain*, Charles Morgan speaks of the seventeenth century as recognizing "an aristocracy of the mind." Find support for this in the essays of Bacon, the *Religio Medici* of Sir Thomas Browne, or the *Areopagitica* of Milton.

7. In an editorial or political speech, point out examples of sweeping generalizations, question-begging words, or name-calling.

8. Find an example of an appeal to loyalties used in such a way as to produce uncritical acceptance of a product or an idea.

9. The following stories are to some extent designed to present a point of view. Do the authors use legitimate means or do they give us characters who are only black or white, or far-fetched situations to support this point of

view? (Page references are to *The Bedside Book of Famous American Stories*.)

Howells: "Edithia" (316)

Cather: "Paul's Case" (681)

Dos Passos: "The Body of an American" (1117)

Caldwell: "Kneel to the Rising Sun" (1218)

See also question 6, Chapter VI

10. Study one of the following plays in the same way. (References are to the same anthologies listed in Chapter VII.)

Galsworthy: *Escape* (T.T.)

Justice (C.D.)

Howard: *The Silver Cord* (C.D.)

Rice: *The Adding Machine* (M.A.D.)

Stallings & Anderson: *What Price Glory?* (T.T.)

Sheriff: *Journey's End* (T.T.)

O'Neill: *The Hairy Ape* (C.D.)

Odets: *Awake and Sing!* (T.T.; M.A.D.)

11. Write a criticism of some poem, short story, play, or novel which seems to you to be insincere or to present biased propaganda.

12. Which of the following seems to you the more sincere? Why? The first is from Robert Ingersoll's speech "At His Brother's Tomb"; the second, a statement by Vanzetti at the time he was sentenced to death.

Yet, after all it may be best, just in the happiest, sunniest hour in all the voyage, while eager winds are kissing every sail, to dash against the unseen rock, and in an instant hear the billows roar above the sunken ship. For whether in mid-sea, or 'mong the breakers of the farther shore, a wreck must mark the end of each and all. And every life, no matter if its every hour is rich with love and every moment jeweled with joy, will, at its close, become a tragedy as sad and deep and dark as can be woven of the warp and woof of mystery and death. . . .

Life is a narrow vale between the cold and barren

peaks of two eternities. We strive in vain to look beyond the heights. We cry aloud, and the only answer is the echo of our wailing cry. From the voiceless lips of the unreplying dead there comes no word; but in the night of death hope sees a star, and listening love can hear the echo of a wing.[12]

If it had not been for these thing, I might have live out my life, talking at street corners to scorning men. I might have die, unmarked, a failure. Now we are not a failure. This is our career and our triumph. Never in our full life can we hope to do such a work for tolerance, for joostice, for man's understanding of man, as now we do by accident. Our words—our lives—our pains—nothing! The taking of our lives—lives of a good shoemaker and a poor fish peddler—all!

That last moment belongs to us—that agony is our triumph! [13]

[12] Ingersoll, "At His Brother's Tomb," *Lectures* (Philadelphia, David McKay Company, 1935).

[13] From *The Letters of Sacco and Vanzetti*, edited by Marion Edman Frankfurter and Gardner Jackson. Copyright 1928 by The Viking Press Inc., New York.

Index

Abstractions, in prose, 118-120
Adding Machine, The, 185, 187-189, 198
Addison, Joseph, 100-101, 106, 108, 212-213
"Adonais," 18, 47, 57
Aesthetic element, 1-2; values, 70-71
Ah, Wilderness, 182-183, 198
Alchemist, The, 197
Alice in Wonderland, 159, 207, 209
All Quiet on the Western Front, 3
Alton Locke, 252
American Language, The, 109
American Mercury, 273
American Scholar, The, 302-303
Anapest, 60-61
Ancient Mariner, The, 37, 43-44, 53-54, 58, 61, 133, 243-244, 290-292
Anderson, Maxwell, 25, 52, 164, 165; use of dialogue, 172-173; theory of tragedy, 184-185; suspense, 187
Anderson, Sherwood, 108, 137, 141
Anglo-Saxon verse, 42; prose, 96-97
Anthony and Cleopatra, 24, 62-63; 180-181, 184
Areopagitica, 114-115
Argument [against] *Abolishing Christianity, An,* 214
Arnold, Matthew, 5, 66, 69, 102-104, 108

Arrowsmith, 130
"A Slumber Did My Spirit Seal," 22
Astrophel and Stella, 231
Auden, W. H., 69, 81-82, 84, 86, 88
Austen, Jane, 140, 145, 153, 236-237
Austin, Mary, 274
Autocrat of the Breakfast Table, The, 204
Awake and Sing!, 190, 199

Babbitt, 144, 284
Bacon, Francis, 132
"Bagpipe Music," 79
"Ballad: The Auld Wife Sat at Her Ivied Door," 209
Ballad, meter, 42-44, 53-54; language, 226
Balzac, Honoré de, 142
Banquet, The, 5
Bartram, William, 37
Barton, Bruce, 92, 276
"Battle Hymn of the Republic," 19
Behrman, S. N., 165
Bellamy, Edward, 132
Belloc, Hilaire, 206
Benchley, Robert, 223, 224
Benét, Stephen Vincent, 110-111, 132, 145
Bennett, Arnold, 275
Benson, Stella, 159
Beowulf, 88
Beppo, 51

Beveridge, Senator Albert J., 250-252

Bible, 5, 246; prose, 111-112

Biglow Papers, 221

Billings, Josh, 223

Biography, 165

Blake, William, imagination, 4-5; anticipates Freud, 6-7; stanza form, 51; use of trochee, 60; use of symbols, 71-77

Blank verse, 24-25, 30, 52-53, 58

Boccacio, Giovanni, 125

Bombast, 252

Book of the Duchess, The, 227

Boswell, James, 101

Brave New World, 15

"Break, Break, Break," 27, 64

Brooks, Van Wyck, 120

Browne, Sir Thomas, 99

Browning, Elizabeth Barrett, 12, 73

Browning, Robert, 26, unusual diction, 34; stanza form, 51-52; 56, 84; grammar, 88; as a dramatist, 167-169

Brush, Katherine, 127, 136

Bryant, William Cullen, 239-240

Buck, Pearl, 129

Bunyan, 3, 4

Burgess, Gelett, 206

Burns, Robert, 86, 215, 265-266

Butler, Samuel, 266

Byron, George Gordon, Lord, 18, 44, 50-51, 61, 210-211; stanzas for analysis, 316-317

"Byzantium," 77

Cabell, James Branch, 121, 144, 147

Caesura, 42, 63

Calverly, Charles, 209-210

Canby, Henry Seidel, 225

"Canonization, The," 237

Canterbury Tales, The, 19

Čapek, Karel, 185

Carlyle, Thomas, 8, 246-247, 205, 207, 209

Carter, Boake, 279-281

Caste, 176

Catalexis, 63-64

Cather, Willa, 139, 283

Cavalier Tunes, 56

Characterization, in fiction, 139-142; in drama, 180-184; conventional, 284 ff.; *see also* Chaucer, Geoffrey, and Shakespeare, William

"Charge of the Light Brigade, The," 62, 232-233

Charley's Aunt, 164

Chase, Stuart, 104-106, 267

Chaucer, Geoffrey, 19, 50; use of feminine rhyme, 59; use of couplet, 69; 71, 86, 108; humor, 216-218, 224; characters, 236, 245

Christabel, 44

"Christmas Carol, The," 133

Churchill, Winston, 11

Cibber, Colley, 212

Clough, Arthur Hugh, 11

Coincidence, in drama, 195-197

Cohen, Octavus Roy, 202

Coleridge, Samuel Taylor, on poetry, 10, 23; 26; language of poetry, 36, 37-38; use of ballad, 43-44, 53-54; aim of poetry, 92-93; 204, 242; stanzas for analysis, 290-292

Collier's, 226

Collins, William, 282

"Come Live with Me," 87

Comédie Humaine, Le, 142

Comedy, in drama, 164

Comedy of Errors, The, 164

Comedy of manners, 164-165

Comic strips, 159

Conflict, dramatic, 169-171

"Congo, The," 26
Congreve, William, 163-164, 171
Connelly, Marc, 186
Conquest of Granada, The, 249
Conrad, Joseph, 127
"Consider This Our Time," 84-85
"Constant Lover, The," 232
Convention, in poetry, 41-42, 47-48; in fiction, 134-136; in drama, 163-164; theatrical, 192-193; *see also* Chap. IX, 225 ff.
Convention and Revolt in Poetry, 242
Cook, Joe, 207
Coolidge, Calvin, 117
"Cop and the Anthem, The," 137
Coppard, A. E., 159, 160, 161
"Cotter's Saturday Night, The," 265-266
Counter-Attack, 232-233
Couplet, 68; tetrameter, 44; pentameter, 45; heroic, 45-46
Cream of the Jest, The, 144
Crockett, Davy, 220
Cross-section-of-life technique, 136, 137, 161
Cummings, E. E., 243
"Cry of the Children, The," 12, 73
Culture and Anarchy, 102, 105
Cuppy, Will, 207-208, 223
Cynewulf, 3

Dactyl, 61-62
Daiches, David, 78
Das Kapital, 5, 88
David Copperfield, 143
"Day of Doom, The," 289-290
"Death of the Flowers, The," 239-240

Decameron, 125
Defoe, Daniel, prose style, 100; novels, 126, 131, 154
Democracy, influence on prose, 108-111
Deor, 13
"Deserted Village, The," 46
"Destruction of Sennacherib, The," 61
Deus ex machina, 134, 195
Development of Modern English, The, 109
"Devil and Daniel Webster, The," 110, 132, 135, 145-146
Dewey, John, 113, 117
Dialogue, in fiction, 147-149; in drama, 169-180
Dickens, Charles, 12, 130, 140, 141, 143, 154, 216, 224, 237
Dickinson, Emily, 241-242, 255
Diction, poetic, 31-36; prose, 111-122
"Disenchantment," 241-242
Disney, Walt, 159, 206
Dobrée, Bonamy, 102, 106
"Dr. Jekyll and Mr. Hyde," 133, 141
Dr. Faustus, 192
"Does It Matter?," 215
Don Juan, 51, 211
Don Quixote, 142-143
Donne, John, 122, 231-232, 237
Dooley, Mr., 221
Doolittle, Hilda, 260-261
Dos Passos, John, 142, 144
"Dover Beach," 66, 69
Dowson, Ernest, 272
Drama, Chap. VII, 162 ff.; definition of, 162-164; types of, 164-167; universal elements, 167-189; special problems, 189-193; values of, 197-200
Dream-vision, 227-228
Dreiser, Theodore, 108, 154-155, 185
Drew, Elizabeth, 77

Dryden, John, 45, 212, 249
Du Gard, Martin, 142
Dumas, Alexandre, 133

"Easter Wings," 243
Ecclesiastes, 270-271
Edge of Darkness, The, 161
Edinburgh Review, 255
Edman, Irwin, 301-302
Education of Woman, The, 100
"Edward," 258-259
Egoist, The, 202
"Eleanora," 146-147
"Elegy Written in a Country Church-Yard," 29, 55, 56
Eliot, T. S., use of images, 35, 79-81, 83; 71; use of symbols, 77; on metaphysical poets, 79
Emerson, Ralph Waldo, 302-303
Emotion, power of, 10-15; intensity of, 20-22
Empiricism, 106
"End of Something, The," 137
Endymion, 45, 56
"English Bards and Scotch Reviewers," 210-211
Essay on Comedy, 219
Essay on Criticism, An, 56, 64
Essay on Projects, An, 100
Ethan Frome, 127
Ethical element, 3-4
Euphues, 97-98
Euphuism, 97-98, 122
Evangeline, 62
"Eve of St. Agnes, The," 47, 54
Excursion, The, 52, 269-270, 284
Experiments in verse, 68-69
Exposition, in drama, 189-191; *see also Hamlet*
Expressionism, 159; in drama, 166-167

"Fall of the House of Usher, The," 244
Faeie Queen, The, 3, 47, 57
Fantasy, in fiction, 159-160
Farce, 164
Farrell, James T., 226
Faulkner, William, 130
"Fenimore Cooper's Literary Offenses," 108-109
Fiction, Chap. VI, 125 ff.; origins of, 125-128; purpose of, 128-129; test of, 129 ff.; elements of, 136-152; schools of, 152-160
Fielding, Henry, 139-140, 154, 216
Finnegans Wake, 157
Fitzgerald, Edward, 8-9, 46
Fitzgerald, F. Scott, 234-235
Fortune, 105-108
For Whom the Bell Tolls, 122, 127, 130, 152, 160
"France: An Ode," 10
Franklin, Benjamin, 204, 222
Free association, 82-84
Free verse, 59, 65-68
"Freezeout, A," 234-235
Frost, Robert, 109

Galsworthy, John, 166, 173-175, 284
"Garden of Proserpine, The," 58
Gay, John, 224
"General William Booth Enters Heaven," 26
Gentlemen Prefer Blondes, 261
"Gerontion," 77
Gerould, Katherine Fullerton, 129
"Getters Not Begetters," 90
"Get There If You Can," 81-82
"Gettysburg Address," 14, 19, 39, 92
"Gnu, The," 206
Goldsmith, Oliver, 46, 175-176

Goldwyn, Sam, 117
Gone with the Wind, 140, 160, 233
"Goody Blake and Harry Gill," 246
Gothic novels, 133
Grapes of Wrath, The, 3, 73
Gray, Thomas, 29, 55, 56
"Great Stone Face, The," 141
Greeley, Horace, 123
Green Pastures, The, 186
Guardsman, The, 194
Guest, Edgar A., 226, 297
Gulliver's Travels, 159, 160, 215

"Haircut," 138, 140, 215-216
Hairy Ape, The, 185
Halleck, Fitz-Greene, 253-255
Hamlet, 36, 132, 141, 162, 163, 166; dramatic conflict, 167-171; exposition, 190-191; 196, 236, 238; restraint, 263; 283
Hart, Moss, 182
Havelock the Dane, 92
"Heaven-Haven," 13
Hemingway, Ernest, 121-122, 128, 130, 137, 139, 147, 226, 282-283
Henley, William Ernest, 66
Herbert, George, 243
Hereward the Wake, 153
Herrick, Robert, 82-83
Herriman, George (Herriman's Krazy Kat), 206
"Hesperidies," 260-261
"High Handed Outrage at Utica," 220-221
"Higher Learning and the War," 113
Hilton, James, 132
Hitler, Adolph, 8
Hokinson, Helen E., 236
"Hollow Men, The," 79-81, 83
"Home-Thoughts from Abroad," 51-52

Homer, 71
Hoover, Herbert, 117
Hopkins, Gerard Manley, 13; versification, 68-69; revolt against grammar, 88-89, 90
Houseman, A. E., 20-21
"How I Create," 223
"How Sleep the Brave?," 282
"How They Brought the Good News from Gent to Aix," 26-27
"How to Tell a Major Poet from a Minor Poet," 222
Huckleberry Finn, 140
Hudibras, 266
Humor, varieties of: boorish, 201-203; wise-crack, 109, 203-204; pun, 204-205; epigram, 205; nonsense, 205-207; mock-heroic, 207-208; parody, 208-210; satire, 210-213; irony, 213-216; kindly, 216-221; absurd, American love of, 221-223; non-sequitur, 223; lasting, 223-224
Humphrey Clinker, 140
"Hunting of the Cheviot, The," 259
Huxley, Aldous, 15, 143
Hydriotaphia, Urn-Burial, 99

"I Hear America Singing," 107, 240-241
Iamb, 59-60
Ibsen, Henrik, 198
Idea of a University, The, 106-107
"Idiot Boy, The," 133, 212, 215, 246, 259
Idiot's Delight, 189, 199
"Il Penseroso," 44, 60
Illiad (Pope's), 45
Imagery, 31-34; connotative use of, 78-82; *see also* Eliot, T. S.
Imagists, 32, 42

Imagination, 4-5, 20; *see also* Truth, imaginative
"I'm a Fool," 137, 140
Importance of Being Earnest, The, 165
"Indifferent," 231-232
Ingersoll, Robert, 115-116, 319-320
Innocents Abroad, The, 220
Isaiah, 20, 23
Ivanhoe, 110-111, 152, 153

"Jabberwocky," 205
Jacob's Room, 156
James, Henry, 136, 155
James, William, 6
Jargon, technical, 119
Jefferson, Thomas, 36
Jeffrey, Francis, 243
Jew of Malta, The, 198
Johnson, Samuel, style, 101-102, 147; on the novel, 126-127, 130, 154; parody of ballads, 210; on restraint, 263
Jonson, Ben, 182, 197, 231
Joseph Andrews, 139
Joyce, James, 34, 121, 156-158
Julius Caesar, 184

Kandel, I. L., 118-119
Kaufman, George, 182
Keats, John, 18; imagery, 33-34; use of couplet, 45, 47; use of Italian sonnet, 48-49; use of pauses, 54; 56, 69; objection to moralizing, 84; Shelley on, 86; economy, 255-258
"Killers, The," 147
King Lear, 6, 86, 263-264
King's Henchman, The, 285
Kingsley, Charles, 153, 252
"Kneel to the Rising Sun," 135

"Knight's Tale, The," 19
"Kubla Khan," 37, 39

"Lady of Shalott, The," 292-293
"Lady or the Tiger, The," 244
Lady Windermere's Fan, 178-180
"L'Allegro," 26, 44, 60
"La Belle Dame Sans Merci," 255-258
Lamb, Charles, 204
Lardner, Ring, 138, 145, 147, 215
Late George Apley, The, 122
Lawrence, D. H., 141
Lear, Edward, 205
Legend of Good Women, The, 227
"Let Me Not to the Marriage of True Minds," 230
Lewis, C. Day, 86-87, 88, 90
Lewis, Sinclair, 108, 141, 147, 154-155, 160, 284
Lewis, Wyndham, 89-90
"Life's Trades," 255
Lincoln, Abraham, 12, 13, 112, 117, 123, 220
Lindsay, Vachel, 26
Literary allusion, 85-88
Literature, Chap. I, 1 ff.; understanding of, 15-16
Local color, in fiction, 139
"Lochinvar," 61
"Locksley Hall," 7-8, 82, 86
Longfellow, Henry Wadsworth, 44, 61, 62, 65
"Look Homeward America," 301-302
"Lost Boy," 149-150
"Lotus Eaters, The," 47
"Love Song of J. Alfred Prufrock, The," 83-84, 85
Lowell, Amy, 32
Lowell, James Russell, 120, 220
Lowes, John L., 37, 111, 242

"Lucy" poems, 43
Luther, Martin, 111
Luxury of Integrity, The, 267
"Lycidas," 29, 59, 65
Lyly, John, 97-98, 122
Lyrical Ballads, 6, 245-246

Macbeth, 2, 71, 230
MacLeish, Archibald, 90
MacNeice, Louis, 79, 86, 88
Madariaga, Salvador, 26
Main Street, 143, 160
Malory, Thomas, 92-96, 125
"Man That Corrupted Hadley-
burg, The," 127
"Man Who Missed the Bus,
The," 141, 159, 161
Mansfield, Katherine, 146
"Marching Along," 56
"Marco Bozzaris," 254-255
"Mariana," 32-33
Marlowe, Christopher, 52, 87,
198, 245, 248-249
"Mary Had a Little Lamb," 31,
43, 54
"Masque of the Red Death,
The," 139, 244
Masters, Edgar Lee, 67, 116
Maud, 252-253
Mayer, Milton, 107-108
Mayor of Casterbridge, The,
135
Mazeppa, 44
Meaning of the Times, The,
250-252
Mein Kampf, 5, 88
Men Like Gods, 227
"Men of Harlech," 19
Mencken, H. L., 109, 121, 273
Merchant of Venice, The, 24,
143, 198
Meredith, George, 201, 202,
219, 221
Merry Wives of Windsor, The,
197

Metaphysical poets, 79, 82
"Midnight Ride of Paul Revere,
The," 44, 61
Midsummer Night's Dream, A,
164
Milburn, George, 148-149
Millay, Edna St. Vincent, 285
Milton, John, 3, 8, 10, 13, 15;
use of onomatopoeia, 26; or-
gan music, 28-29; use of
rhyme, 30, 59; 44; blank
verse, 52-53; experiments in
verse, 65; 71, 73; use of allu-
sions, 88; prose, 99, 114-115;
changes sonnet convention,
238-239; 245, 246; Dr. John-
son on, 277-279
Milton (Blake), 75-77
"Modern Novel, The," 126
Modest Proposal, A, 11
Mol Flanders, 126, 160
Molnar, Ferenc, 194
Moon Is Down, The, 127
Moore, George, 39, 90
Moore, Thomas, 60, 296
Morris, William, 132
"Morte d'Arthur," 94-96
Much Ado About Nothing, 182
"Municipal Report, A.," 137
Music, in poetry, 22-31; in
prose, 113-116
Mussolini, Benito, 8

Nathan, Robert, 159
Naturalism, in fiction, 154-155
Neo-Platonism, 74
New Testament, 39
New Yorker, The, 236
Newman, John Henry, Cardinal,
106-107
Newton, Isaac, 70
"Night," 51
"Night Club," 127, 136
"Nightingale, The," 207-208
Norris, Frank, 245

Not to Eat Not for Love, 150-152

Novella, 125

Novelette, 128

"November 1806," 10

"Nun's Priest's Tale, The," 207

"Ode to a Nightingale," 35

"Ode to the West Wind," 54-55

"Ode Written During the Negotiations with Buonaparte . . . ," 250

"Ode Written in the Beginning of the Year 1746," 282

Odets, Clifford, 166, 186, 190, 199

"O, Bury Me Not on the Lone Prairie," 56

O'Casey, Shean, 165

Of Mice and Men, 160

Of Thee I Sing, 198

O. Henry, 136-137, 222-223, 229

"Oh, Breathe Not His Name," 296

"Oh Hush Thee My Baby," 87

O'Hara, John, 219

"Old Man's Comforts, The," 208-209

Old Wives' Tale, The, 275

"On the Grasshopper and Cricket," 48-49

"On the Late Massacre in Piedmont," 10, 239

O'Neill, Eugene, 166, 182-183, 185

Onomatopoeia, 26-27

Oppenheim, E. Phillips, 133

Origin of Species, 5, 6

Originality, 38, 39; *see also* Chap. IX, 225 ff.

Othello, 230

Ottava rima, 50-51

Our Town, 133, 189, 193, 244

"Over the Hill to the Poorhouse," 59

"Owl and the Pussycat, The," 205

Pope, Alexander, 45-46, 51, 56, 64, 125, 208, 212-213, 218-219, 222

"Population Going Down," 104-105

Prayer Book (Anglican), 21, 246

"Prejudice the Garden Toward Roses," 118

Prelude, The, 52

Pride and Prejudice, 140, 143

Princess, The, 29

Propaganda, Chap. XI, 267 ff.

"Prophecy of a New Era," 66

Prose, Chap. V, 92 ff.; historical development, 96-111; qualities of, 111-124; *see also* Chap. VI, 125 ff.

Psalms, 9, 18, 112, 270

"Pure poetry," 39, 90

"Purple Cow, The," 206

Pamela, 126, 153

Paradise Lost, 13, 28-29, 43, 52-53, 60, 71, 133

Parker, Dorothy, 147

Parody, 187, 208-210

"Passionate Shepherd to His Love, The," 87

Pathetic fallacy, 252-253

"Paul's Case," 139, 140

Pauses, 63-64; *see also* Keats, John

"Peter Bell," 246

Phraseology, poetic, 34-36

Piers Plowman, 118, 227

Pilgrim's Progress, The, 3, 227

Pinero, Sir Arthur Wing, 176-180

"Pioneers! O Pioneers!," 67-68

Pippa Passes, 167-169, 172, 191-192
Pit, The, 245
"Pit and the Pendulum, The," 130
Plato, 5
Platonism, 74
Plot, 136-138
Plautus, 219
Poe, Edgar Allan, 34, 95, 130, 139; striving for effect, 146; lack of reality, 244; stanza for analysis, 296
Poetry, nature of, Chap. II, 17 ff.; Coleridge's definition, 20; form and function, Chap. III, 41 ff.; stanza forms, 42-52; variations within stanza, 53-59; types of feet, 59-63; interpretation of, Chap. IV, 70 ff.; Newton's definition, 70; poetic methods, 71-91
Point Counterpoint, 143
"Poison Tree, A," 6-7

Quatrains, 46-47

R.U.R., 185
"Rabbi Ben Ezra," 34
Rape of the Lock, The, 45-46, 207, 222
Realism, in fiction, 154-155; in drama, 165-166
Rehearsal, The, 101
Republic, 5
"Requiesat," 103-104
Restraint, Chap. X, 248 ff.
Reunion in Vienna, 165
Rhyme, 30-31, 56-59; royal, 50; feminine, 58
Rhythm, of verse, 22-26; of prose, 117
Rice, Elmer, 166, 185, 187-189

Richard II, 14
Richardson, Samuel, 126, 127
Rime of the Ancient Mariner, The. See Ancient Mariner, The
"Rip Van Winkle," 133, 141
Rivals, The, 165, 182, 189-190, 197
Robertson, Stuart, 109
Robertson, T. W., 176
Robinson, E. A., 52
Robinson Crusoe, 126
Rogers, Will, 220, 221
Romanticism, in fiction, 152-153; in drama, 165
Romeo and Juliet, 190, 262
Romains, Jules, 142
Ross, Leonard Q., 224
Rossetti, Dante Gabriel, 210
Roosevelt, Franklin D., 124
Roosevelt, Theodore, 118
"Rose for Emily, A.," 130
"Rousseau," 120
Roxana, 126
Rubáiyát, The, 8-9, 46-47, 63
Ruskin, John, 3, 252
Ruth, 113

Sabatini, Raphael, 134
Sandburg, Carl, 67, 241
Saroyan, William, 153-154
Sarton Resartus, 246-247
Sassoon, Siegfried, 215, 232-233
St. Paul, 276
Saturday Evening Post, The, 226, 234
"Say Not the Struggle Naught Availeth," 11
Scansion, 59-63
School for Scandal, The, 164
Scott, Sir Walter, 61; prose style, 110-111; on Jane Austen, 145; 160; lack of economy, 256-259

"Sculptor's Funeral, The," 283
"Second Inaugural Address," 112-113
Second Mrs. Tanqueray, The, 176-180, 191-198
"Secret Life of Walter Mitty, The," 144
Sentiment and sentimentality, 261-266; in fiction, 153-154
Service, Robert W., 226
Shakespeare, William, 6, 14; styles of blank verse, 24-25; imagery, 32; 36; sonnet, 48-50, 69; use of by MacNeice, 86; 88; on Euphuism, 98; 132, 141, 143, 159; use of dramatic conflict, 167-171; use of chorus, 180-181; characterization, 181-184, 186; exposition, 189-190; clarifying the action, 190; 197, 198, 203, 216, 219, 221, 224; use of sonnet, 230; characters, 236-238; 245, 246; restraint, 262-264, 275
"Shall I Wasting in Despair?," 232
Sharp, Becky, 135, 140, 143
Shaw, Bernard, 171, 172
She Stoops to Conquer, 175-176
Shelley, Percy Bysshe, 3, 4, 18, 35, 47; use of terza rima, 54-55; use of Spenserian stanza, 57; use of symbols, 73; on Keats, 86
Sheridan, Richard Brinsley, 182, 189-190, 197
Sherwood, Robert, 165, 189, 199
Short story, 127-128
Sidney, Sir Philip, 231
"Simon Lee," 27-28
Sincerity, 123; Chap. XI, 267 ff.
Singe, John M., 165
Sir Fopling Flutter, 165
"Sir Patrick Spens," 43, 259

"Sire de Maletroit's Door, The," 138-139
"Skyscrapers," 67
"Slumber Did My Spirit Seal, A," 22
Smollett, Tobias, 140
"Snow Bound," 64
"So, We'll Go No More a Roving," 317
"Song of the Militant Romance," 89
Song of Solomon, 112
"Song: The Sunlight on the Garden," 86
"Song to Celia," 231, 237
Sonnet, Petrarchian, 48-49; Shakespearian, 48-50; as conventional form, 228-229; see also Milton, John
"Sonnets on the Punishment of Death," 48
Southey, Robert, 208-209, 243, 244, 249-250
Spectator, The, 100-101
Spender, Stephen, 69, 88
Spenser, Edmund, 230-231
Spondee, 62
Spoon River Anthology, 67
Sprung rhythm, 68
Stanza forms, 42-55; "Fourteener," 43; Spenserian, 47-48, 57, 86
Stein, Gertrude, 244
Stockton, Frank, 244
Strange Interlude, 166
Stephens, James, 26
Steinbeck, John, 73, 127, 153, 160
Stevenson, R. L., 138-139
Stowe, Harriet Beecher, 12, 128
Strachey, Lytton, 233
Stream of consciousness, 155-159
Strife, 173-175, 183, 284
"Strike Churl," 89
Structure, in drama, 185-188

"Student in Economics, A," 148-149

Style, prose, 145-147; derivative, 121-122; "door banged," 106; see also Prose, historical development

Suckling, Sir John, 232

Suckow, Ruth, 140

Suggestion, in poetry, 84-85

Sullivan, Pat (Sullivan's Felix), 206

Surrey, Earl of, 245

"Susan and the Doctor," 140

Swift, Jonathan, 11, 214, 215, 216, 219

Swinburne, Algernon Charles, 58

Symbolism, in poetry, 71-78; in fiction, 141-142

"Tables Turned, The," 31, 84

"Tam O'Shanter," 215

Tamburlaine, 248-249

Taming of the Shrew, The, 164

Taylor, Jeremy, 99

Tennyson, Alfred, Lord, prophesies air war and league of nations, 7-8; onomatopoeia, 27, 29; imagery, 32-33; 47; use of dactyls, 62; technical skill, 65; Auden's use of, 82; moralizing, 84; Day Lewis' use of, 87; use of Malory, 94-96; on war, 232-233; use of pathetic fallacy, 252-253; stanzas for analysis, 292-293

Terence, 219

Terza rima, 54-55

Thackeray, W. M., 140, 145, 154

Theme, in fiction, 129, 142-145

Thoreau, Henry, 312

Three Men on a Horse, 164

Thurber, James, 144, 220, 221

"Tiger, The," 63, 71-74

Time Machine, The, 166

"Tintern Abbey," 31, 246, 268-270

"To a Skylark," 73

"To Autumn," 33

"To Caroline," 316-317

Tobacco Road, 143-144, 276

Tour de force, 244

Tristram, 52

Tristram Shandy, 140, 153, 205

Trochee, 60

Troilus and Criseyde, 50

Trollope, Anthony, 153

"Troy Town," 210

Truth, imaginative, 132-134; fictional, 130-132; dramatic, 193 ff.

Twain, Mark, 127, 220, 224; prose style, 108-109

Twelfth Night, 163

"Twenty Grand," 139, 147

Typhoon, 127

"Ulalume—A Ballad," 296

Ulysses, 156-158

Uncle Tom's Cabin, 12

U.S.A., 144, 145

Unintelligibility, cult of, 90

Utopias, 132

Vanity Fair, 129, 140, 143

Vanzetti, Bartolomeo, 122-123, 320

Vaughan, Henry, 78-79

"Verses on the Death of Dr. Swift," 216

Vicar of Wakefield, The, 153

"Villanelle of the Poet's Road," 272

"Vision of Judgment," 281

"Vision of Judgment, The," 51

Volpone, 182

"Voyage to the Houyhnhnms, A," 215

Walden, 4, 312
Waiting for Lefty, 186
"Wanderer, The," 12-13
War and Peace, 128
Ward, Artemus, 220, 222
Waste Land, The, 88
Way of the World, The, 164
Weller, George Anthony, 150-152
Wells, H. G., 227
Westward Ho!, 153
Weyman, Stanley, 133
Wharton, Edith, 127
"When Icicles Hang by the Wall," 32
"When in Disgrace with Fortune and Men's Eyes," 69
"When Lilacs Last in the Dooryard Bloom'd," 14
Whistler, James McNeill, 204
White, E. B., 222, 312
Whitman, Walt, 14; versification, 66-67; 107; originality, 240
Whittier, John Greenleaf, 64, 109
Wiggelsworth, Michael, 289-290
Wilde, Oscar, 178-180, 204, 205
Wilder, Thornton, 189
"William and Helen," 256-259
Winchell, Walter, 226
Winterset, 25, 52, 172-173, 185, 187
"With Rue My Heart Is Laden," 21

Wither, George, 282
Wodehouse, P. G., 216
Wolfe, Thomas, 122, 146, 149-150
Woods, William, 160
Woolf, Virginia, 129, 155-156, 160
Word-sound, in poetry, 28-30
Wordsworth, Dorothy, 37
Wordsworth, William, 4; on materials of poetry, 6; on intellectual sensitivity, 21, 22; 26; use of unsuitable music, 27-28, 31; use of Dorothy's *Journal,* 37; 43, 48, 52, 65, 69, 71; use of Platonic imagery, 74; moralizing, 84; on Burns, 86; on language, 103; 133, 212, 213, 243; originality, 245-246; 259; sincerity, 268-270; use of propaganda devices, 284
"World, The," 78-79
"Wreck of Old 97," 43
Wright, Fredrick Tappan, 132
Wyatt, Sir Thomas, 245

Yeats, William Butler, 75, 77, 165, 248
Yellow Book, The, 272
You Can't Take It with You, 182
"Youth in College," 105-107

Zola, Emile, 155

(1)